FIGHTING BULL

To Gary,   9th September 2011

FIGHTING BULL

Best wishes

NIGEL FARAGE

Nigel Farage

biteback ˇˇˇ
^^^

First published in Great Britain in 2010 by
Biteback Publishing Ltd
Heal House
375 Kennington Lane
London
SE11 5QY

ISBN 978-1-84954-039-1

10 9 8 7 6 5 4 3 2 1

A CIP catalogue record for this book is available from the British Library.

Set in Bembo

Printed and bound in Great Britain by TJ International Ltd, Padstow, Cornwall

CONTENTS

ACKNOWLEDGEMENTS

I have been on the road for over a decade and owe an incalculable debt to my family, who have made huge sacrifices yet somehow kept a warm, welcoming place in the nest against my occasional visits on leave. The small parts which they play in this book reflect my neglect, not the parts which they have played in my life. I must also thank the extended family of dedicated UKIP supporters whose time, creative skills and passion have sustained me through thick and thin. Of all my colleagues and friends, three who have fought unwaveringly at my side warrant particular mention. David Lott – he of the one-man-and-his-horsebox crusade - John Whittaker and Graham Booth have remained loyal over many years and have kept me laughing under fire. Without Annabelle Fuller's perceptiveness and goodwill and Mark Daniel's unfailing flair and imagination, this story would have been considerably duller.

PART I

I

WHY'S WALLY?

Who – or what – dunnit?

That seems to be the question on most people's minds when they ask about my life off the political stage.

Obviously detective-novel enthusiasts or *Where's Wally?* hounds, they are convinced that somewhere, hidden amongst all those commonplace milling memories and confusing clues, there lurks 'the answer'.

I suppose the question is: 'What turns an alarmingly normal, cricket-loving middle-class English boy into a full-time troublemaker, leader of a rabble in revolt against a mighty empire, thorn in the flesh of Presidents and Prime Ministers and spokesman for an entire generation of libertarians and democrats?'

Or, as a man with glazed, cobwebbed eyes rumbled at me in a Westminster bar the other night, 'Oi, Nigel. 'Ow'd you get to be so, like, totally doolally?'

Well, welcome to *Why's Wally?*.

Enjoy the hunt.

For myself, I don't believe the quarry exists.

I was an alarmingly normal, cricket-loving Kentish boy – albeit a bolshy, argumentative and perverse one. I remain an alarmingly normal, cricket-loving Kentish boy, as bolshy and argumentative as ever.

There were two horrific moments for which I will forever remain grateful, moments which did not so much change me as cause me to review my priorities and so irrevocably to alter my course, but those occurred when I was in my early twenties and confronted by imminent death.

I do not believe even these made me significantly doolallier than before.

They merely woke me up to the fact that I wanted something more on my gravestone than 'fed, drank, made money', that we English boys and girls were under threat and that, if further generations were to enjoy all that I had, someone just had to stand up and fight.

And, being doolally, I reckoned it might as well be me.

*

> Sexual intercourse began
> In nineteen sixty-three
> (Which was rather late for me). . .

It may have been bad timing for Larkin, but it was perfect for me. Because, in direct consequence of this admirable innovation, I emerged – as ever at the forefront of fashion and technological advance – into the light of Farnborough Hospital on Friday 3 April 1964.

The following day, the Beatles made history by occupying the top five places in the US Billboard charts. I claim no responsibility for this almost equally impressive demonstration at once of British supremacy and of the fact that the sixties were now truly underway.

I also therefore know far more precisely than most people where I was on 22 November 1963, the day that Kennedy died. My mother had no doubt shed tears with the rest of the world for the promise and the naive but inspiring dreams which perished with its fallen king.

I opened my eyes, then, on a world at once looking to the future and counting on the young, breaking free of the cautious conventionality instilled by two World Wars but now aware that there was no magical silver bullet which could not be counteracted by one of copper-jacketed lead.

Materialism – some would say realism – had already lurched hawking and cursing into the reveries of the sixties.

My parents – or, more exactly, my mother, because my father was busy earning a lot and spending a lot more in the City – took me home to Downe, a still-enchanting village in the North Downs of Kent.

Downe is one of those place-names apparently designed by the devious British to confuse foreigners. The village is set in a wooded valley in a ridge of chalk downland (by which we mean uplands of course) which terminates abruptly in the White Cliffs of Dover.

Just to add to the confusion, its most famous resident, Charles Darwin, lived at Down House, Downe, which he called Down House, Down because he refused to accept the slightly chi-chi 'e' appended to the village's name. My family home backed onto the grounds of Darwin's. It was a pair of Victorian semi-detached workers' cottages which, by the time I arrived, had already grown into what estate agents would call 'a desirable residence with two acres of garden' and would in time acquire a 'substantial' in the description as the two became one and extensions were tacked on until now it is a seven-bedroom 'villa', whatever that may mean.

I therefore spent the first summer of my life beneath rowan trees in my Silver Cross pram, reflecting, no doubt, on the virtues of natural selection (of which I was living proof), in what was, in effect, Darwin's garden, and was pushed along the Sandwalk where he had done his best thinking.

Now I think that this, unlikely as it sounds, really did have an influence on me. Darwin's status has since risen to that of a prophet, but, back then, he was, for the bulk of the general public, merely an illustrious but contentious figure. In Downe, he was ours.

There were villagers whose grandparents had worked for him and his family, whose grandparents had played cricket with him or had been members of the 'Darwin Coal Club' and remembered him with affection. We were aware of him and loyal to his memory, much as many Christians grew up with unthinking loyalty to creationism.

Certainly a central tenet of my convictions since then has been that whatever has evolved is superior to, and fitter to survive in its peculiar environment than, that which is designed by one hubristic age (let alone an alien culture) on a drawing-board.

As 'Radical Jack' Durham said at the time of the Great Reform Act, demonstrating a similar ecological concern for indigenous forms:

> I wish to rally as large a portion of the British people as possible around the
> existing institutions of the country. . . I do not wish new institutions but
> to preserve and strengthen the old. Some would confine the advantages of
> these institutions to as small a class as possible. I would throw them open to
> all who have the ability to comprehend them and vigour to protect them.

Our weights and measures system, over which our supporters fought so long, gallant and victorious a battle against dirigiste idiocy, are a minor but significant case in point. It may indeed be simpler for the cerebrally challenged to work in decimal because they can count on their fingers and, where necessary, toes.

Our ancestors, however, did not sit down cackling, intent on devising a system of measures in multiples of twelve which would thoroughly confuse children and idiots. The system evolved from use and is, in consequence, more user-friendly, adaptable and natural than its alternative, which was designed (along with a ten-day week made up of ten-hour days and 86.4 second minutes. Ah, sweet simplicity!) by Napoleon's bureaucrats.

Or take the most successful medical innovation of the twentieth century – which is. . .

. . .well, penicillin has a claim, but no human brain invented and developed that. It was merely discovered. The other great life-saver was developed by a pair of very sick lay-people who got together one day and compared notes, then allowed the experiences of other sufferers to complete the job. It has saved the lives of millions. It is called Alcoholics Anonymous.

I had cause to be grateful to AA very early in life.

As I sat there in that Vanden Plas coachwork sarcophagus, ruminating on mysteries somehow too deep for speech and accustoming myself to life, my father was making a determined attempt to kill himself just 20 miles away in the City of London. He solemnly swears that the two things were unrelated.

He was twenty-nine years old and doing precisely what I was to do – having what he felt sure was a 'good' time amongst the boys in the City.

He was seldom at home, so he contrived that trick which so many fathers worked back then. He appeared from time to time, expensively dressed and telling glamorous stories, whilst my mother, who had to deal with workaday problems like nappies and mounting bills and suffered the additional disadvantage of being there all the time, paid the proverbial price of familiarity.

Guy Farage – the name alone surely indicates his mother's Georgette Heyer-style aspirations on his behalf. No. Hang onto your hats: Guy Justus Oscar Farage. . .

A man with such a moniker would have been welcomed at the gaming-table by Percy Blakeney, Brigadier Gerard or Sidney Carton.

He would of course be a dandy – and yes, with his handmade shoes and Savile Row suits (worn, of course, as per stereotype, with the obligatory bowler hat and brolly), my dad is remembered as the best-dressed man on the stock exchange at that time. He would be a gambler – and yes, he took exceptional risks, some of which actually came off. He would be a toper.

But of course, Miss Heyer's bucks had extensive lands and holdings. Guy Farage had neither. They disported in a regulated and structured society, he in a curious era where social strata were melting and melding and the universal aspirations of his childhood – military, class-ridden, Edwardian – were being displaced by rude, laid-back, liberal, hippy values. Many of the prettiest girls and fanciest motors seemed suddenly to belong to the smelly-socks brigade, which was outrageous.

Ten when the war ended, twenty-five when the sixties dawned, he saw his heroes age by half a century overnight.

And in truth, his temperament was not that of the successful aristocratic buck who, having sowed wild oats, could settle to the care of his estates. He was sensitive and compulsive. Trained to aspire, he aspired with all his heart and soul, not as a passing diversion. He collected miniatures and antique silver, butterflies and moths – an acceptable foible in a Heyer hero – but he became expert in them and collects them and loves them to this day. His games were not kept compartmentalised – discreet diversions, unrelated to real emotions – but absorbed him.

And, whilst many of his fellow City stockbrokers drank prodigiously but retained control, he plunged into that world and found that he no longer knew which way was up.

Of course, I knew nothing of all this. Even had I been older and more capable of understanding, this was an era in which such things were not discussed, at least not in my family. Damn it, we weren't even allowed to discuss World War I because it had been nasty and embarrassing and several members of both sides of the family had fought in the trenches.

I knew only that my father was generally absent somewhere mysterious and represented better food, fancier presents, exciting tales and convivial company whilst my mother was the kind, dutiful person who performed the altogether duller tasks of dressing and feeding me on a day-to-day basis.

This put-upon soul was an exceptionally glamorous twenty-five years old.

I know now about the crippling loneliness which is perhaps the worst aspect of life with an alcoholic as, night after night, he sank into the arms of his great, obsessive love. He did not lose his charm or his wit when sober – all that comes much later in the alcoholic's decline – so there was always hope that tonight he would be the loving, responsive person whom he showed to the world by day. And every night, as he telephoned with another incredible tale about working late or as he passed out making a noise like riffled cards intermingled with whale-song in his armchair, that hope was dashed again.

I know now about the worries which must have grumbled like thunder throughout her slumbers and sometimes awoken her as searing lightning – the debts piling up, the continuous worry about his personal safety and the children's future should he not return.

I know now about the need – in those days also the bounden duty – to cover up for him. 'Exhausted. . .', '. . .slight cold. . .', '. . .terrible drugs from the doctor. . .', '. . .Well, why shouldn't he let his hair down after all that strain. . .?' '. . .Yes, but he's always been a cavalier type. It's one of the things I love about him. . .'

*

I was barely toddling when my brother Andrew was brought home and took his place in my Silver Cross.

He was totally unworthy of that hallowed position. His thoughts, so far as I could tell, were not interesting at all. He seemed to think exclusively of his physical requirements, which was very tedious. It made one doubt natural selection.

Thanks to that natural self-interest, no doubt, he now earns in a month what I earn in a year and is a generous and amusing companion.

As my father's problems worsened, it fell to my mother to tell us that we could not have this or that treat and to nag us about thrift. This only served to make my father's appearances more wonderful.

Most middle-class families in those days had some sort of staff – a nanny, an au pair or at the least a daily cleaner. We could not afford them, so, as mum tended Andrew, I found myself more and more at liberty.

I wandered, at first around Down House and what is now Downe Bank Nature Reserve, then further afield. I wandered, I chattered away equally to people and animals I met in my wanderings – and I rummaged.

I suppose it came from my collector father, this rummaging thing. By the age of eight, I would not leave the house without a fork and a trowel with which to hunt for treasure. I have many of the treasures thus uncovered to this day: clay pipes, coloured glass bottles, possets, lead soldiers, coins and fragments of pottery and masonry. I still spend many a holiday on battlefields, recreating in my mind the tawdriness, the terrors and the occasional squibs of everyday human magnificence and picking up relics. Even in childhood, I never hankered after hoards of gold. I just wanted to feel the connection between me and the land and the people who had come before me.

Weird child.

Only two things drew me back home: food and cricket.

At the end of 1968, I remember thinking, 'This has been the most important year EVER, and there will never be another like it.' As it happens, I was not so far wrong, but I blush to admit that the Tet offensive and the student unrest in France and Chicago had quite passed me by.

I was aware of the deaths of Martin Luther King and of Bobby Kennedy and (an instant hero by merit of his charm, his fiery delivery and his quickness on his feet. I had never witnessed a top-class lawyer in action before, and brain and tongue working so in synch struck me as no less a marvel than a leisurely cover-drive in response to a John Snow thunderbolt). I was aware of the Soviet invasion of Czechoslovakia. Every child was. We understood about bullies.

Above all, however, this was the year when I became self-aware and England failed to recover the Ashes, even though John Edrich, Geoff Boycott, Colin Cowdrey, Tom Graveney, John Snow, Alan Knott, Derek Underwood et al., plainly the greatest cricketers EVER, all performed prodigies.

1968 was also the year in which I discovered Europe.

We went to Portugal, which was obviously the best country EVER.

My father had decided that what we really needed to make everything better again was a couple of weeks on the Algarve.

I had not flown before – even visited Heathrow before, nor knowingly visited London – so even the airport was an exotic foreign country. There were girls with architecturally unstable cairns of hair and black eyes that looked like Dennis the Menace's dog Gnasher. They wobbled about the terminal on smoked-glass egg-timer legs.

'Lady Madonna' and Gary Puckett's 'Young Girl' were bouncing out of the PA system, Viscounts and Stratocasters whining on the tarmac outside. It was all so. . . *modern*. I ate my first Wimpy hamburger and chips washed down with Coke. I vomited for the first time in – well, really quite near – a public convenience.

This was living.

In Portugal, there were old women dressed all in black, stray dogs on the streets, goats on the hillsides and young women dressed in almost nothing on the beaches.

I was four. Food still had precedence over young women. There was lots of garlic – still then a culture shock inspiring jokes about bad breath and kissing and displays of gastronomic machismo. A steak proved to be fish – fresh tuna, which was alarming but good – and they had vicious trick sausages which pretended to be the bland, soft things provided by Messrs Walls but turned out to be chewy and to bite back.

There were also ingenious sardines which had somehow escaped their tins. The correct masculine thing here was to crunch them, bones, burned skins and all, whilst females and infants grimaced and said ooh.

I already knew my role. Because my dad, my glamorous, beautifully dressed, funny, generous, adventurous dad – well, what else could all those prolonged absences mean save adventure? – was my model, I crunched the skin and bones and said that it was good, and was rewarded for being like him with some strange lemony biscuits which seemed to be called lavatories.

I said that they were good too. In the shiny black-and-white picture, my mother is vaguely smiling amidst all the laughter as she sees another potential ally going over to the other side.

*

I was not only talking by now, I was talking volubly. In fact, I considered a moment not filled with piping Farageisms wasted – unless Brian Johnston or John Arlott were doing the soundtrack, in which case a respectful silence was required.

The retired Indian Army neighbours, therefore, the gardeners at Down House, the village idiot (yes, every village had one back then and provided casual employment for him or her before the state tidied them into its solicitous bins) and every kind old lady foolish enough to ask me how I was, all heard at length my views on 'abroad', on which I was now an expert.

Abroad (except for sausages which were just mean) was good.

I have never changed my views on that. I have spent a huge part of my life – working and leisure – on the mainland of Europe, enjoying the food, the company and the diverse cultures and exploring the churches, the battlefields and the people.

It would be many years before I began to explore Britain with the same enthusiasm and so came to marvel at the astounding diversity of culture, landscape and language contained within our own shores.

And that, of course, has been another major factor in my battle against the growth of the European soviet – the love for Europe's astoundingly rich diversity and the respect for each cultural phenomenon, each custom, rite, dialect, foodstuff and cultural or genetic characteristic which has grown naturally from its very special and very peculiar environment. Each, it seemed to me, deserves to be protected no less than each local species of flora and fauna.

They are already threatened by globalisation of course – my Lisbon airport now boasts a McDonald's and a Pizza Hut and offers Lacoste,

Swatch, Tie Rack and all the other usual brand-names which render it indistinguishable from any other airport in the world. That, until a major upheaval, is an unfortunate and inexorable fact of life.

But as every other man-made union of nations in the world fragments agonisingly back into its constituent parts – the USSR, the states of the Eastern Bloc, Yugoslavia (even Italy's union now hangs in the balance and I am none too sanguine about the United States); as our own home nations (Scotland, Northern Ireland, Wales, Cornwall. . .) assert their autonomy and demand self-determination; as even the smallest regions promote the integrity of their home-grown foodstuffs and identities amidst the homogenising tide – now a strange group of bureaucrats and outdated idealists seek to smear them all into one featureless landscape.

They call it a 'level playing-field'.

Just think of that.

Mountains, hills, moors, pastures, deserts, coastlines, fishing-grounds – all levelled (and marked with 'No Dogs', 'No Smoking' and probably 'No Heavy Petting' signs) so that orderly men in cities can play a silly game according to man-made rules.

I knew even then that I wanted diversity to thrive.

I did not know – I would not have believed – that anyone would try to take it away from me.

*

The arguments were as muffled as no doubt the sex had once been. The grief and anger were manifest only in the stutter of the salt cellar on the tabletop, the occasional pan banged that little bit too hard, the light laugh swallowed that little bit too quickly, the honed knife-edge momentarily ringing beneath the velvet in answer to a child's daft question.

We sensed it, of course, Andrew and I, and like all herd animals exposed to frailty in their leaders, no doubt asked more daft questions than were needed and punished my mother for her inattention by dangerous and downright stupid behaviour.

The word 'divorce' was still terrifying, the concept louche, American, all but unthinkable. Divorce happened to Zsa Zsa Gabor and Burton and Taylor, but not to respectable English boys like us, and yet. . .

No. It was impossible.

But we were gently but suddenly told that dad would no longer live with us. Considering that he had been absent more often than not, this information was strangely distressing.

I assume on reflection that the decision was a mutual one and equally painful for both of them. Mum, however, quite properly played blithe and careless in front of us, so I concluded that, with gross *lèse-majesté* and want of concern for her offspring, she had kicked him out and did not care.

At a time, then, when she most needed support, I was as aloof, distant and disapproving as a strutting little five-year-old can be.

I was the man of the house now, and, like my father, my place was not at the hearth but out there delving in ditches, dung-heaps and dust-heaps for treasure. I was busy.

I was not big enough to be much help, perhaps, but my mum had some preposterous idea that I might at least run errands, lay tables and empty bins, for example, or hold the trug as she gathered fruit or flowers.

She clearly did not understand that I had far, far more important things to do.

*

You see what I mean? Normal family, normal problems, normal silliness, normal failures. Nothing much happened. Everything was normal, almost by law. That's how things were back then before 'it' was all allowed to hang out and each upheaval was promoted to a trauma.

God knows whether such a culture of denial was healthier than today's, in which people post their period pains and hangovers as headline news on Facebook and consider the death of a soap-opera star or a disturbed princess grounds for prolonged mourning and therapy.

In truth, I have much admiration for my parents and their stoicism. I believe that their insistence on seeing only surmountable molehills probably really reduced the mountains in their way, and that their view of themselves and of their emotions as transient and peripheral rather than central to existence was beneficial to them no less than to others.

On the other hand, I bitterly resented the censorship which had kept me in the dark until the sudden announcement of the *fait accompli*. God knows what I thought I might have done had I known, but at least I would have understood more and not taken sides on a facile 'doer' and 'done to' basis as I then did.

Whether in consequence of the censorship to which I was then subjected or no, the whole of my life since then has been ruled by the conviction that there is nothing which should not be discussed and, where possible, tempered in the furnace of debate.

This was about to become an unfashionable principle.

In my early childhood, every playground rang to the dictum 'It's a free country!'

'You can't do that!'

'It's a free country.'

'You'll get in trouble. . .'

'It's a free country.'

The words ring hollow today.

Even children do not believe them any more.

Back then, we chanted them or sullenly mumbled them because they were the distillation in everyday terms of everything which our parents and grandparents had fought to preserve. They were our consolation for the costs of war.

In other cultures, we knew, censorship had been imposed by main force and dissent punished so soon as expressed. This was still the case in the Soviet bloc. We in Britain, however, could say what we would, however contentious or absurd, so the suffering had been worthwhile.

Absurdity, indeed, was the ultimate rebellious celebration of that freedom. *The Goons* were seditious. Fools had as much right to speak, albeit amidst mockery, as Fellows of All Souls. After all, as we were assured, 'they all laughed at Christopher Columbus when he said the world was round' and so on, and 'the fool who persists in his folly becomes wise'.

It was for no one man, no one class and no one age to decide with certainty who was the fool.

Now, however, the talk was of 'D' Notices – edicts prohibiting the publication of news. Soon the earnest anoraks were telling us of opinions, 'You can't say that.'

Soon after that, the anoraks, by dint of their earnestness, were in power.

Laws were made prohibiting historical debate, personal opinion – even scientific findings – if they ran counter to the views of the urban minority or risked causing 'offence'. As ever, the circumscription of liberties was justified in the cause of our own welfare.

Freedom of speech no longer extended – no longer extends – to those deemed fools.

Of course, when the fool can freely speak even his small portion of a mind, he is challenged, derided, corrected. He may even learn.

When he is forbidden to speak, he learns nothing. On the contrary, he harbours and husbands his delusions and rightly resents their suppression. He privily seeks out those who share them. They argue that fear, not reason or justice, motivates the censors. They come to despise the law and all authority. They are marginalised.

Freedom of speech and belief is not subject to approval by a transitory authority. It is absolute or it is nothing.

Such was and remains my conviction.

And oh, it has got me into some delicious trouble.

*

There were times when we were not allowed to see dad. This was further evidence of my mother's iniquity (well, how the hell was I to know? I only knew the laws of cricket and had a child's highly developed sense of fairness). Would James Bond be banned from seeing his own children?

In fact, Guy Farage did at last prove a hero worthy of my mum and even of my illusions. In 1971, at the age of just thirty-six, he knocked the booze and started afresh.

He had, I later discovered, lost his position at the Stock Exchange (No. They do not punch a hole in your bowler and break your brolly *à la Mary Poppins*, but it must have hurt none the less) and attempted to eke out a more meagre and solitary existence by buying and selling antiques.

In 1972, the Queen opened the Stock Exchange Tower on Threadneedle Street. Sponsored by old friends who knew of his ability, a scrubbed and newly sober dad was ushered back onto the trading-floor where he belonged. He is still a stockbroker to this day.

As for mum, she too found her level and attained her deserts. We had all been conned – dad no less than the rest of us – by that glamorous, seductive, rakish, old-fashioned image. After years of having to be the sensible and stoical one at home, never knowing when or if her husband would return and, if he did, in what condition, she found love with a local businessman sober, sensible and sound enough to allow her to be the impulsive, creative, fey partner. She married Richard Tubb in 1971.

In her sixties, she discovered that she had a gift for public speaking and is now much sought after on the halls – town and village, that is – lecturing on local and natural history, Darwin and the like.

The greatest effect of the impending divorce on me (or so I thought at the time; the Freudian *Why's Wally*ers may dissent and may even be right) was that it blighted my first years at school.

I was sent at the age of four and a half to Greenhayes School for Boys on Corkscrew Hill in West Wickham. Today it seems incredible, but there was not one other child in my year who came from what was then known as a 'broken' home.

Divorced people had been admitted to the Royal Enclosure at Ascot since 1955 (though still debarred from the Queen's Lawn), but the Farages were not in that fast set. In my world, divorce was shameful and squalid, and the fact that my parents were indulging in it made me the object of unwanted and intrusive sympathy from adults and of the sort of awed and disapproving curiosity from other boys which would have been afforded to a murderer's or lunatic's child. It was as if the taint might rub off on them.

And I, of course, being argumentative, filled with a sense of injustice and accustomed to being heeded, shot my mouth off. I was as good as – no, better than – they. Divorce was normal – maybe even obligatory – amongst us er. . . top, very clever. . . er. . . top people.

This was no more the right approach for a bright little squit turning up at a traditional English prep-school than was the casual avian equivalent of 'Hi, guys. How's it hanging?' with which dodos greeted humans.

Neither dodos nor I had encountered unpleasantness before. We were both to encounter plenty.

English prep-school education at the time was a daunting gamut whose effectiveness depended in large measure on the teachers. You learned your social skills by trial and often painful error and the bulk of your academic skills by rote. I attended two. They did much the same things very differently. For some things – the learning of dates from the arrival of St Augustine via Magna Carta, Bosworth Field and so on to the outbreak of World War II, the list of British monarchs from 'Willy, Willy, Harry, Stee. . .' down to 'Four Georges, William and Victoria', the inevitable recitations of times-tables, declensions and conjugations, I have had cause always to be grateful. They furnished the matrix in which further knowledge and experience readily lodged.

When it came, however, to recalcitrance or inability – the birthrights of most boys – teaching methods were often less efficient. Board-rubbers flew with an accuracy and slippers were wielded with a vim which testified to the teachers' proficiency on the playing-field rather than in academe.

There was a deal of bellowing which served only further to confuse the confused. Our wrists grew strong through the writing of lines, which did nothing to inhibit their use in more natural – though no more productive – activities as we reached puberty.

Cromwell plainly encouraged his reputation as an occasional whimsical consumer of Irish children. No doubt my teachers too emulated and parodied their Dickensian and Hughesian archetypes. Unfortunately, some of them forgot that it was parody and found that it answered deeper needs and insecurities.

The experience with the teachers at that first school was alarming, but I was resilient and bright. The experience with the other boys initially gave my confidence a serious blow. 'Not before time,' some might say – and yes, I am sure that I must have been a cocky little sod, sorely in need of challenging, but this was an unanswerable challenge born of ignorance and prejudice. It taught me to bob and weave, how to appease (which did not come naturally) and when to attack (which did).

I remained at Greenhayes for just two years. I was then removed because of a rumour about the headmaster's extra-curricular activities. They said with knowing nods that it was 'the usual thing'. It seemed strange to me to be spurned for anything so usual.

I moved to Eden Park, an academy run by the fearsome Mrs Mallick, a war widow who, amongst her other impressive skills, killed wasps with her bare hands. The education here, however, which included meticulous attention to elocution, was really very good and the teachers imaginative and encouraging. I started to breeze.

Talents and passions tend to be governed by the law of supply and demand, so a boy or girl who is persuaded of the rarity of a facility in playing the flute, say, or in chess, in consequence nurtures and develops it and eventually allows that ability to ordain the course of his or her life. I have met many people destined, in the world's terms, to be failures because their parents or teachers have expressed unwarranted awe at a minor talent.

On the other hand, I have known others who never cultivated considerable natural gifts because they were never made aware of their rarity and value.

I found most things easy.

I could see the ball clearly in cricket, knew the classic shots from my television-watching and reading of Sir Don Bradman's book, rehearsed them, thrilled to the experience of playing a well-timed off-drive or square-cut and seeing the bobbing ball cleaving a green path through the dew on its way to the boundary.

I thought, 'OK, that was great. What's next?'

At eight, I took up golf. That, of course, would never be consistently easy. Had I the time, I would still be regularly engaged in that eternal quest for an illusory perfection, but again I could readily strike the ball true and could readily take on board the instructor's advice and adapt my swing as necessary. My mother's new husband was my first such instructor. He played off a handicap of seven and gave me a great deal of patient encouragement.

Academically, I proved quick and slick rather than brilliant – a superior jack and sometimes minor master of all trades – save maths which defied, taunted and tormented me.

I flirted with a hundred subjects and pastimes but fell in love with none of them. None became an overwhelming preoccupation, nor was I concerned to excel at them. They were merely amusing features of the curriculum or of daily life, and I rummaged through them and collected information and skills just as, in the holidays, I rummaged through the dust-heaps and collected stray artefacts.

Gradually, my academic facility, my impertinent blitheness and, above all, my sporting prowess sent me bobbing uncomfortably to the surface. After three or four years of being overawed and hesitant, I became a social animal. I was on top again.

I sat Common Entrance a year early. My maths was still weak, but my mother was told that I made up for this with an exceptional essay entitled 'What I Did Last Weekend'. There was enthralling adventure and action in there – my brother and I had been staying with an aunt and uncle in Hampshire and had waded into mud so deep that we had had to abandon our embedded wellies and leap for the verge in stockinged feet – but the examiners were most impressed by my account of the table which my relatives kept – the fine wines and fabulous food. I may have gone a little overboard with the larks' tongues and sweetmeats from farthest Araby, but I definitely conveyed the fact that they laid on one hell of a spread.

So I squeaked in by merit of my ability with words and love for food, wished Eden Park farewell and entered Dulwich College at the age of ten. My parents were delighted. There were Dulwich connections on both sides of the family.

My premature arrival was also, I think, characteristic. Others with my acumen might, with a little work, have won brilliant scholarships. I did things very easily and proficiently but was in far too much of a hurry to worry about your actual excellence. Had I stayed on for an extra year at West Wickham, I would simply have grown restless. I doubt that I would have improved my Common Entrance results by a single percentage point.

I just mastered something and wanted to get on at once with the next project.

I was in a hurry not because I had any more idea than a rushing river where I was bound, but just because I had exhausted the possibilities of the previous place.

Eddying was tedious, stagnation death. Moving on, babbling and sometimes sparkling, was just what I did.

2

DULWICH

Dulwich, alma mater of Raymond Chandler, P. G. Wodehouse and, most impressively to me, cricketer and commentator Trevor Bailey, was not terrifying at all, but I was properly terrified.

It was not terrifying because it was well-accustomed to tending and nurturing every sort of boy yet invented, and young Farage was perhaps not quite as exceptional as he believed.

I was terrified because it was enormous and teeming with huge and very active boys and young men. There were countless buildings in which to get lost, countless traditions to absorb, countless terms to be learned.

Most public schools are isolated like Ampleforth or, at the least, like Eton or Marlborough, self-contained villages in their own right, attached to towns which need not be visited by pupils from one year's end to the next. Dulwich is almost unique in that, for all its extensive grounds, it is very much a part of south London life.

There are many day-boys, like me, who commute from other parts of London and the Home Counties and so must negotiate the Tube and bus systems and the more or less mean streets on their way to and from school.

There is a very high proportion of pupils on bursaries or scholarships, often from deprived or ethnic minority backgrounds. I hazard that, in the early seventies, there were few state schools outside the major cities with so broad a cross-section of cultural and racial backgrounds represented amongst the pupils.

We were linked by excellence – or, in my case, proficiency. Our homogeneity was elective, not inherited or enforced. I learned from my Ghanaian and Indian friends and they, I suppose and hope, from me. There was no childish assertion of cultural autonomy as in so many minorities today.

Dulwich may have been different in these ways from the majority of English public schools at the time, but it was no less exacting – it has always been in the top 2 per cent academically – and it tolerated fools no more gladly than others. '*Amo, amas, amat*, that's all you lot are good for,' physics master 'Sniff' Hart told us when we were being more than usually obtuse. 'To be at Dulwich College, you have to be in the most intelligent 2 per cent in this nation. Well, if you're the cream of England, God help the milk.'

A Brixton boy who had won a scholarship to Dulwich and who on his death left a large sum of money so that others might have the same opportunities, Hart never foresaw that the milk and the cream might be homogenised by edict.

Dulwich also retained the eccentricity of many English public schools. After my first ever assembly, at which I regarded the gowned, moustachioed masters with the trepidation with which the limping faun no doubt regards carrion crows, I set off for my first class. It happened to be PE.

PE was the province of Regimental Sergeant Major T. E. Day, familiarly known to all as 'Ted'. Ted wore a pencil moustache which looked like two printed ticks upside down and a baggy, polo-necked blue tracksuit in which his puffed-out chest showed to impressive effect. He also carried on a lanyard an impressive bunch of keys with which he threatened to cosh us.

Off-duty, however, he was transformed.

He lived in Dorking. Every morning, he dressed in a dark suit, a spotless white shirt, a regimental tie and highly polished brogues. A bowler hat covered thin hair which gleamed like wet dolphin skin. He marched to the station, flourishing his umbrella like a swagger-stick, boarded a train to Victoria, hailed a taxi out to Dulwich and, once arrived, hung his Dorking personality on two hangers and donned the track suit.

Every evening, he went through the same process in reverse. We conjectured, of course, as to his other correct uniforms – the striped Victorian bathing-suit for the bath, the mess tunic and black tie for bangers and mash in the kitchen, colour-coded French letters for Mrs Ted. . .

On that first day, Ted took us for a run around playing-fields, along bright pavements and back around the muddy fields again. I had never been a runner and was one of the youngest in today's field. Although I started amongst the leaders, I soon dropped back and was forced to study the asterisks of other boys' arses as they drew further and further away. I finished in the last five, with only fat boys for company in humiliation.

We were not only humiliated. We were also scared. Of non-existent frogs.

We had heard what Ted did to slackers. He led them, it was asserted, to a deep, steep, mud-streaked trench close at hand. 'Right!' he would bawl. 'Seeing as you gentlemen 'ave not seen fit to exert yourselves to the uttermost, you will now crawl up and down this 'ere ditch until you 'ave found a frog, whereupon you will be permitted to return to the school and an 'ot and soothing shah. Trouble is, unless I am much mistaken, there ain't no frog!'

At a later PE lesson, when asked to project myself at the vaulting-horse, I grew windy and kept nipping back in the line. In my defence, I was tiny and the horse seemed a veritable Clydesdale. Ted spotted my backsliding and asked me what my problem was. 'I can't do it, sir!' I gulped.

'Do you know who the last person was who said to me, "I can't do it, sir?"' demanded Ted.

'N-no, sir.'

'It was 'Edley Verity,' he said (Hedley Verity was a famously unflappable Yorkshire and England left-arm spinner who had been killed during the Allied invasion of Sicily). '"I can't do it, sir! I can't do it, sir!"'e said. And I said, "You will do it, Verity." And 'e did. And 'e broke 'is leg. Now, off you go!'

This was just the start. Almost all the teachers at Dulwich when I arrived were veterans of World War II, tough, opinionated, cavalier, articulate, outspoken and very good at their jobs. That is, they amused and inspired. They made their lessons memorable.

They knew the value of red herrings and, so far from resisting our attempts to distract them, encouraged ventures into byways because they provided context for highways. Their terms of reference were not restricted to their own subjects. English lessons were enriched by references to French and history, say, and maths enlivened by reference to horseracing odds. They expressed personal opinions, which meant that we came right back at them with our own. Debate was encouraged.

Of course, I subsequently learned that such broadcast teaching is efficient only for us fertile sods, if you see what I mean, and not for stonier soils, but Dulwich, as I say, did not tolerate fools gladly or slow its pace to match that of the sluggard. Like 'Ted' Day, it simply encouraged you to catch up with the leaders and gave you the means to do so.

Occasionally we had supply teachers, fresh from university, who relied upon endless Xeroxed notes. We scorned them, yawned through their classes and did badly in the exams for which they were meant to be preparing us. It was noticeable, however, that those habitually at the bottom of the class fared far better when imagination was curbed.

Today, the pendulum has swung entirely towards the college-trained spoon-feeders to the detriment of those who prefer to hunt and to forage for themselves. Personality and personal experience are no longer considered assets in the teaching profession nor originality in exam candidates. Target-led, production-line education is the norm.

Again, diversity is reduced and the world, for all the levelness of its playing-fields, thereby diminished.

Anyhow, the system suited me down to the ground. I was recently invited back to Dulwich as a guest-speaker and was delighted to encounter a new breed of teacher who corresponded to neither of these models yet possessed the best attributes of both. It is still a very fortunate school.

A week after I arrived there, the Master, David Lloyd, addressed the school. 'There are those,' he warned, 'who do not realise how fortunate they are nor how seldom if ever they will again have such an opportunity to feast on knowledge and experience as during these few short years. They drift through their years at Dulwich and only afterwards realise that they have wasted a great gift. Do not drift through your days at the whim of the breezes. . .'

I remember thinking, 'Dear God! He's right! I've been here ages and have achieved nothing. I've been drifting. Never again. . .'

Only later did I realise that my overwhelming guilt was a little premature, being occasioned by just five days during which I had learned, amongst other things, the geography of the school, the whereabouts of my classrooms, the names of my contemporaries, prefects and teachers and much more.

Nonetheless, I resolved to make up for lost time. I had been busy since I was a toddler. Now I had cause to be busy day in and day out. I was up before daybreak, spent twenty minutes on the train reading Ian Wooldridge and catching up on homework, then walked to school from West Dulwich Station. Aside from lessons, snatched meals, daily games and Corps, I doubt that there was a single school club which I did not visit and from which I did not derive something.

Theatre, art, music, debating, model-railways, numismatics, philately, film and oh so many others briefly commanded my attention. Characteristically, I joined nothing. Only the Combined Cadet Force (CCF), in which I was an ardent member of the army section, cricket and golf, in both of which I grew ever more proficient and soon represented the school, occupied me throughout my school career.

I attended every lecture on politics, philosophy and current affairs given by visiting speakers and was prominent when questions were invited from the floor. Red Ken Livingstone addressed us and was assailed by a fervent Farage. Enoch Powell visited in 1982, a day before his seventieth birthday, and dazzled me for once into awestruck silence. I helped to found the Investment Society where we pooled modest sums and traded, through my father's agency, on the stock market.

I was convinced that all this feverish activity constituted the sort of progress which Mr Lloyd had exhorted. It was to be many years before I realised that I had merely been drifting after all, albeit with random trips in the jolly-boat to a thousand atolls.

Others found islands to their liking and built and farmed on them. I just visited them. I enjoyed the scenery and the natives then set off again. I was still rummaging, sightseeing, acquiring acquaintances, knowledge and mementos.

Others had vocations. I had vacations.

And all the while I was reading with a similar want of discrimination or direction. Some called reading work. I just did it whenever I wasn't in company, and didn't much care what it was, just so long as I was visiting someone else's world or acquiring his or her understanding or skill.

One day, all this would prove phenomenally valuable. I love people. Canvassing and campaigning are not just means to an end but ends in themselves. And I derive no satisfaction from just pressing the flesh and passing on. However briefly, I like to engage with those whom I meet in my wanderings and to learn from each of them. The quickest way to achieve this is through their passions.

Dog-racing? Pheasant-breeding? Led Zeppelin? Christian Science? The Marx Brothers? Flat Earth Societies? Bring 'em on. I have been there. I have shared your enthusiasm.

There was another benefit from this amateurish Grand Tour. The gauche, argumentative infant soon became thoroughly clubbable. I got on well with my seniors and was cultivated by them as a no doubt amusing and provocative clown or precocious performing and yapping terrier.

The yapping – and occasional growling – occurred when anyone tried to deny me knowledge or to put one over on me or others.

Whenever I encountered interventionist authority, I was at the forefront of the dissidents. Whenever I encountered unthinking acceptance of doctrine, whether about the news or history, I challenged it fiercely. Whatever my own views. I would champion any neglected damsel in distress amongst ideas against the dragons of prejudice. I fought fiercely for anarchy, CND doves and warmongering hawks, Christianity, atheists, the pro- and anti-abortion (NOT pro-choice and pro-life) factions, feminism, chauvinism. . .

This was not mere puppy play-fighting. I had discovered in myself a passionate loathing for received opinion. The era of doctrinaire liberalism was dawning, and I despised views acquired free with chart records or designer jeans and sloppily dribbled or spewed forth without fear of challenge. I required terms defined and postures defended against dialectic and invective as ferocious as I could muster.

Above all, perhaps, I despised the conflation of trite aesthetics and ethics. The fact that something was distasteful or offensive did not make it unacceptable. Sex, birth and death – anything other than the status quo – are distasteful and offensive to the burgeoning, alienated middle classes. The easiest way to their approval was to fulminate against these without thought. I could not manage it. I must temper every view in the furnace of argument.

Aesthetics, after all, are the slaves of mere fashion. Sentimental squeamishness has in its time justified racism, the condemnation of homosexuality, the censorship of all good journalism, the sequestration of the old and the disabled, the routine cruelty of the battery farm because no-one wants to acknowledge that meat comes from living creatures, the hanging of the innocent brunette and the sparing of the wide-eyed blonde though guilty as sin, the assumption that the Comanche was a savage and the man in the white hat a hero. . .

Yes, Farage was 'off on one' again, to the glee of my schoolfellows and the embarrassment of my teachers.

Today, such childish amoral 'morality' has primacy. Wring the neck of a free-range bird for the pot or use a four-pound hammer and a razor-sharp knife on your pig and you are a wicked brute. Buy a plastic-wrapped pink thing which lived its entire life eating shit in darkness and your conscience can remain untroubled. The supermarkets demand and receive huge benefits from the EU and a government which presumes to ban the ritualistic bio-control of hunting. Senility and death are nasty, so confining our old people in homes is nice. Go figure.

Of course, the facile assumed that such passion indicated that I was in favour of everything for which I argued. I was pro-hunting, smoking, abortion, the needless splattering of the brains of helmetless motorcyclists and no doubt suicide in my time. In fact, I was at the time agnostic about pretty much everything. I only knew that no-one was going to cheat me by daubing a vexed and important subject with sticky pink frosting and declining to discuss the alternative because it was not considered 'nice'.

Where had this zeal sprung from? I don't know. Maybe it did have its origins in my experience of unjustifiably assumed authority at prep school or in the 'none of your concern' attitude with which my parents had attempted to defend me from knowledge for my own good but which had in fact left me flailing in the dark. Maybe it was the combination of my limitless inquisitiveness and the 'Because we say so' which then greeted all childish enquiries.

I like to think that it was simply a keen critical faculty and a highly developed sense of justice and fair-play. No-one should ever be denied an audience nor any idea denied consideration, whether by law, by jackbooted stormtroopers or by a smug elite. No-one was ever going to tell me what to think.

Others rebelled by growing their hair or shaving it, by flouting conventions of dress or speech, I by declaring the freedoms of fools, especially since there has never yet been a great idea which was not once deemed folly.

I was fourteen when, one lunchtime in the school library, I came upon John Stuart Mill's magnificent statement of those freedoms in *On Liberty*. I felt as if, having lived an entire life amidst aliens, vaguely persuaded that something was amiss, I had at last come upon another of my own kind.

> The only purpose for which power can be rightfully exercised over any member of a civilized community, against his will, is to prevent harm to others. His own good, either physical or moral, is not sufficient warrant. He cannot rightfully be compelled to do or forbear because it will be better for him to do so, because it will make him happier, because, in the opinion of others, to do so would be wise, or even right. . . The only part of the conduct of anyone, for which he is amenable to society, is that which concerns others. In the part which merely concerns himself, his independence is, of right, absolute. Over himself, over his own body and mind, the individual is sovereign.

These instantly became sacred words. They remain sacred. Self-determination – the freedom of all save minors and the mentally incapable to go to hell in their own way, however apparently ill-advised, without interference from others – remains at the heart of my moral beliefs and was to become the core principle of my politics.

For politics were, willy-nilly, to enter my life.

*

Dulwich was a school at which politics were not merely theoretical or academic. They were real and alive all around the school. They seethed and burbled in its corridors. As I have said, many pupils were on bursaries and came from widely diverse backgrounds and nationalities.

In 1981, the economic and social tensions resulting from mass unemployment, shoddy policing and racial intolerance were to explode into riot in Brixton, just down the road. The police used the college as their base throughout the disturbances. Some 279 police and forty-five members of the public were to be injured and over 100 vehicles torched.

For those who read of the riots, it was no doubt a simple matter of law-abiding and lawless, white and black, native and immigrant, right wing and left. We knew better. We had Asians, Afro-Caribbeans and the children of the unemployed amongst us, and there was nothing predictable about their political affiliations or tribal loyalties in Britain.

No matter what your affiliation, what your loyalties, it was hard to be proud or hopeful in late-seventies Britain. Politicians still postured absurdly in the fairy-tale guises of working or upper class and declared themselves left or right wing. They maintained these sad, hackneyed roles at the expense of pragmatism and common sense.

Encouraged by such play-acting, the trades unions threw their weight about – Cnuts, feverishly building, at huge expense to others, futile breakwaters against an irresistible tide. Their equally foolish opponents adopted the wicked, moustachio-twirling baronet role from melodrama. The result was a paralysed nation.

In order that we should keep bearing children, maintaining the law, watching *The X-Factor* and the like, humans tend to forget or to downplay past pain and so, when crippled by opium addiction years later, we accuse the doctor who first prescribed morphine. Whatever the views of Margaret Thatcher today, few can deny that she and her reforms were desperately needed back then.

In 1978, as the Winter of Discontent loomed, Sir Keith Joseph, the initial architect of Thatcher's success, came to Dulwich to address the school.

Joseph's was a lucid intellect, which is probably why he would never seek the highest office. He also had impeccable manners.

His vision was limpid and beautiful. Citing the example of British Leyland, he argued vehemently against public ownership of industry (not least because industry cannot wait around for public and bureaucratic sanction for every move nor be subject to just such vote-hungry posturing as was then petrifying public services). He damned the self-feeding, infinitely proliferating quangos which had sprung up under a Labour government ruling by patronage and appeasement.

He envisaged a Britain – and so Britons – free to deal as they would with one another and with the world. He had that trust in the people which, though sometimes misplaced – and that is the cost – is the *sine qua non* of democracy. Ultimately, the people and the market will regulate themselves.

I had never joined anything in my life, but the following day I joined my local Conservative Party.

It is almost as hard for those who were not there to understand the gloom into which the nation was plunged as it is for us to understand how otherwise intelligent people espoused Marxism or Fascism in the thirties or, indeed, shoehorned Britain into the 'Common Market' in the aftermath of World War II, firmly convinced that they were justified in deceiving the public because they were ensuring world peace.

The echoes today are striking. At the end of the seventies, worldwide unemployment soared. The energy crisis sent oil prices sky high. The price of gold attained a record high point and the US dollar plunged to an all-time low. The troubles and the outrages continued in Northern Ireland and the European Court of Human Rights found Britain guilty of maltreating prisoners there. Public service strikes saw unburied corpses and garbage piling high. Only the rats have it down as a boom year.

I was never to be an ardent Conservative activist. I helped out at a couple of election nights. I attended a few functions. As an individualist and a libertarian, however, I was an enthusiastic supporter of Maggie and a believer in the self-reliant, self-determining society which she envisaged.

One of our history masters at Dulwich declared that, no matter what their guiding principles, the British remain temperamentally divided by one crucial distinction: we are always Cavaliers or Roundheads.

The Roundheads, of course, were characterised in *1066 and All That* as 'right but repulsive' because, having faith in their own rectitude but not in other people, they saw fit to impose their ideas upon everyone else. There were almost as many of these dry as dust dirigistes in the Tory party as in Labour. Maggie, however, was a Cavalier in their midst, and I, an individualist and an anti-authoritarian, was ardently pro-Cavalier.

When, in May 1979, she became Prime Minister, it was as if the pebble-dashed back wall onto which our windows had for years looked out had been demolished to give us glimpses at least of rolling hills and a bright sea.

And we who were young could actually set forth that way. . .

Aside from my passionate defences of just about any defenceless cause, which drew requests for temperance and some exasperation from my seniors and teachers, my greatest transgressions in my undistinguished school career involved alcohol. I suspect that this was due not so much to genes as to another legacy from my father – the association of alcohol with independence and adulthood in defiance of domestic restraints.

I was only in the fourth form when my friends and I pooled our money and brought a half-bottle of Teacher's whisky into school. We met early by the cricket pavilion on a misty September morning. Impatient and heedless of proprieties, we thought it best to dispose of the evidence there and then.

We felt very warm and contented as we heard the headmaster's admonitions at assembly that morning, and we bellowed 'Jerusalem' with unwonted fervour – all save Winterbourne. Winterbourne's internal organs were evidently more fragile and startled than ours. They did not know what to do with such sudden stimulation. To our horror, the boy turned white, clutched at his stomach, winced, lurched and collapsed like a stringless puppet.

They gathered about him, teachers and matrons, and they performed a rapid and accurate diagnosis. One whiff of Winterbourne's breath would have given the game away.

An unnecessary but exhaustive enquiry was launched. It was principally unnecessary because our colour was high, we were shifting from foot to foot and repeatedly swallowing jagged chunks of nothing and our breath too must have stunk of Scotch and Maclean's spearmint. Nonetheless, procedure must be followed, the empty bottle retrieved from behind the big roller, evidence sought and justice seen to be done.

At lunchtime, we found ourselves in the anteroom to the Middle School headmaster's study, overseen by his secretary. We shrugging shoulders every minute or so, tapped our feet and considered the pattern of parquet very seriously.

I was the last to go in.

It was bravado rather than any desire to emulate that lickspittle brat Washington which saw me crossing my legs, soigné like, and explaining, 'Well, sir, it was a beastly cold morning and there was some whisky, so I just thought it would be a good idea – you know – to have a couple of nips to keep out the cold before plunging into the fray.'

'Who supplied the whisky?' demanded Mr D. V. Knight.

'Oh, sir, you know I can't tell you that.'

The other boys were staggered when they heard what I had done. 'You're in the shit,' they told me. 'Why admit it, you berk? We just denied it straight out. He can't prove anything.'

That evening, we were summoned once more to face judgment.

Again for some reason I was the last to be admitted. I sat there in the twilight hearing the swish and the thwack of the cane. My fellows emerged one by one, biting their lower lips and flapping their fingers. I braced myself, adjusted my waistband to no obvious effect and entered the headmaster's room.

Classic stuff – hackneyed but effective for all that: Knight standing there chiaroscuro, the light from his lamp picking out the gilt on the leather desktop, dabbing the tweed lapels, his cheekbones and his brow, streaking the folds of his gown and outlining in silverpoint the cane which should, it seemed to me, be smoking. My arse twitched. My genitals bunched. My stomach whimpered.

'Farage,' he said after a suitable pause. 'I am not entirely sure what I should do with you. You are a bloody fool like the rest of them, but you're the only one to own up. Get out of here and please do your best to develop some sort of a brain. . .'

I obeyed the former order at once. I have falteringly attempted to obey the latter.

Certainly I have never had cause to question the wisdom acquired that day. True power is arbitrary, and, when you're firmly and unequivocally hooked, the best policy is to laugh and leap into the frying pan. Wriggling is tiring, futile, inelegant and irritating.

I am still vaguely ashamed of my next alcohol-related transgression.

It was CCF field day, and Simon Pipkin and I were appointed to the very important role of emergency support services. This meant that, whilst the rest of the army section yomped around on the South Downs, attempting to find their way back to base by means of compasses, a map, trigonometry, the growth of lichen and trails of breadcrumbs or something, we were meant to occupy a position outside a red phone-box in anticipation of calls informing us that they had fallen down crevasses, been savaged by dormice or whatever.

In our defence, it was a sweltering hot day, so the dangers of hypothermia, avalanche and ice-related injuries were small. The dangers of sunstroke were real, but we felt that we were exposed to them as much as, if not more than, our harder-working fellows. There was, too, no entertainment beyond watching sheep up there in that desolate spot. A thoughtful eighteenth-century person had, however, taken mercy on the traveller and built a pub up there.

We manned our position gallantly until roughly eleven o'clock in the morning. At that point two things happened almost simultaneously. The pub's front door rattled and swung inward and we, who had studied the subject in our First Aid manuals, detected unquestionable symptoms of sunstroke in ourselves. There was the rasping throat, for example. We agreed that we both had that. The delirium seemed to be kicking in early too. We were both hallucinating, mostly about beer, and I said that Pipkin was gibbering. He was of the opinion that it was I.

We were vital components of the orienteering exercise. It would have been totally irresponsible of us to have risked collapse and death by the roadside. We could always return to the phone-box from time to time. If anyone were dying, they would just keep trying, wouldn't they. . .?

So we swaggered into the pub in our battledress, ordered what we felt to be the certain cure and, for want of stretchers or truckle beds, sprawled on a banquette.

There was, I believe, a period of euphoria, but we knew this to be a common feature of delirium. We ignored it.

By two thirty, our worst fears were realised. We were both drooling and feeling queasy. Our faces were very red, our eyes blurry. We adjourned to the beer garden. We kept taking the medicine.

By five thirty, when the school coach came to pick us up, it was clear that we had made the right decision, because all the other boys, though dust-coated and complaining of sprains and bruises, were evidently hale and well, whilst Pipkin and I were falling about and vomiting copiously.

School coaches did not run to loos in those days (and that, on reflection, is a very odd sentence). We vomited principally, therefore, on the upholstery, our kit and our clothes. Just occasionally and for variety, we vomited on other people's kit and clothes.

Major Tony Salter plainly had no medical knowledge whatever. Our explanations did not impress him. He was crimson with anger. He was about to send us to the headmaster, which would have resulted in suspension or even expulsion, but I remembered the lesson learned two years ago.

'Oh, hell. I'm sorry, sir,' I said. 'But it was infernally boring up there, and having the pub right next door. . . Well, it was too much. We blundered badly. I'm sorry.'

It did the trick. Salter's lips twisted for a while like caterpillars racing. He frowned very sternly. His medal-ribbons continued to rise and fall, but their motion seemed to slow. Then I glimpsed the ghost of a smile at the corner of his lips. 'Farage, Pipkin, you are loathsome and lowly specimens of a very low life-form. . .'

'Yes, sir.'

'And you have let the side down not only badly but, which is worse, conspicuously badly.'

'Yes, sir. Sorry, sir.'

'Nonetheless, I grant that the temptation placed in your way was considerable and it was improvident and discourteous of us not to have foreseen it. Whilst I MIGHT. . .' – he raised his voice above another snakepit susurration of 'sorry, sir's – 'Whilst I might have excused a visit, albeit illegal, to the pub, the inability to hold your drink and your consequent releasing of it all over our vehicle and kit is inexcusable. Do I make myself clear?'

'Yes, sir. Sorry, sir.'

'Drink providently, boys, and do not run before you can walk, or, in your case, stagger before you can march.'

Our punishment, fittingly enough, I suppose, consisted in a great deal of mind-numbing square-bashing after school.

I seriously considered the army as a career after that. I even went for an interview with a view to taking a short-service commission. Although I was eager to leave school, which seemed to me to have given me all that it could, I suppose that what I really wanted was merely to continue it in another form – the unchallenging camaraderie, the duties performed with undeserved ease, the travel, the jaunty social life. I was directionless. I merely wanted amusement and challenges to overcome.

Two things dissuaded me, thank God, from entering a peacetime army.

One was my total inability to obey orders without question.

The other was that the City, that Emerald City which had inspired my dreams since infancy, was now booming and glittering as never before.

And it wanted me.

*

I was of course replicating my father's initial disastrous career, though, thumb in bum, mind in neutral, like most adolescent boys, this did not cross my mind.

The City had always been for me a fairy-tale playground, an Oz in which vast sums were won and lost and somewhat smaller but in scale equally impressive sums were spent on good times. The City was anything but domestic; it was, by definition, anything but suburban. It was the heart of things, and the richest, best oxygenated blood bubbled there.

Just as, in early childhood, I had rejected the comforts of the hearth to go acquisitively rummaging about the countryside, so the army and the City represented repudiations of a mother's concerns, of the siren songs of women in general. (Playful girls were somehow not included in this category. I could respond to their song, moor overnight and weigh anchor the next morning.)

And my mother duly played her part. She made my replication of my dad's career a certainty by expressing her concern. She wanted me to stay on at school and go to university, acquire specific expertise in specific subjects, develop sensitivity, become someone. She thought that I would make a good barrister, which, as she pointed out, was a service, still earned lots of money and left the door open should I wish to change direction and go, for example, into politics.

I laughed.

I was not concerned to perform a service. I had no desire to enter politics. I did not want to take instructions from anyone. I did not see the future as a small steam train on which I might play a useful part as stoker or steward. It was a giant, thundering, brightly lit express and it was pulling away from the station right now. Maggie was taking care of the driving. All I had to do was jump on and open the champagne.

It would bear me to — well, where? I did not really consider. Boxes at Royal Ascot came into it, and long days at Lord's catching glimpses through mint-leaves and ice of Viv Richards, smiting like the Old Testament God.

The idea of spending three years at university, 'faffing around' as I called it, whilst the train raced on was quite ridiculous.

A similar argument weighed against that short-service commission. By the time that I emerged from army or university, my contemporaries would be driving Porsches and would be on Roederer Cristal drip-feeds. I knew the rate of attrition in the City. I expected to be burned out by the time I was thirty — burned out, but very, very rich.

So, as I polished off my O-levels with accustomed ease, I was nipping up to town to eye up the terrain. My father and my seniors at school who had gone on before welcomed me. They took me to Gows in Old Broad Street where I ate dozens of oysters, drank champagne cocktails and relaxed amidst brays, barks, guffaws and good yarns.

I paid visits to the Stock Exchange, Lloyds, discount houses, looking for my niche. I knew just one thing. I did not want to be known as 'someone's boy', and my father was a well-known character on the Exchange. . .

The solution was found, as so many solutions are, on the golf course and on the doorstep.

West Kent Golf Club undulates between our house and Downe village. I was playing off a handicap of four at the time, and one snowy afternoon shortly before Christmas I found myself pitted against Bob McPhie. I barely knew him. I had no idea what he did beyond the usual 'something in the City'. He was just 'something in the City' and a familiar face on the golf course. As we played, I outlined my ambitions to him on clouds of vapour.

We stomped back into the clubhouse rubbing our hands and shedding balls of ice. We ordered pints of Shepherd Neame, knocked back the first round in a single draught, then settled down in armchairs to thaw out and drink at leisure.

'Tell you what,' said Bob (though at this stage I still called him 'sir' like any well brought up boy), 'I happen to be managing director of a little concern called Maclaine Watson on the London Metal Exchange. I think it might suit you. Why don't you come up and take a look in a couple of weeks?'

I went home. I researched the Metal Exchange. I grew more and more excited. Christmas seemed interminable. I was grumpy and impatient. I really could not see why goodwill to all men, glockenspiels and filthy mulled wine could not be put in cold storage until my important business was done.

They say in the country that, if snow remains beneath the hedgerows, more will come to pick it up. The snow melted, but lacy tatters remained beneath the hawthorn and holly bushes well into January. I discounted the old country wisdom.

The evening before I was to head up to London, I polished my black brogues. I starched and pressed my sharpest shirt. I hung a dark suit and a neutral silk tie on the door. I set my alarm. I have never slept much, but the prospect of tomorrow's adventure meant that I grabbed just four restless hours before I got up. Perhaps I could catch an early train and stroll around the City a bit before keeping my appointment.

The air tasted of batteries. I groaned. I looked out on blackness, but through the swirling strobe lighting of a blizzard.

The garden was already fat with snow. I switched on the radio. '. . .blizzard. . . only essential journeys. . .' said the man cheerily. 'The following roads are impassable. . . cars reported stuck overnight. . . and here's the Pretenders' latest, "Brass. . ."'

I dressed hurriedly. I had difficulty with the cufflinks because my hands were shaking so much. I went downstairs and opened the front door. Snow swirled in and pattered on the flags. I looked out at the lane.

There was no lane. Drifts had turned a sunken lane into a sporadically broken ramp to the sagging, surprise-by-death-mid-dribble hawthorns and willows.

It all depends on your point of view, I suppose. We now see the young Farage at his most determined or, as it now seems to me, his most demented.

It had surely been possible to call Bob McPhie, explain the situation of which no doubt he was already well aware, and postpone my visit until another day.

Not I.

I pulled on a tweed cap and a Barbour. I placed my shoes in a carrier-bag.

And I walked six miles in the darkness to Orpington station.

No. That is a euphemism. I staggered, plunged and slithered six miles to Orpington station. I ingested a great deal of snow en route. I spat out still more. My trousers and socks became drenched, my eyelashes became beaded, but I made it to my train in time.

And oh, it was worth it.

The Metal Exchange is the last remaining market to retain Open Outcry Trading – deals shouted out on the floor. I loved the hubbub, the urgency, the sudden ripples that spread through the crowd in response to tremors thousands of miles away. It was the purest theatre, filled at once with high drama and with comedy.

I was shown around the offices. They were old-fashioned, collegiate, informal and friendly. I must have been glassy-eyed when at last I sat down opposite Bob at the Paris Grill on London Wall. He pointed out to me the neckties which decorate the walls, all cut from customers by waiters on special occasions. We ordered smoked salmon and chargrilled fillet steak béarnaise with chips and two bottles of Beaune. I was in the leafy suburbs of heaven, following the signs to the City Centre.

'Well, old chap,' said Bob as we reverted to port. 'If, after you leave school, you should want a job, there'll be one waiting for you at Maclaine Watson.'

Suddenly, I was full of peace, merriness and goodwill to men. My future was assured. All my Christmases had come at once.

*

I was sixteen then. I considered that I had outgrown school.

I sat my A-levels and acquired undistinguished grades in history, geography and economics.

I was unconcerned. I knew where I was going.

One or two teachers deserved better reward for their faith in me. In particular there was my inspiring history teacher, David Gregory, who awoke a passion for history which has remained with me to this day, and my headmaster – 'The Master', as he was called – David Emms, who, to the astonishment of my peers and the outrage of many in the staff common-room who particularly deplored my spirited defence of Enoch Powell, made me a prefect in that last year, .

In my leaving report, David Emms wrote: 'Life at the school will not be the same without him,' which could be read as a tactful statement of the obvious but which I hoped and believed to be approving and just mildly regretful at my departure. It was. I spoke to him at the Founder's Day lunch in 2009. He told me that he had voted for me in the European election. I felt really rather proud at that.

For now, I just wanted to get cracking. Almost all my contemporaries were going on to university. Many were taking a year off in which to travel and learn languages. I could not believe that they could be so profligate with their youth.

I nearly attained glory for the school through golf. I was captain of the school team. Throughout a busy fixture-list in the Lent and summer terms, we did well. One of the principal events was the national schools' championship, sponsored by Aer Lingus. We won our way through to the regional finals at Foxhills in Surrey and had good reason to expect that we would acquit ourselves well here too.

The course was waterlogged. A stiff, rain-speckled gale buffeted us from every direction. We waited in hope that the weather would ease. If anything, it got worse.

At last, it was resolved that the event would be reduced to a nine-hole strokeplay contest. The brief day was drawing to a close as I came off the eighth green to be informed by Giles Jackson, the master in charge, that I only needed a par four on the last hole to take what was almost certainly an unassailable lead.

I drove. The contact was sweet. The ball soared and sped towards the green. Then the wind woofed and pounced. The ball veered to the right. If it had done as it was told, it would have ended up on a cosy green carpet. As it was, its disobedient behaviour left it in deep, drenched scrub, nestling up against a steeply sloping shard of flint.

I was going to say that 'it all went downhill from there on'. I wish it had. I might have putted it for the same score or even less. As it was, I took a sorry double-bogey six and finished in joint fourth overall. Traditionally, the winner of the event received a golf scholarship at Arizona College.

I might never have made it as a top-flight golfer, but it would have been an adventure. I suspect that I would have accepted. I suspect that I would have enjoyed the States. It is no consolation, I am sure, but when the EU Commissioners curse the name of Farage and wonder how I ever came to be the bane of their otherwise cushy lives, they can blame it all on the English weather and a Surrey flint.

3

LUCID BUT AGGRESSIVE

On 1 September 1982, I strode into Maclaine Watson, shed my suit jacket and deposited a gold pen, a lighter and two packets of Rothmans on my desk.

'Hmm,' said a nearby colleague approvingly. 'Good start!'

We worked beneath a strand of tobacco smoke. Our conversations were punctuated with the 'pft' sound as cigarettes were pulled from our lips. We worked hard, but we did not consider it work any more than a Tudor monarch arose from bed and groaned, 'Oh, no! Not hunting again!'

Because that was what it was – hunting, with all the speed and risk and demands upon your intuition and nerve which the word implies.

And, like Tudor hunters, having amassed a goodly quarry, we adjourned to the tavern. It was a bit like hunting too because there were days when, barring freak events, there would be no scent and all the world's traders would have gone to ground. On such afternoons, our office – no, the entire Exchange – was like the *Mary Celeste* and there was a constant surging, heaving swell in the pubs, wine-bars and restaurants.

On good scenting days, however, the floor was in full raucous cry and we, the huntsmen, hollered into our telephones over and over and whooped on the rare occasions that we laid them down. The coverts were busting with game, and when, late at night, we finally turned homeward, a fine bag of small fortunes was hanging in the larder.

To my no doubt puerile, materialistic mind, this was very heaven, though the serpent had already entered the garden (I sometimes wonder if this is why creationists cling so tenaciously to their improbable doctrine as literal fact rather than as beautiful myth, because it casts men and women as children trespassing against a stern but kindly parent rather than as autonomous adults entitled to take risks and accept consequences).

Maclaine Watson was a very old-fashioned, liberal, English outfit. It had lately, however, become a wholly owned subsidiary of Wall Street's Drexel Burnham Lambert, whose 'No guts, no glory' motto was to inspire the barely fictional character Gordon Gekko in *Wall Street* and was to lead the company to sensational bankruptcy in 1990. We had a free rein for now, but the Americans were already in situ and plainly regarded our easy-going but efficient style with misgiving.

I started out as a backroom boy and spent five months on warrants at an income of £4,000 per annum. Although I memorably lost a silver warrant worth £90,000, which was never found despite a thorough ransacking of the building, I did well and was soon moved to the front office where I could schmooze clients, find business and, best of all, authorise trades.

At the age of eighteen, I was handling millions and drinking more or less continuously.

Of course, everyone was drinking more or less continuously. The City then was staffed largely by Essex wide-boys whose ambitions were measured in sports cars, and public-school dropouts, either too thick or too sharp and bloody-minded, like me, to stay on the slow but steady travelator to respectability. I did not quite belong in either category. I got on well with both.

I mistrust nostalgia. Not long ago, I was on a beach in north Cornwall on a sunny but sporadically cloudy day when a prone sunbather murmured sleepily, 'I can remember the days when a patch of blue like that would have lasted an hour and more. . .'

There was a mumble of agreement. I too knew exactly what he meant. Then a tiny giggle bubbled up. It took a while before the absurdity of the statement percolated through the sun-drenched brain-cells, and then even the speaker had to acknowledge that skies had probably not gone downhill since the good old days.

Nonetheless, I, in common with all old City hands, am nostalgic for those days when we floated on a smoky golden haze of champagne vapour and anyone could affix a brass plate to his front door declaring that he was a trader in futures.

Competent cavaliers thrived, just as competent cavaliers fare well as officers in wartime and with imaginative and discursive teachers, just as the Vincent Mulchrones – well, the one and only Vincent Mulchrone, but he had his fellows if not his peers – caused sober hacks in Fleet Street to essay alcoholism just in case it was the secret. It was an era of 'wrong but wromantic' excellent amateurs, where today we are ruled by 'right but repulsive' college-spawned clones.

The age of mediocracy was dawning.

I acknowledge, however, that the rate of attrition was high. Many friends from that era who existed only to earn now exist only in urns, having burned up twice. Their livers rotted, their flash cars crashed or they sought more enduring oblivion, this time without hangover.

That's OK. They chose to enter the Darwinian gladiatorial arena. They knew the potential costs and would have rejected protection had it been offered. There were others, however, at whom the right but repulsive mediocrats will with some justice point – the parents, widows, children and the aspirants who copied them though plainly unfit – who were caught in the flames as they crashed and burned, but then the same is true of service personnel and steeplechase riders. Again, freedom is not negotiable.

We all drank far, far too much according to the advice of those who claim to know best. Some few of us (it has been roughly 10 per cent of the population ever since that notable lush Noah) had that gene which makes one drink too many and a thousand not enough. The worst of it is that we never know until it is too late whether we are of that cursed number.

I was far luckier than I deserved. Given my father's experience, I should have been alert to the danger of alcoholism. It never crossed my mind. At eighteen, I was drinking throughout the day and night, but youth and adrenalin sustained me.

What was my motivation at that time?

I have many friends whose dreams are filled with wicked women. Their ambitions, when distilled, consist very largely of non-specific sybaritism. These took holidays in the Maldives, dreamed of yellow Lamborghinis and owned gadgets that did nothing much but did it ever so cleverly.

I have friends with clear visions from childhood of the rectory with five acres, a few children, an Aga and a couple of salmon-pools. These took Scottish fishing lodges and spent their weekends with tinkly girls in broderie anglaise petticoats.

I fancied a bit of all these. I liked girls – the wicked and the tinkly variety – but as extra-curricular diversions. I liked country sports. I enjoyed luxuries, but only briefly. The notion of a day's, let alone a week's, sybaritism was horrific. Somewhere at the back of my mind was the awareness that one day I would want children and a country house, and that a woman would presumably be necessary for both, but my idea of fun was trading, drinking and trading some more. I wanted life to be one long boys' club jamboree with occasional bouts of conkers on the Exchange.

I was, in short, a puerile sexist in a puerile sexist world.

Oh, I was never a raucous, discourteous 'Hooray Henry'. I was too well brought up and perhaps marginally too bright and too sensitive for that. I was as clubbable as ever, and aware of others' feelings. I simply was not particularly interested in sensual pleasure or in the emotional nakedness necessary for intense personal communication. I preferred the city (or dress or morning) suit which symbolised and assured my cherished independence.

I discovered girls, of course, but even then I was principally concerned only to check that the experience was as pleasant and jolly as anticipated, then to get on with more important things. So I added girls to the list of pleasures (somewhere below trading and convivial drinking and way above, say, television or sleep) to be attended to whenever there was a moment spare. There would be time enough for such weakness when I was ill or old.

Some might accuse me of being scared. I, though no doubt less qualified than some, humbly suggest that I was bloody terrified.

I knew nothing of women (it should be remembered that they were only just beginning to enter the City. Nowadays, if I am scared, it is for far more realistic reasons) and I dreaded domesticity, which seemed to me slow death.

Maybe some will suggest that my subconscious retained the infantile conviction that my father had been harshly judged simply for being a good and gallant chap, and that I was not going to go the same way. Again, some seem to have plausible intuitions, though the thought certainly never then crossed my conscious mind.

All I knew was that, whilst conquests and associations with women were widely thought to confer the laurels of virility, they seemed to me to unman good men. That Antony had seemed like a thoroughly good sort – a toper and a bull-trader – until he started getting all unguent with Cleopatra, and several of my seniors similarly became cautious and sober so soon as they fell into the trap.

I had worlds to conquer. I considered not one of them well lost for a woman.

It was, then, some will persist, my own susceptibility rather than females per se which scared me. . .

I wish that 'some' would shut up.

Who invited them anyhow?

*

By 1985, I was earning £20,000 a year and still living – or, at least sleeping for an hour or two a day – at the family home.

In October of that year, the International Tin Agreement, a unique worldwide commodity pact which, since 1956, had sought to stabilise the supply of and the demand for tin, exhausted its credit and collapsed. Tin was delisted. The London Metal Exchange faced massive lawsuits from creditors. We brokers were owed hundreds of millions. The phones stopped ringing. There was nothing for us to do.

If I believed that a divinity given to vulgar and profligate drama was shaping my ends, I suppose I should have considered that to be the first indication that not only I but the games to which I had thus far dedicated my adult life were vulnerable and mortal.

If warning it was, I ignored it. I was a high flier. Another meeting on the golf course had opened up the prospect of a job at Rouse, who had a far broader portfolio and so offered me a greater understanding of financial markets. I was to accept the offer the following year at an increased salary with a very attractive bonus-scheme.

On 25 November, I enjoyed a very good, very hot curry over a prolonged lunch. In the evening, I engaged in a ferocious pub argument about the Anglo-Irish agreement, sustained, as was only decorous and fair, by English ale and Irish whiskey.

I was of the opinion that Thatcher and Co. had betrayed the Unionists. With what passes for maturity, I acknowledge that the declaration of an end to a blood feud is the prerogative of a truly strong ruler and is always painful, but it still hurts to consider the vile murderers who walked free and crowing from gaol after mere months. I believe that the new generation of trigger-happy pseudo-Republican punks believe themselves validated by that pact.

Right or wrong, I was, as ever, fighting my corner with particular vigour and enjoyment that night. It was an inconclusive but enjoyable bout, and I then decided that perhaps I should honour my mum's house with my presence for a few hours.

I emerged at Orpington station still rehearsing arguments in my head. I remember lighting a cigarette and stepping from the station into darkness. I remember the soft veils of rain dragged along the street, the squirming pools of light beneath the lamps. There was speckled breeze in my hair and on my cheek. The pavement rustled beneath my feet as though wrapped in clingfilm.

I swaggered down to the pelican crossing. I grasped the lamp's stalk and swung myself into the street.

I remember nothing more.

Others do. The couple sheltering in the shop doorway, the man walking his bull-terrier down the opposite pavement, the driver of the Volkswagen Beetle – they remember the tritone whine of brakes, the thud, a shout from somewhere. They looked up or span around.

And they saw a man fly.

I am told that I – or a body which had lately been mine but was by now unoccupied – did it beautifully. There was, they say, no ungainly flapping or flailing. I appeared composed, almost relaxed. Had style judges been there with score-cards, I would have been awarded an 8 or even (so the girl of the couple says, but maybe she's just being nice) a 9. I vaulted that VW fully extended, without touching the bonnet or the roof. The parabola of my flight perfectly matched the famous curve of the car.

It was the landing which undid all that good work. Even in the high-risk, flashy, modern school, landing directly on the head is not considered stylish. It causes a certain. . . crumpling. The smooth line which I had thus far described became a sort of fractured swastika, an angular scribble on the wet pavement.

At the time, style no longer mattered much to me.

INTERLUDE

They gathered a week later in the thirteenth-century church of St Mary the Virgin in Downe.

Of the fifty or so mourners who turned up to pay their respects, only three – my parents and a tall, blonde model called Vanessa whom I had met in a wine-bar the previous week – did not have hip-flasks in their pockets. Vanessa did not have a hip-flask in her fox-fur jacket because you don't put champagne in hip-flasks and all those burly men in dark blue cashmere were just dying to give her a drink.

They winked at one another in the porch, murmured things like 'If it had been a Testarossa, OK. . .' and 'Dark suit, dark coat, bit pissed. Shouldn't think the poor bugger behind the wheel saw a thing', 'Who's the foxy bint with, then?', 'Heigh-ho. 'Nother one bites the dust. . . Way it goes. . .'

They then took up the approved position in the pews – hands clasped before their groins, faces downturned – and heard a eulogy by a vicar who had mugged up on his subject the previous night.

'Nigel was so full of promise and energy. At twenty-one, he was about to take up a new job which paid more than the entire tower restoration

fund, which is ridic. . . splendid. Just think of that. Who knows what heights he might have attained had he lived? Millions surely awaited him, fast cars, big houses, marriage, maybe children. . .

   'But it was not to be. A very seriously slow car was to snuff out the bright, feverishly flickering light which was Nigel Farage. I am sure that he would have been glad to think that he was heading home when the accident happened, back to the family house which he so seldom found time to visit save for three or four hours' kip, but near which he will now sleep in unwonted peace and in perpetuity.

   'What can we say about this remarkable young man? Everyone liked him. At the pub, the golf-club and at least one church fête which he attended, he talked to everyone with such ease and understanding of their interests. Miss Maitland recalls his enthusiasm for, and understanding of, her bantams. Colonel Brereton tells me that he never knew a man so young yet so knowledgeable about fishing. The professional at the golf-club assures me that Nigel might have been truly exceptional had he devoted himself to the game. . .'

   And so they laid this paragon in the graveyard and returned to the City to get very drunk (and, in at least one instance, also laid) in my memory, and the stone subsequently raised above my head read 'NIGEL FARAGE, 1964–1985'.

   And then, since the stonemason was absently taking dictation, 'ER. . .'

OK. I do not ask you to believe that I awoke, Scrooge-like, from a reverie of my own death and was instantly transformed.

I wasn't dead (there is another sentence which I seldom have cause to write), in part thanks to Adolf Hitler's pet designers and their invention of the motorised computer mouse *avant la lettre*. A vertical radiator grille would surely have killed me.

I wasn't even strictly unconscious for long. My notes, of which I caught a glimpse in hospital, declare me to have been 'lucid but aggressive' as the ambulance decanted me from a very wet impromptu nativity scene on the pavement into A&E at Bromley General. My doctor on the night tells me that, when first he approached me to perform an examination, I told him, 'Oh. Right. Yes. Listen, mate. Get me a cab, will you? I've had quite enough of this, thanks,' before passing out again.

They could not operate on me until my blood alcohol levels had declined, so they sedated me, for which, I think, I have cause to be grateful because I was a right mess. Then, I assume, came the general anaesthetic and the hours under the knife.

I was very surprised when at last I awoke. I did not really do hangovers at that age, but if this was what they were like, temperance suddenly seemed alluring.

First there was that sensation of something bound very tight about my temples. Then there were the discords inside my skull. For some reason, you never get a tuned-up orchestra playing a lush, harmonious, Brahms symphony-type chord. You always get the oboes and clarinets with frayed reeds tuning up whilst an obsessive timpanist pounds away. I was getting the Portsmouth Symphony orchestra let loose in the Radiophonics Workshop.

The certainty that you are dying because of acute but obscure pains and wriggling things in chest and bowels? Check. And the dead leg because you've been lying on it for too long? Check.

I was mildly surprised that the leg was in that position, though.

Perhaps above all, my mouth was causing me distress. This was in part, I was to discover, because all my teeth had been knocked loose. It was also in part because I had had a very hot curry and a great deal of drink last night and nil by mouth thereafter, leaving my mouth feeling like Queen Nefertiti's gusset.

I opened my eyes. Only one opened. The other appeared to be buried beneath a lot of upholstery which had not been there before.

The monocular view explained a certain amount, which was nice.

The explanation wasn't.

*

No, the reason for the daft little fantasy section above is simply that that was what was playing in my head in quiet moments over the next three months, during which I was occasionally visited, occasionally fed semolina (for a long time the only solid food permitted to pass my lips) and spent much of the time fretting.

First I fretted because they thought that I would lose my left leg which was pretty much pulverised to north and to south. If they saved it, they said, I might just be able to walk – well, OK, hobble – short distances, but even that would take a long time.

I fretted because I was not at work. Billions were being made, and not by me.

I fretted because I could neither laugh nor cry because of the broken ribs, nor turn over and curl up in a foetal position because my left leg was raised high above me. My recovery position was that of a chorus girl in Pompeii when the lava hit.

I fretted because of tinnitus which continued after the orchestra had left and continues to this day. Though some may dissent, the doctors assure me that my graceless landing on the kerb had caused no enduring brain-damage once the cuts were healed and the swelling went down. The echoes, however, persist. Dwarves mine for gold in there, and occasionally whistle happy diatonic tunes. . .

Above all, I fretted because of the Halford Hewitt.

It is given to few fully to understand the intensity of that fretting. Only sixty-four schools play in the matchplay foursomes tournament for the Halford Hewitt Cup, which takes place at the Royal Cinque Ports and Royal St George's (known to all simply as 'Deal' and 'Sandwich') every April. Others wait poignantly outside, their privileged noses pressed against the pane, yearning in vain for admission.

As for us whose schools are eligible, we spend the winters doing sit-ups and playing solo surreptitious rounds of golf in the freezing dusks or dawns in hope of the call from our Captains. If that call does not come, we conclude that our active lives are done, don slippers and lay in supplies of Viagra and cadet Country Cousins.

I was hoping to play for Dulwich this year. Instead, I was in traction mumbling on semolina. I resented this.

The funeral scene was just light relief from all this fretting. At first I blamed all the mourners (and particularly Vanessa) for being so insincere.

Slowly, however, the ridiculous notion percolated through to me that perhaps I was missing something, that I might have given a little more of myself to my endeavours to date, that perhaps I wanted more from life before the next car hit me.

It was only a thought, but it was a new one on me. . .

It was a good thing that I had generous friends with a better line in medicines than the doctors. They saw no reason to bring mere grapes, skins, pips, stalks and all, when they could bring them already stripped down and distilled to their very essences. They brought them in quantity. I was soon providing medicinal cheer to the other poor sods in my ward, more hopeful than confident that I was helping them rather than killing them but, as ever, allowing them to make that decision for themselves.

What? I am meant to have renounced my wicked ways and become an ascetic saint overnight because of a mere prang?

Look, the people who wrote the Bible didn't concern themselves much with psychological verisimilitude. Papyrus was expensive and time short, what with the Second Coming and Armageddon expected just as soon as they'd swept the wrong sort of sand off the rails. It was easier for them to stick to the headlines.

A lot of miracles might not have been quite so miraculous if we'd had detail. The evangelists might have gone into other recorded cases of catatonia, novel resuscitation techniques, Lazarus's hangover, the therapy which he had to undergo and what his wife and the life-insurance companies had to say about it all. But no. Lazarus dead, Lazarus alive. That's all we get. Miracle.

So we know that Saul (a European Commissioner if ever there was one) ran into some pretty impressive *son et lumière* stuff on his way to Damascus and subsequently decided that maybe these Christians were on to something, but the notion that he at once gave up all his former convictions, ambitions and friends is just downright silly.

At a guess, he drank rather more than usual, told himself that he must have eaten some dodgy matzos, found that the fun had gone out of a good stoning, became thoroughly grouchy and had to fake his laughter when they told the one about the praetor, the Philistine actress and the

X-shaped cross, discussed the whole business with his mistress and only over months or years became a pain in the arse within the Christian camp rather than without.

Augustine's 'Make me good but not yet' is far closer to the mark, to judge by my own experience and all the recovering alcoholics, junkies and reformed rogues whom I have encountered. We all live by our faiths, however mundane, and if Saul abandoned his and his fellows for the sake of a few fireworks (like formerly Eurosceptic politicians within days of winning power), he was a berk. Had I been the ghost of a Christian put to the sword by him, I would have been affronted to have died for convictions so paltry.

So the novel experience of being tenderised by a car may have been instructive and thought-provoking for me, but it did not cause me to renounce my loves and loyalties to date.

It caused me immediately, however, to do two things which thousands of wounded soldiers have done in reality and in fiction. First, I fell in love with a warm smile, competent, jolly affection and Nature's guarantee of a future: my nurse.

Well, Carol Vorderman (*Countdown* was the daily boon amidst the drabness) and my nurse. . .

Carol was not available, so my nurse bore the brunt.

I don't want to imply that Clare Hayes was merely a symbol, nor that I fell for her solely because her warmth and vivacity contrasted with the monochrome routine of hospital life. She was a great girl who was to make me happy for several years. At twenty-one, however, immature and only barely aware of prospects beyond those on my very near horizons, I was unfit for marriage and would surely never have considered it had it not been for my brush with death.

I left the hospital in late January, still in a full cast. I was to remain in half-plaster until November.

My brother Andrew was now working for a paper company near Waterloo and was the proud owner of a 2CV. He therefore chauffeured me daily to and from my work. This gravely circumscribed my social life. As I half-sat, half-lay in the back seat of the Gallic rattletrap, I thought that, were we to have an accident, I would be lucky to have ten mourners. To have started the job with a VW Beetle and to have finished it in a 2CV would surely have marked me forever as a failure.

I saw a lot of Clare that year, but then I could not spend much time in pubs and bars, not dressed up as a chalk with my younger brother, constantly checking his watch, in attendance.

That divinity which shapes our ends and in which I do not believe now got seriously cross with me. He or She had gone to all that trouble, admittedly on a pitifully low-budget, with the late-night car accident, and I appeared to have paid no attention.

'OK, then,' they said on Olympus or wherever they meet these days, 'let's see if the little bugger gets *this* message!'

I went to work on Boxing Day 1986, just one month after the plaster was at last removed. On my return to Downe, I hobbled on that atrophied leg into the Queen's Head. I had got as far as 'Good evening, and a Happy—' when an invisible larding-needle was stabbed directly down through my kidney and into my left testicle. I said something memorable like 'Fuck!' and doubled up in excruciating pain.

Back in hospital, I was painfully examined by four doctors. They resolved that I was suffering from testicular torsion, also known as 'Winter syndrome' because scrota which have sagged in warm beds tighten abruptly when their owners arise in the cold air, causing snarled up spermatic cords to tighten into blood-knots.

I was about to be wheeled into theatre when an Indian consultant (upon whom may eternal blessings shower) stepped forward and dissented with the diagnosis. Surgery was cancelled. I was released. The pain, which had abated by then, returned. My left testicle swelled up, first to the size of a golf-ball, then to that of a tangerine.

I went to my GP, who was baffled. A City colleague reminded me that my terms of employment included comprehensive BUPA cover. I took a taxi to Harley Street. I was given an ultrasound scan. The consultant shook his head slowly, clicked his tongue and told me, 'Oh, Mr Farage, I do hope you're not planning to go anywhere too quickly. . .'

I had testicular cancer.

In early February 1987, I was admitted to the Princess Grace Hospital in Marylebone, I signed a form consenting to any mutilation deemed apt and went under.

Last time I did this, I awoke monocular. This time I awoke monorchid.

I knew, of course, that Nature (again I was grateful to evolution) doubled up on truly vital organs such as kidneys, lungs, ovaries and testicles, providing us with a spare of each against just such emergencies. I didn't need two, but I had quite liked the sense of security which the extra one had provided, besides which, as Eeyore had said of his tail, I had been attached to it. Nonetheless, when they offered me an artificial one to supply me with greater social confidence, I refused.

I had had a teratoma ('monstrous tumour' in Greek). These not only have a nasty habit of moving about the body at alarming speed but tend to like company in the lymph-glands and other areas. I was advised that I was likely to have secondaries in my lungs and stomach. I underwent a comprehensive CT scan.

I believed that I was going to die.

In common with all others so persuaded, I thought this unfair. I reflected on all the things that I was never after all going to be able to do but which I had hitherto assumed to be my birthright. These included being married and having children. Clare had the misfortune to be the only one of my friends not only to be female, attractive, affectionate and on the spot but to be able to treat my afflictions with brusque professional amusement rather than with terror or hilarity – which I suspect to be the same things.

On Friday 13 February 1987, I was sitting with Hugh LeFanu, a friend and fellow broker, watching the racing in my private room. We had cigarettes and large straight malts in either hand. Peter Harper, the oncologist, strolled in. He leaned back against the wall and waited politely as Peter O'Sullevan gabbled the last rites over several hundred of our pounds. Then he stepped forward. 'You will be delighted to know, Mr Farage,' he said with a small smile, 'that the scan has uncovered no further anomalies. You have, for now, the all-clear.'

Hugh whooped, slurped more Laphroaig into our glasses and pressed a toothmug of whisky on the consultant.

'Hmm,' said Harper. 'Some of my patients after such an experience spend the rest of their lives drinking carrot juice and avoiding all excess. A few go the other way. I suspect that you belong in the latter category.'

He then laid down the conditions of my release. Instead of chemotherapy, I was to turn up at London Bridge Hospital twice a week at 8.00 am to have my alpha-fetoprotein count taken. Should it rise by an iota, I would be whisked back into hospital and subjected to every indignity which technology had yet devised.

In early March, I played thirty-six holes with such proficiency and bloody-mindedness that I was selected to play for Dulwich in the Halford Hewitt.

I was back on track.

*

No Pauline conversion, then, but my time in the sidings had given me pause in more senses than one. The next five years were to be a bid at compromise, an attempt to persuade myself that I had been right and was just fine as I was, thanks.

I bought a house. Clare moved in with me. We were happy.

But then, we were both working full-time and I was on a roll, so happy was easy. Our news, on the rare occasions when she was not in the hospital and I neither on the exchanges nor in the bar, was consistently exciting. In that same year, my colleague Charlie Vincent and I were charged with setting up a metals department. My annual income rocketed. Clare believed my constant absence to be the normal price for such rewards.

By the following summer, she was pregnant and we married. Our son Sam was born in January 1989. This was an unparalleled joy for me. I don't want to bore those who have had the experience, but it is strange and sobering to feel your heart wrested from you by main force as that negligible little thing slithers into the light, flexes its fingers and commands your allegiance for life.

I now officially had everything. I was still fretting.

4

'SOVEREIGNTY WILL CEASE'

Those in search of seamless progression will note that, in this account of the first twenty-five years of my life, there is no mention of the European Union, though in its various guises it had been a fact of life since my ninth year.

In common with just about everyone with more soul than a Swiss roll, I had railed against unnecessary regulations and interference. After 1986, the City became more and more regulated and it was clear that the days of the cavalier free trader were numbered.

Emptor did not have to *cavere* quite so much (or so it seemed. The crash of the noughties shows that, on the contrary, regulation affords a dangerously specious sense of security) but talent, intuition, flair and fun were all but outlawed.

This was the nature of 'big bang'. It brought huge sums of money into the economy and established Britain as a dominant player on the global market. At the same time, it marked the end of the gentlemen's club which had been the City and the cold, grey dawn of corporatism.

My new employers, R. J. Rouse and Co., had started out as a coffee and cocoa broker and, when I joined it, was owned by Mercantile House and run by a very English retired colonel called John Barkshire, who was still occasionally to be seen wandering through our offices, murmuring encouragement to the gold-braceleted Essex boys and the chalk-striped public-school dropouts barking into the phones.

Shortly afterwards, however, Rouse was snapped up by the French corporate giant Credit Lyonnais. A senior French executive swaggered into the dealing-room and demanded of one of our broadest, brashest bond-traders, 'What grade are these staff on?'

'Yer what?' came the response. 'Nah, mate, we don't do that stuff round 'ere. Way it works is, either they make money or they fuck off.'

Worse still, every aspect of human life in Britain was becoming the subject of homogenising intervention.

Not just my market – the financial – was being prowled by unimaginative jobsworths intent upon standardisation, but the very street markets where I bought my morning apple, the pubs where I ordered a pint and a homemade pie and mash, the builders and plasterers whom I engaged to improve my home, the police officer who had greeted me every morning outside the tube station but was now usually absent, proving compliance by filling in forms, even Clare and I as we tended Sam when he had croup – all of us must kowtow to regulations and procedures intended, so they said, to protect us.

The defining moment for me came in October 1990. We were drinking in Corney and Barrow's on Old Broad Street one evening after work when news came through that we had joined the European Exchange Rate Mechanism. All my colleagues were incredulous.

I was incandescent. I am told that I spent the rest of the evening fuming and spitting like a very hot fire of green timber. 'What sort of stupid, asinine moron *is* this Major. . .? This *cannot* work. . .! This *will* not work. . .! This will be a *disaster*. . .! Yes. Another pint please. . . This Major man is *certifiable*. . .! What does he think he is *doing*. . .? Oh, hello, Kit. Good day? I cannot *believe* it. . . Stupid! Stupid! *Stupid!*'

I became a well-known ERM bore, a soothsayer and prophet of doom. It was obvious to me that this was going to end in disaster, so how was it possible that not merely the Tories but Labour and the Lib-Dems, the CBI and most of the trades unions were in favour of what Norman Tebbit called 'the Eternal Recession Mechanism'?

I knew at least that ERM would prove short lived, but the constraints of corporatism were increasing daily and looked to be set in stone. There was much reason to resent such impudent and pointless regulations, and I resented them all the more when told that they emanated from Brussels – that they had sprung, that is to say, not from the will of my own people, aware of and concerned for our very specific needs, but from an alien group of appointed bureaucrats no more concerned for, or knowledgeable about, our cultural traditions and immediate practical requirements than I for Greek shepherd songs or the preservation of a seventeenth-century rebel leader's birthplace in Bari.

This was long-range, one-size-fits-all colonialism – entirely contrary to the British tradition – and driven, if by anything more than the bureaucrat's desire for homogeneity and tidiness, by a nebulous concern for our own welfare and a misplaced notion as to how that might best be served.

And every time we allowed someone the right to 'protect' us, we conceded another power of self-determination and hammered another tack into the coffin of individuality and freedom.

I vaguely concluded, however, that this was the way of the world and that the people had chosen to enter this bondage. That was what everyone told me. Live with it, Farage. It's a fact of life.

But I had not adolesced and spurned the loving but oppressive protectiveness of a mother only to sink back unquestioning into childish dependence. I had not developed skills, intuition and a gambler's sixth sense only to find them deemed dangerous criminal traits.

And if my favourite costermonger or my pub landlord found a source of russets or steak which tasted better and cost less than the approved varieties, if my builders wanted to offer me a special deal or the police officer to use his initiative or local knowledge to break ranks and warn off a potential mugger or to turn a blind eye to an otherwise law-abiding lock-in at a local pub, or if Clare knew of an old treatment for croup as yet unapproved but effective, I wanted the freedom to avail myself of them and considered myself adult, autonomous and so able to assess the risks.

In November 1988, Margaret Thatcher had made her famous speech in Bruges in which she precisely encapsulated my personal feelings, declaring, 'We have not successfully rolled back the frontiers of the state in Britain only to see them reimposed at a European level.'

As I tried to be a dutiful husband, sitting in the car whilst Clare shopped for baby bric-a-brac, then, with ever greater disbelief and anger, on trains and in my every spare waking moment, I read up on the history of the EU.

I found myself growling a lot.

The EU had been designed to be an accepted fact of life, I discovered, creeping in as imperceptibly as, and no more to be questioned than, the seasons.

In common with everyone born after 1957, I had never been asked whether or not I approved of the steady but sure surrender of the British people's self-determination to an alien bureaucracy. Even my parents' generation was asked only if they approved, after the event, of membership of a 'Common Market'. No mention was made then of a mighty, wealthy, corrupt, overweening, distant EU which would presume to regulate every aspect of our lives.

The submission of the British people to undemocratic rule has never once been democratically sanctioned.

This was always the plan. The will of the people and peoples of Europe was irrelevant to Robert Schuman, Jean Monnet, Paul-Henri Spaak and their brethren who first concocted the plan of a European superstate. In common with most idealists and socialists, they believed the people to be servants of the state (and so, implicitly, of the state's senior 'servants') rather than vice versa.

In the wake of two devastating World Wars which had had their origins in Europe, they were resolved – no doubt sincerely – to attain their vision (one curiously akin to that of the drooling John Lennon) at any cost. The end justified any means.

The western European supranationalist project was conceived at the same time and for much the same reasons as that initiated by the Eastern Bloc.[1]

---

1. I have my own conviction, irrelevant to the battle in hand, that the EU project was born at the Battle of Verdun. The German strategy was to 'bleed France white' – a deliberate policy of attrition. The industrial might of two great countries were pitted against each other on that small ring of hills to the east of Verdun. After this, the Champagne offensive of spring 1917 led to mass mutinies and France was never to be a serious player again. When the League of Nations was founded Jean Monnet was its first Deputy Secretary General. Unsurprisingly perhaps, given the extent of the carnage at Verdun, his philosophy appears to have been 'If you can't beat them, join them'.

The nation was an outdated notion, nationhood and national identities the principal obstacles to peace and enlightenment. Russia was hugely more powerful than her neighbours, so she tried to impose unity by main force, repression and doctrinaire ideology. We have seen the results.

The EU's founders obviously had to be far more cautious. Those two wars, after all, had been consequences of one European nation's attempts to impose her will upon the others, and the two biggest nations, France and Germany, had been humiliated and hobbled. Theirs, then, must therefore be a slow, softly-softly approach. They would be patient. Like their more easterly brethren, they would recruit agents in high places. They would lie and cheat as necessary. They would conceal their true intentions.

Although it is a fundamental principle of anthropology that a people or race is what it deems itself to be, although the peoples of Europe severally deemed themselves autonomous, and although democracy is founded upon the principle of self-determination, this self-anointed group of singularly pragmatist dreamers resolved that nationhood must die.

Democracy and diversity were the price that must be paid for peace.

They thought that a small price.

By now I was howling in fury and disbelief.

You think this paranoid raving? So did I. It had to be. There must be some mistake. I read on.

OK. Consider the words of Arnold Toynbee, another of the EU's architects:

> If we are frank with ourselves, we shall admit that we [perhaps the first-ever mention of this shadowy, undefined 'we'] are engaged in a deliberate and sustained and concentrated effort to impose limitations on the sovereignty and the independence of the fifty or sixty local sovereign independent states.
>
> The surest sign that this fetish of local national sovereignty is our intended victim is the emphasis with which all our statesmen and publicists protest with one accord, at every step forward that we take, that the sacred principle of local sovereignty is not really being encroached upon. It is just because we are really attacking the principle of local sovereignty that we keep on protesting our loyalty to it so loudly.

To all Britons who, over the decades, have heard their statesmen, Tory and Labour, falsely professing this loyalty again and again as we slip further into the maws of the Leviathan, these words are both prophetic and deeply shocking. Here we see explicitly outlined the vilest and most dishonest strategy – to betray the very people to whom politicians owe their power and privileges in a cause which those people do not share and is not demonstrably in their interests.

Toynbee continues with a frankness which subsequent federalists have seldom shown:

> We are at present working discreetly but with all our might to wrest this mysterious political force called sovereignty out of the clutches of local national states, and all the time, we are denying with our lips what we are doing with our hands – because to impugn the sovereignty of local national states is still a heresy . . . Sovereignty will cease in fact if not in name to be a local affair.

Monnet too assumed a power which no-one had ever given him. He declared any public understanding or debate of the 'fusion' project to be simply 'counter-productive'.

These people – this international 'we' – had somehow appointed themselves adoptive parents to the peoples of Europe. They knew what was best for the children. How we were led and by whom was no longer our business. We were to be seen and not heard.

As Raymond Barre, Heath's contemporary and Prime Minister of France from 1976–1981, put it, with an arrogance worthy of a late Bourbon king, 'I have never understood why public opinion about European ideas should be taken into account.' And let them eat cake to you too, Prime Minister.

Democracy was explicitly repudiated. And these people appointed their successors and they theirs to this day. The European Commission, fount of all patronage and of 75 per cent of our laws,[2] has never been elected by the people of Europe. They are self-appointed, self-perpetuating autocrats.

The more I learned, the angrier I became. These people had only had

2. A recent study of German law concluded that 84 per cent of that once proud nation's laws emanated not from its democratically elected Bundestag but from the self-appointed, unrepresentative EU Commission.

power in their own nations thanks to the democratic process. Having attained it, they proceeded to use that power to strip their employers of their wealth and their power in the service of their own very dubious ideals.

The mid-1930s were a memorable time for Mephistopheles. They were holding a bonanza, bargain-basement, never-to-be-repeated, everything-must-go soul-sale at the Oxford and Cambridge branches (some less impressive bargains were also to be had in the minor university towns).

Three years after Toynbee wrote those shameful words, and at the very moment when Philby, Burgess, Blunt and Maclean in Cambridge were being recruited by Moscow, Edward Heath was being groomed by Alexander Lindsay, Toynbee's Marxist and federalist successor at Balliol College, Oxford.

Blunt and Burgess were homosexual, Maclean bisexual. This is often cited as a reason, in that age of prejudice, for their sense of alienation from their class and nation. Heath, so far as is known, was asexual, but he was certainly a resolute misogynist. The Cambridge Five were gifted and socially adept. Heath was neither.

The greatest difference, however, lay in the fact that Heath was recruited to serve a foreign power which did not yet exist. No charge of treason admitted of such a case. The Cambridge mob fled to Russia to avoid life imprisonment. Heath could have fled only to Nephococcygia – Cloud Cuckoo Land.

One month before Heath was elected Prime Minister (which means 'first servant', but no-one seems to remember that), he was briefed by Monnet. He then set about forcing the British people into the European Union by hook or by crook.

It took a hell of a lot of crook.

Heath followed Toynbee's and Monnet's instructions to the letter. He lied and lied and lied in order to impose their will upon his people. He maintained again and again that the EEC was no more than a trade association. A government White Paper assured us that 'there is no question of any erosion of essential national sovereignty', and Heath himself declared in a television interview, 'There are some in this country who fear that, in going into Europe, we shall in some way sacrifice independence and sovereignty. These fears, I need hardly say, are completely unjustified.' He knew that destruction of national sovereignty was the ultimate purpose. He admitted as much in retirement.

Had this been any other contract, it would have been null and void because entered into on the basis of wilful misrepresentation. Had it been a marriage, it would have been annulled. The seducer lied throughout his wooing in order to get his hands on Britain's wealth, body and obedient service.

Peter Thorneycroft, Heath's colleague in the Royal Artillery and in the Conservative Party, openly declared their shared contempt for the democracy to which they owed their positions: 'It is as well to state this at the outset – no government dependent on a democratic vote could possibly agree in advance to the sacrifices which any adequate plan for European Union must involve. The people *must be led slowly and unconsciously* into the abandonment of their traditional economic defences, *not asked* [my emphasis].'

Or, in other words, 'The people are morons. We are intelligent. We have no intention whatever of serving them. They have elected us because we cleverly conned them, but they cannot be relied upon to run their own lives. We will therefore lie to them.'

If this is not a valid parsing of Thorneycroft's words and the European integration policy of both Labour and the Tories to this day, I would be very grateful if a senior politician of either major party would afford me an alternative interpretation.

They know my address. I am not holding my breath.

My blood was by now boiling. Just who did these people think they were by their own admission to blindfold their masters and lead them into sacrifices which they would never otherwise be willing to make? How could men afforded huge power and wealth by democratic process so sneer at democracy and use that power to undo it?

So determined was Heath to win his place in the history books that he gave away without mandate or popular sanction the entire British fishing industry and the world's richest fishing-grounds in exchange for British membership of the EEC.

He and his ministers lied about this too. The convenient acquisition of 80 per cent of Europe's fish-stocks and the destruction of a British industry employing not merely 30,000 fishermen but their wives, children and all engaged in boat-building and maintenance, fish preparation and curing and related trades was not even included in the treaty.

It was thus a totally illegal bribe – part of the *acquis communautaire* as they politely called it – given by a British public servant without the authority of the British public in order to obtain his own way. It was as if a valet had given away his master's Rembrandt in order to get laid.

The loss to the British economy, to traditional communities and to employment was far greater than that suffered because of pit closures in the mid-eighties, and, where British mines were genuinely unprofitable, British waters were still teeming with fish and demand was higher than ever. Where British mineral deposits remain undamaged, giant French and Spanish trawlers now hoover up the contents of the oceans, destroying fish-stocks built up and nurtured over millennia, and British fishermen throw back, dead, up to five times the number of fish that they land.

Viruses do not exterminate their hosts. Farmers and fishermen do not destroy their own stocks because they know that they will provide a livelihood to their descendants. When let loose in others' territory, however, why not use slash and burn rather than husbandry?

It has been an ecological cataclysm and a wanton destruction of a priceless natural – and national – resource.

It was not necessary for me to be a bolshy bugger or a dedicated sea-angler (though I am both) nor to feel obscure frustration with my life to date (which, it is now plain, I did) for me to become very angry at all this. I – we, my children – had been cheated and betrayed for someone else's dream.

OK, OK. Take a pull, Farage. That was a shameful historical fact like, say, slavery. There are quite a few of them. We must indeed live with them and move on.

But slavery was long since proscribed. This was – this is – still going on. Year after year, more powers of self-determination were signed away to the corrupt, monolithic project, and we taxpayers are paying £45 million a day for the privilege.

The Tories modelled themselves, it seemed, on their most famously unsuccessful leader to date – Neville Chamberlain. They kept returning from negotiations in Europe waving scraps of paper and claiming that they had won great victories – only for us to discover that they had in fact conceded more sovereignty.

The Lib Dems were wholly sworn to the European project – surely inconsistent in a party claiming ancestry from the Whigs, a party with those two words in its name, a party whose heartlands are the farming and fishing-dependent West Country and a party professing ecological concerns.

And Labour? Well, Labour were initially quite properly opposed, but who now remembers Tony Blair's sincere pledge to his electors in Sedgefield in 1983 that he 'would negotiate a withdrawal from the EEC, which has drained our natural resources and destroyed jobs'? Certainly not Blair when once elected. His conversion really was overnight. He did not even, like the Tories, pay lip-service to British sovereignty.

Under Kinnock, Labour underwent a miraculous transformation similar to Blair's. It was apparently somehow left wing and right-on to be pro-EU and thereby right wing (very possibly fascist) to be opposed. Thus is the language reconstituted. It is now right wing to assert the power of the people and left wing to kowtow to unelected oligarchy.

The trick here is brilliantly simple and depends upon a two-party system. The Tories will strike anti-EU poses, make anti-EU noises and promise referendums whilst remaining committed to the cause of integration and signing the bulk of the articles of surrender. Labour will more aggressively and openly side with Brussels.

Euroscepticism thus becomes a feature of Conservative old fartery and Europhilia an espousal of modernity and egalitarianism. (Modern? A pre-war trading-bloc run by authoritarian bureaucrats? Egalitarian? A self-perpetuating, dirigiste oligarchy which explicitly rejects democracy? Pah, and maybe even – yes, why not? – pshaw!) The electorate therefore swings from one to the other, with the young and idealistic who reject Toryism forced into the Europhile camp whilst Toryism offers a spurious refuge to those seeking security in the old ways and values. (Old ways? An unelected body assuming power over our people as surely as any invader?)

There was no other way on offer.

I grew angrier and angrier. No-one – not one of the parties purportedly representing the will of the British people – was offering a voice to the view which I heard daily expressed at work, in bars and in the sporting-field. The newspapers and the other media simply disregarded the plaints of the farmers, fishermen and small business people losing their livelihoods due to the EU. The subject was like race or death. It was taboo. Its very discussion was embarrassing and disreputable.

And, as has been established, if a subject's very discussion was embarrassing or disreputable, I wanted to discuss it. In depth.

Yes, but what about the much-vaunted advantages in trade? Here above all I was surely qualified to judge. London, after all, was the world's biggest marketplace and I a coster at its heart. I traded with the entire world. Telephones shrilled like ululating squaws in those days. Each time I snatched up the receiver I had no idea whether the caller would be in Stockholm or Santiago.

And just as a tsunami of new technology was making global communication and trade instantaneous, these political Cnuts were leading us into a restrictive trading-bloc which ignored the wider world! What advantages could we possibly derive from that? This was Wellingtonian Toryism in the face of progress. Britain has yet to find a Brougham.

Mexico, I discovered to my fury, actually had a better trade deal with Europe than we, yet it had not conceded its power to make its own laws or to set its own interest rates.

I made deals daily with an independent Switzerland which had declined not only membership of the EEC but even of the European Economic Area yet still traded freely with every other nation in the world.

In fact, all four members of the European Free Trade Association (EFTA) – Iceland, Liechtenstein, Norway and Switzerland – do more trade per capita with the EU than does Britain. Switzerland, like Liechtenstein one of the world's great financial centres, does twice as much trade, yet was not paying billions a year to be bogged down by regulations and pointless paperwork and sacrificing democratic government.

We had sold our birthright for a mess of potage.

And fifth-rate, stinking, mass-produced, toxic potage at that.

5

ESCAPE PLANS

In the European elections of 1989, I voted Green.

Well, why not?

Thatcher by now resembled a hard-pressed aurochs beset by bull-terriers, barely able, for all her might, to lumber through the forest for the Howes, Hurds, Heseltines and other bloated terriers nipping at her heels and dangling from her throat. Her anti-integrationist stance was admirable but futile whilst the rest of her party persisted in 'denying with our lips what we are doing with our hands' as per Toynbee's prescription.

I might have been a Thatcherite but I certainly was not a Conservative if this was what Conservatism entailed. Labour and the Lib Dems both dutifully sang the old tunes of their respective clans but had abandoned the massed choirs to perform their own inharmonious descants.

The only party then avowedly Eurosceptic and consistently principled were the Greens, not least, perhaps, because they had never had a sniff of power in Britain.

Besides, I am a green at heart. I firmly believe that we should all cultivate our own gardens and that the greatest danger comes from those so alienated as to be bent on saving the entire planet according to one philosophical or political prescription.

People always scoff at nimbyism, but, if everyone were nimby and nurtured and defended their own with the love, dedication and knowledge only possible for locals, the entire world would be at once vibrant, diverse and healthy. A mother loves her own child and knows its peculiar needs. She can only vaguely wish well to children in general. A farmer loves his land and stock. He can only hope for the best for an entire planet or for animals in general, and trust that those who understand specific species and habitats will care for them as well as he.

Supranationalism has been justified and billions spent on the decidedly dodgy premise that human activity is responsible for global warming. Whilst I'm all for common sense and buying local and seasonal (blessed diversity again), I am firmly convinced that all that time and money should have been devoted to allotments, sinking wells and teaching children to skin Thumper and eat ears and trotters rather than insisting on imports of hormone-stuffed patties made with prime cuts thousands of miles away.

Again, I suppose I come back to the same thing. The individual and his or her own community are best able to react appropriately to their own circumstances in accordance with their needs, priorities and conventions.

I still find it incredible that anyone purporting to be green can subscribe to standard provision for multiple diverse habitats with peculiar needs, but, of course, the Greens, having attained considerable clout in the EU Parliament, have also now become ardent supporters of the empire.

After casting my vote, I popped into the George and Dragon in Downe. When Bob Brett, the local Tory organiser, heard of my change of heart, he very nearly collapsed and had to be revived with ardent spirits.

My vote was, personally, a hugely significant break with the past. I was striking out on my own, no longer finding refuge in the compromises offered by conventional parties. I was drawing inspiration directly from values which I had cherished since childhood, regardless of the disapproval or incomprehension of my peers. So much at least had been changed by the accident and the illness.

My new-found convictions did not, of course, mean that I no longer sought the company and support of my fellows. I simply married the two things. In that same year, I founded a luncheon-club called the Column Club. We met at Simpson's Tavern in Cornhill on the first Monday of every month. The criteria for membership were an appreciation of things

British (with particular reference to cricket), a resilient liver and a hearty appetite, and a deep mistrust of the European Union.

Aside from this new-found restlessness and a conviction that something must be done (which did not yet equate with 'I must do something') little in my life had changed. I was making a great deal of money. I was drinking and gambling it away as fast as I made it. I was still screwing up my marriage because I simply forgot it 90 per cent of the time. I was occupied and preoccupied.

So successful was the slow-creep strategy of the EU's planners that at least 80 per cent of my friends and associates broadly agreed that it was a baleful influence upon our lives but for all that accepted it, much as we might accept the existence of an epidemic – not worth fighting save with a rabbit's foot and a prayer.

I think it was then that I first became aware of the truth contained in Milton Friedman's phrase 'the tyranny of the status quo'.

It was not until 1991 that I encountered others who not only felt as I did but were prepared to do something about it.

*

Our second son, Tom, was born in that year. Our marriage, I think, was already dying.

How could it not be? I was never at home.

Commodities trading is like trench warfare. On a quiet day – and there were sometimes quiet weeks – there was a breathless hush in the trading-rooms and, although we stayed close at hand, we were out in the pubs, drinking, spread-betting on just about everything and playing practical jokes on one another.

Then the bombardment started. And all hell broke loose. Phones shrilled for split seconds before they were snatched up and millions were fired about the globe. Larynxes and nerves were worn threadbare as hour succeeded hour and deal succeeded deal. Oh, it was very heaven.

But then, I was twenty-seven. What on earth had made me suppose that I could be a devoted husband and father at that age when death or glory awaited me on the field of battle and companionable carousing with my comrades when at last the New York silver exchange shut its doors at 7.25 in the evening?

Oh, yeah? You're forty-five now. And you're fit for marriage and parenthood, are you?

Look, I enjoy a good heckle, but these 'some' are getting on my nerves. Could you lock the doors this time?

*

Thatcher had been ousted and Maastricht loomed, a treaty which would enormously enhance the powers of the European institutions and effectively destroy the sovereign status of member-states.

Consider. It established European citizenship and laid down the agenda for the introduction of a European currency. It actually ceded in perpetuity the sovereign powers of the Queen in Parliament to an unelected body in Brussels.

It turned the entire British constitution on its head.

Now, it is grammatically nonsensical and wholly illegal for a constitution to be altered by a constitutionally elected government. It can be altered only by the will of the people who gave those temporary leaders their power.

And no British political party intended to challenge these impertinent usurpers who were about to sign away what was not theirs. Some Tories dared to object, but John Major called them 'bastards'. In the words of Sir Peter Smithers, secretary general of the Council of Europe, 'When the Maastricht Treaty was before Parliament, John Major forced it through by ruthless whipping and unacceptable personal pressures.'

So much for the 'niceness' of a Prime Minister principally remembered only for that quality and for adultery whilst espousing 'back to basics' to the people. So much, too, for democratic representation.

When, therefore, I saw an advertisement in the London *Evening Standard* for a meeting of the Campaign for an Independent Britain at Westminster Central Hall at which Labour's Peter Shore and the Conservative John Biffen would be speaking, I went along in hope that I might learn something new or that someone could reassure me that I had read the whole situation wrongly.

Shore was a superb speaker. There were several hundred people in the audience. So far from reassuring me, he confirmed all my worst fears. The forthcoming treaty, he warned, would sound the death-knell of democracy. He advocated voting Labour. Biffen was less impressive but agreed that the treaty was an irrevocable renunciation of Parliament's powers and of democratic process. He said that we should vote Tory. Both men declared the EU to be a distant, inefficient, unresponsive and unrepresentative system of government.

The meeting was thrown open to questions from the floor.

'If we're all agreed that the system is wrong,' said one man, 'why don't we simply get out and return to governing ourselves?'

There was a deal of shuffling and mumbling on stage. Biffen gave it as his opinion that we should reform the EU from within rather than talking of withdrawal.

At that, another man sprang to his feet. He would later become a close colleague and loyal friend. He was a Sussex maths teacher, by name John Harvey. 'Exactly how are we meant to reform the EU when we have a joke Parliament that refuses to represent its people?' he asked. 'And how can we make our will count for anything when qualified majority approval is needed for any change? I will stand as an Independent in the next election. It's not much, but it's all I can do.'

There was a cheer and an outburst of applause.

Another man stood. Scruffy but suited, with a pink marshmallow face, a boyish smile and a shock of surprisingly black hair, he declared above the hubbub, 'No need. I intend to start a party which will lead Britain out of this mess. If you professional politicians won't take that responsibility, we will.'

Soon afterwards, the meeting broke up. I, in common with many others, made my way towards these two men. I was inspired to meet for the first time people who not only shared my convictions and my awareness of the urgency of the situation, but were prepared to do something about it.

I shook the black-haired man's hand and murmured something about helping if I could. I ascertained from those around that his name was Dr Alan

Sked. He lectured in European history at the London School of Economics and had written quite a lot of books which I hadn't read, including *Great Britain and the Continental Revolutions of 1848* and *The Decline and Fall of the Hapsburg Empire, 1815–1918*. I felt still better about my own incredulous research. Here was a man who should know better than most others the nature and the extent of the EU threat, and he was taking it as seriously as I.

Sked was persistent and persuasive. Every halfway personable enquirer was at once recruited to stand for his 'Anti-Federalist League'. These were the founding members of the General Committee, which soon became and which remains the National Executive Committee.

Some, notably John Harvey, who has been the party's most adept fixer and editor of the newsletter and Gerard Batten, a BT sales executive who is now my colleague in the European Parliament, are still prominent in party affairs. Others such as Sked's academic colleague Dr Helen Szamuely (who fancies that she was just Sked's token female and whose sharp brain was a sore loss to the party) soon fell by the wayside.

For all his bids to obtain active supporters, the League was Sked's invention and was intended to be made in his own academic image. Its name was modelled on Cobden and Bright's Anti-Corn Law League, an organisation so successful that it achieved its ends and so its effective demise in the 1840s. Cute, and no doubt impressive to Sked's colleagues, but not, perhaps, an allusion which would find resonance with the British public.

This, I confess, was my stated reservation from the outset. Sked seemed bright, sincere and affable, but soft, unworldly and strangely spoiled. He was accustomed to the autonomy of the academic – self-reviewing, unaccustomed to being edited or criticised save by his acknowledged peers – and I doubt that he acknowledged peers outside his own field. He was autocratic in style and a seriously bad organiser.

Hugh Moelwyn-Hughes, a solicitor from south Wales and another stalwart of the party from the outset, met Sked in 1992 and was at once asked to draw up a constitution for the then League. He did so with professional meticulousness, taking care to cover all the bases and assuming that many of the clauses would be amended in the course of subsequent debate. Sked took one look at the impressive finished document and declared it 'far too complicated.

'So I went away, and this time I wrote the whole thing in the form of one-liners. Gross oversimplification, of course, but again I assumed that discussion would supply the necessary detail. I was asked to present it at a meeting at the LSE, and turned up to discover that Sked, without telling anyone, had invited members of the public along. He had also failed to tell the technicians that we would need a table and some chairs, so I had to sit on a dusty stage like a student at a poetry reading, proclaiming what had been intended to be a discussion document to an audience of complete strangers. One Tory heckler there jeered at my every word. It was the most embarrassing evening of my entire life.

'So that version of the constitution was also rejected out of hand and the solution was that Sked wrote his own, which was very self-serving indeed, but was passed by a new and nervous committee.'

Others claim that Sked was a good orator. Again, I disagree. He was brilliant at exposition but wanted passion and responsiveness. He did not listen to others or venture into milieux other than his own. He therefore found it difficult to translate his high-flown theories into terms which reflected popular concerns. I shared his convictions and applauded his initiative, but the League seemed to me destined to be yet another short-lived special interest pressure-group.

I was considerably more impressed in truth by John Harvey and by another supporter, Major Michael Kelly, a charming and able man who knew a great deal more about administration and motivating all ranks than Sked and who would certainly have contested the leadership of the League had he not been struck down by a heart attack.

I was merely gratified to have my conclusions confirmed. I returned to work.

I noted with interest that Sked stood on an Anti-Federalist League platform in Bath in 1992 against the then Tory Party chairman, arch-federalist and later EU Commissioner, Chris Patten. Patten was trounced by the Liberal Democrat candidate, which was cause for celebration, but Sked, though attracting far more indulgent attention from the media than we were able to command once an organised political party, was trounced by everyone, polling just 117 – 0.2 per cent – votes.

I was, I thought, by now far too busy to get involved in what seemed to me, in Sked's hands, a hopeless cause. I was working – and, yes, playing, but the two were inseparable – a fourteen-hour day. Instead, I resorted to the businessman's usual salve for his conscience. I pulled out the chequebook, scribbled, 'The Anti–Federalist League' and 'Fifty pounds only' and popped it in the post on my way to the pub.

*

For all my resistance, the gods had not given up on me. Sked's letter of thanks was brief, but he suggested that I might like to lend him a hand at the Newbury by-election in which he was also standing.

I mused upon this unlikely suggestion. I discovered that he was absolutely right. I needed a break, and this was my sort of break – a frantically busy one involving a lot of fresh air and a vast number of people, leafleting, knocking on doors, being roundly abused by total strangers and, on one memorable day, chauffeuring Enoch Powell, who came down to speak in support of Sked and his embryonic League.

I collected the great man (and, for all his want of diplomacy and his occasional errors, I apologise to no-one for maintaining that he was a singularly great man: principled, with a formidable mind, the courage of his convictions and enduring independence of spirit) at 33 Eaton Place. He elected to sit beside me, forcing Sked into the back. As I drew away from the kerb, he enquired, 'And what is your intended route to the M4?'

I sort of nodded in the vague direction of Brompton Road and nervously mumbled something or other.

'I have a daughter who lives in Chiswick,' said Powell. 'Follow my instructions.'

As we entered Sloane Square, it was 'Take the fourth exit', then 'I generally find it better to be in the middle lane here. . .' This was Brigadier Powell, and I, the poor untrained orderly driving him, found the experience considerably more nerve-racking than my driving test.

We stopped off for dinner before the main event. Powell had a glass of wine which, he claimed, was of the first importance before a speech. After the meal, I lit a cigarette. This was considered normal in those days, save by Powell, who regarded the cigarette with disgust. The clock ticked on and I suggested that we should leave for the venue. 'No, no,' he said with a wave of his expressive hands, 'better to be a little late. It is all part of the act.'

We reached Newbury racecourse to find a small crowd of communist demonstrators tipping paraffin over Union Jacks and setting them on fire. They instantly spotted us and my heart sank. One hefted a large wooden stave, snarled and strode towards us. He swung at the rear wing. There was a bang and a crunch and the car rocked. In time, I would worry about what Credit Lyonnais Rouse were going to think about their new Mercedes. Right now, I was wondering how much damage a similar blow might do to Enoch's cranium or mine.

He was totally unmoved. 'Get the car as close to the door as possible,' he said calmly and almost cheerfully, so I calmly and almost cheerfully did as I was told.

The previous autumn, Powell had been diagnosed with Parkinson's disease. There was no indication of debility or hesitancy tonight. His speech was fiery and colourful, logical and persuasive. Aside from one meeting of the Bruges Group, this was to be his last public appearance.

He was an astonishingly focused man. Now that the day's work was done, he was at liberty to enjoy himself. On the way back, he was chatty and cheerful. He had a profound faith in the British electorate which he had famously declared in his great speech on House of Lords reform in 1968: 'As so often, the ordinary rank and file of the electorate have seen a truth, an important fact, which has escaped so many more clever people – the underlying value of that which is traditional, that which is prescriptive. . .' I shared that faith, but wondered whether today the British people really believed in themselves any more. He was confident. 'Look at the Falklands,' he replied.

That meeting, with a man who had achieved so much and sacrificed so much for his principles, awoke all sorts of aspirations in me which I had not even acknowledged before. It inspired me. Public service was not just about kowtowing to a party line.

One man who would not have recognised a party line had it been drawn in blood was R. E. G. Simmerson, who gratefully sprang to our support in Newbury. 'Reg', as he was universally known, was – well, single-minded. Some might prefer the word 'obsessive'. Maybe history will see him as the Baptist, crying out in the wilderness. Certainly he was way ahead of his time.

Reg had left the Tories in 1961 over the first application to join the EEC. Euroscepticism brought him and his wife Betty together. They travelled to Brussels to throw ink over Edward Heath as he signed the Treaty of Accession and spent a night together in the police-cells.

Reg was to stand in twenty-one by-elections, a record beaten only by my old friend Lord Sutch and Wing Commander Bill Boakes. An ambitious cricketer's dreams would include run-totals larger than the numbers of votes which Reg generally polled, though once, when he had the backing of the Cheshire Cricket Club captain, he topped 1,000 votes in Macclesfield.

Most candidates wheedle and toady to voters, at least until they are elected. Not Reg. He assailed them. I remember being with him when a mother passed, innocently going about her business with a couple of toddlers. 'Ah, yes!' he roared, and pointed. 'You'll notice when VAT is extended to children's clothing!'

She started, recoiled, hastily gathered the children to her and scurried away.

Reg's by-election innings had been cut short by emphysema, so he was delighted when UKIP appeared. He died in 1999. Betty invited Sked and me to speak at his funeral. I was honoured to accept.

I spent a total of eight days down there in Newbury, explaining the cause on doorsteps, in coaching house bars and in village halls, watching the electors' faces turning from incredulity or dismissiveness to shock and anger.

Too often, the anger was swallowed and replaced with resignation. 'Well, there's nothing we can do about it now', 'Our hearts are with you, but we'll still vote Tory because we don't want to waste our votes' or even, astoundingly but repeatedly, 'It's all right. We're voting Lib Dem. They agree with you about Europe. . . don't they?'

I wanted to pick up these well-meaning and credulous good people and shake them, shouting, 'That is not how democracy works! Use your vote to express your feelings, not to win an election! One vote for us means one more reason for the liars and cheats to tread softly! Don't you see that they depend upon that attitude of resignation? Stand up and be counted! Fight! Your children's freedoms depend upon it!'

I didn't, of course. I just smiled and nodded and thought, 'Dear Christ! They really haven't a clue what's being done to them in their own name. . .' but then, neither had I until the gods stepped in with their beetles and testicles jokes.

But every widening of the eyes as realisation dawned, every gritting of the teeth as anger gripped, every good wish and assurance of support was to me exhilarating as the moment when a fresh-run spring salmon hits or a resistant goddess strikes her colours and reaches out a hand. I was able to get through to people and the message was at once important and pressing.

I was hooked.

*

I was invited to join the 'General Committee', soon to become the National Executive Committee. I accepted. I caused the occasional stir amongst the dry academics and professionals by swanning in, glowing like a pippin in a striped blazer and flannels after a day at Lord's and from time to time behaving really quite disrespectfully towards Sked.

In those days, my rare holidays were expensive and impressive expeditions with friends – game-fishing in Africa, following the England cricket team to Barbados and the like. I had also started 'Farage's Foragers' on the Western Front battlefields.

Farage's Foragers were four-day historical and gastronomic feasts organised by ex-Royal Marine Lieutenant Colonel David Storrie and his wife Linda, who looked after the wounded each morning. For several years, Professor Richard Holmes was our lecturer. I don't spend much time being wistful, but thinking about those expeditions does it every time.

I was away on one such holiday when, in September 1993, the historic meeting was held at which the League became a party.

The meeting had been called 'to discuss the items left unresolved from the last meeting on 6 August' at which it had been agreed that the League should 'take on the name and structure of a populist party' in order to fight the 1994 European elections.

Although this was an obvious and necessary step for a body intent on the assertion of democracy, I suspect that it had remained unresolved at the earlier meeting because Sked did not want his infant adolescing and moving beyond his control. As Moelwyn-Hughes remembers, 'He refused to believe that anyone had skills other than his own or that, if they had, they had value. He could not delegate. Everything was always about Alan, and all decisions must be referred to him. He was certainly no administrator, and, as soon as this was pointed out, he flew into a fury.'

All the other committee members, however, wanted the League to grow up and go to war. Gerard Batten even wrote a paper proposing that members should stand for the European Parliament but should, if successful, refuse to take their seats just as Sinn Fein had refused to take up theirs at Westminster.

There was a lengthy debate about the name of the new party. John Harvey insisted that it be short, self-explanatory and unambiguous. 'The British Independence Party', 'The British Independence League', 'The Independent Britain Party', 'British Democracy', 'The British Democratic Party' and 'The British and European Freedom Party' were all rejected, not because of post-imperial guilt on the part of members, which, quite properly, did not exist, but because such neurosis was widespread elsewhere and because other organisations such as the vile British National Party had already tainted that once proud epithet. Besides, we were eager to stress the Union.

'The Freedom Party' was attractive, but, although I was a libertarian to my fingertips and would have welcomed the chance to fight for the nation's cross-dressers, swingers, naturists, prostitutes, adult nappy-wearers, consensual cannibals and the like who would no doubt have flocked to our fold, they might have been a distraction from the main agenda, and not all committee members were as generally libertarian as I.

'The Majority Party' surely cursed itself as, proverbially, does naming a racehorse 'Hard to Beat' or 'Lightning'. We were prepared for embarrassment, but did not need to add that assured by 'Majority Party, two votes' at the election count. Nor, for that matter, did success offer easier prospects. 'John Bloggs, MP MP for Milton Keynes' did not trip off the tongue.

'The Reform Party' and 'The Resurgence Party' would have rung down the ages had we triumphed, but in truth they belonged in the history books. They were altogether too magnificent and, like many magnificent phrases, too vague (think of all those wonderful battles fought for the non-specific *la gloire* and *l'honneur*. . . Then count French battle honours).

Nobody much wanted 'UK' or 'United Kingdom' in the party's name. It is cumbersome and enables the unthinking to associate us with British supremacists. We were not a nationalist group, but believers in self-determination for all people, peoples and cultures. On the other hand, we happened to be British and happened to be battling in this instance on our own behalf against a specific threat in an international arena.

'UK Independence Party' was resolved upon quite simply because it succinctly declared our origin and our principal aim. Further resurgence and reform must wait until our own nation had won freedom from the EU. From the outset, the committee decided that they would refer to the Party by its acronyms. 'United Kingdom' would not be used on letterheads or in conversation. We would be the UK Independence Party or UKIP.

So far, so good.

Now the enduring headaches were set in place. Sked's hasty Constitution, affording an absurd degree of security of tenure to the leader, was adopted. The General Committee named itself the Executive Committee and limited itself to fourteen members (of whom, it appeared, I was one), and the party would hold an annual conference during the traditional autumn conference season.

On to battle-plans. UKIP would contest the 1994 European elections. Gerard Batten and John Harvey would recruit eighty-seven candidates. Gerard would also approach wealthy individuals and organisations for badly needed financial support.

He had already written to one James Goldsmith, the ultimate 'wrong but wromantic' gambler, asset-stripper, buccaneer and cosmopolitan lone wolf who had already supplied considerable funding to the European Foundation, a Eurosceptic think-tank. Goldsmith had replied, 'I am grateful for your suggestions. However, I will continue to fight for the cause, but on a non-party-political basis.'

He must have kept tabs on this insolent new grouping, however, and observed its rise because, of course, in the 1997 general election, his short-lived Referendum Party was to steal much of our thunder, supply a focal point for Eurosceptic feeling in Britain and, incidentally, prove a rich source of talent for UKIP.

My absence meant that I also missed the first skirmish in another dispute which was to torment us in years to come. It was, of course, purely academic, even fanciful at the time, but the committee now considered just what it would do should we manage to return members to the EU Parliament.

Sked was adamant and high-principled. In taking his seat, a member could be seen as legitimising the parliament and British participation in the European project, which our members could evidently never do. The seat must remain vacant. John Harvey suggested that successful candidates should visit Brussels just once, make a speech demanding independence and retire to Britain.

Helen Szamuely, a woman and so, for all her brilliance, never so academic or so principled as to abandon pragmatism, held, as would I, that the voters deserved something more than a high-minded and ultimately impotent gesture in exchange for their votes, and that a UKIP MEP would be uniquely privileged to increase public awareness of the corruption and waste in the parliament.

I had set off on holiday with a passionate hobby. I returned to find myself on the Executive Committee of a national party, committed to fighting every election. It was as though I had bought a small salamander for amusement and company and had seen it grow into a fire-breathing dragon with a prodigious appetite.

But then, this unlikely Saul was finally coming out to himself and to the world as a committed Christian. I cursed it and the demands that it made on my time and my wealth, but I dearly loved my pet dragon.

This was the year when the new life began.

To start off with, I had finally resolved that I could no longer even pretend to be a corporate man.

What had been a two-man metals-trading desk at Rouse had grown into a large department. My disenchantment had grown with it, and now politics was eating deep into my few leisure hours.

As so often, the catalyst for change came unheralded, unbidden and at first sight unwelcome. It took the burly form of my good friend Joe Corazza.

Joe, for many years a client, is, if such a thing can be conceived, a sort of G. K. Chesterton writ large, amplified and speeded up. He has a lion's mane of fair hair, a walrus's moustaches and a voluminous figure. He is a fine shot and an ardent fly-fisherman who, in those days, smoked sixty or seventy cigarettes a day, had a phenomenal capacity for drink and expressed his forthright views on just about anything without much in the way of diplomacy or restraint.

Joe came to town and we lunched, as ever, at Sweetings, a wonderful old fish restaurant on Queen Victoria Street. We began with a few pints of Black Velvet. Then there were West Mersea oysters, then Cornish brill, then soft roes on toast, all washed down with Chablis. Everything was going swimmingly until the first decanter of port thumped onto the table. I cannot remember if it had one successor or two, but it may just be that our intake that afternoon was a trifle excessive by the standards of the modern City.

It was somewhere in there that Joe suggested that I might take him down onto the London Metals Exchange trading-floor as my guest.

Knowing Joe as I did, I am sure that I should have – and, had we been a little less convivial, probably would have – resisted more firmly. As it was, I thought, 'Oh, what the hell? He's a good client. Damn them if they can't take a joke.'

They couldn't.

My confidence had drained away a bit by the time that we got there. I stood on the exchange floor in silence, almost frozen to the spot as Joe careered about, jovially abusing all and sundry there. He plainly felt that unseen clients on the ends of telephone lines were not getting value from their brokers and therefore shouted his own colourful additions to the conversations into the receivers. At last, he was bustled out by concerned officials.

My bosses at Rouse were unamused. For a moment, I thought of protesting my innocence. After all, I had done nothing wrong beyond inviting the wild man in. . .

It's. . . sort of true. I was. . . sort of innocent. After all, I had not known for a certainty that Joe would kick up on the trading-floor and I had not encouraged him. . .

Hmm. I don't believe my own protestations. In retrospect, I would class it as brinkmanship. I had known that things must change.

Fun and flair had fled the City. We were answerable to joyless and talentless people. All right, it was a little like those dreary teachers with their Xeroxed notes, under whose tutelage the average and subnormal did really quite well whilst the gifted and the maverick lost all their verve and enthusiasm, but I had come to the City in search of originality and inventiveness from no matter what source.

If the newspaper seller outside the offices heard a rumour, I wanted to hear it, because, if it tallied with my intelligence and inspired guesswork, I would act on it. I was good at reading the water, sensing the barometric pressure and picking the right fly to catch the very biggest fish. In the brave new world where everything was under the control of the water bailiffs, I was now expected to snooze on the bank whilst the stake-nets in the estuary scooped up an approved poundage of minnows and fry.

I had known that Joe was a bull beyond my control and that the trading-floor, once a bullring, had been converted into a china-shop. I had known that Rouse was in the midst of a serious financial dispute with the Exchange. If he had not run amok that day, something else would soon have happened to precipitate my departure.

As it was, my well-behaved masters at Rouse thought it provident to show me the door. 'Work hard – play harder' was no longer a motto which worked here. You worked as you were instructed and your play, if you knew how to play, should be discreet and unrelated.

I had friends and admirers who sympathised. I received job-offers. I turned them down. I knew that I was unemployable. I was henceforth going to be my own boss. Under the banner of Refco, who were happy to let talent flourish on its own terms, I founded Farage Futures.

My political career started, fortuitously, at the very moment when Britain first rumbled the nature and the scale of the EU's plot to acquire control. I could never have become involved as I did without the relative freedom (I was now twice as busy, but on my own terms) and the high income afforded by running my own company, so the EU Commission can add Joe Corazza to its blacklist of 'Those Who Made Farage Possible'.

And then my marriage, which had been on ice and torpid with its claws bound for so long that we had both forgotten that it was alive at all, at last expired. We were both in love with other people, which only means, in truth, that we were both thinking and feeling like single people and so did what comes naturally.

If there be such a thing as an amicable divorce, this was it, not least because it made so little difference to our lives. There were no arguments about access or money. I recognised that I had made not the slightest effort to sustain the marriage. Clare had quite properly made a life for herself without me. At her request, I bought her a new house and she moved out with the children.

Henceforth, I had access to Sam and Tom every weekend. I had no idea how to cook and no interest in theme parks. Fishing and cricket, my old passions, came to the rescue. The boys became expert sea-anglers and dedicated cricket fans, and I know as well as Gordon Ramsay how not to ruin a fresh cod, bass or bream.

Public awareness was not, I think, on Conservative MP Stephen Milligan's mind as, bound, gagged and clad only in stockings and suspenders, he died of auto-erotic asphyxiation in his Chiswick home. It was the sad destiny, however, of this former president of the Oxford Union to contribute more to public awareness – albeit of a very arcane nature – by the manner of his death than by his work in life. His death also put an abrupt end to John Major's 'Back to Basics' campaign and left the parliamentary seat of Eastleigh up for grabs. I jumped at the chance to contest it and so became the first candidate ever to stand for UKIP.

The Tories were running scared, so delayed the by-election until 9 June in order that it coincided with the European election, in which I stood for the angler's celestial constituency (or, as one wit had it, the *tinea cruris* seat): Itchen, Test and Avon.

I simply loved the hustings. All that interaction brought out the best in me. The reactions of the people of Eastleigh to the brash new interloper on the electoral scene were much the same as those which I had encountered when canvassing for Sked: a lot of goodwill, broad agreement and persistent fear of a 'wasted vote'. In the end, I won just 952 votes – 1.4 per cent of the ballot. I narrowly beat Screaming Lord Sutch, founder of the Monster Raving Loony Party. The seat went to the Liberal Democrats on a 16.3 per cent swing from the Conservatives. The Conservatives lost a crushing 26.5 per cent of their vote.

As we waited for the count that night, David Sutch (who campaigned for such important causes as all-day opening for pubs, more than one Monopolies Commission and the like) swayed up to me and said, 'Oi, Nige. Let's go for a drink, shall we? The rest of this lot are a bunch of wankers.'

Who could resist such an invitation? We returned to the stage just in time for the announcement of the result.

The film of that announcement was to be shown many hundreds of times as an illustration of the Conservatives' woes. There, alongside the grave-looking candidates of the main parties were Sutch and Farage, looking slightly pink and not at all reverential.

I had to develop a little more high seriousness – but not much – in my later political career.

In all my years of canvassing, though I have encountered the usual grumpy old buggers who quite reasonably and indiscriminately threaten all politicians with Rottweilers, hunting-whips, the contents of chamber-pots and so on, I have rarely met a normal voter who grew angry at our policies. That is the exclusive preserve of professional politicians (such as Tony Blair) who for some reason grow apoplectic at the mention of us.

This is, I think, strange and significant.

Things were very different in the European poll, whose result was announced on 12 June. Here the 'wasted vote' crowd felt freer to express their sympathies, and 12,423 of them or 5.2 per cent, voted for me.

This established a pattern which has remained constant over the decades. Small parties fare ill in national elections under our misguided three-party, first-past-the-post system. Tribal loyalties prevail one way or another, so electors tend to vote for or 'against' a particular candidate, and voting against the candidate in the black hat invariably means voting for the guy in the white.

In the European elections, however, they feel free to express their personal views and preferences. It has been amongst UKIP's intentions from the outset to re-engage voters in the process of their own government and to overthrow the two-and-a-spare hegemony of British party politics. After some years of wrestling with prejudice and fear of Italian-style, writ-in-water, permanent coalition government, I have no hesitation in acknowledging that proportional representation is, though flawed, a more representative system than our own.

In that 1994 election, which was still first-past-the-post, we had twenty-four candidates and won 157,000 votes – 3.3 per cent of the vote in the seats where we stood. Not bad for a special interest group which had only been a political party for a scant few months.

We had also attracted attention. When we were first told of our party political broadcast, we anticipated telephone enquiries and asked who would be taking them. 'Oh, I'll do that,' said Gerard Batten. 'Give them my home number.'

I winced. I stared. I contrived to conceal whatever disdain might have crept into my voice as I insisted that it might be a better idea to have extra lines installed in my Eastleigh election office.

The broadcast itself was also amateurish – a five-minute Talking Sked. Sked had ignored Andrew Alexander's advice that he should get a haircut. The Muppet-like stormcloud atop his head was therefore a major distraction from the good sense that he spoke. Several people who tuned in believed that they were watching a sketch from *Not the Nine O'Clock News*. It nonetheless attracted 30,000 enquiries. The phones rang continuously until 3.00 a.m., when we had to give up.

This was another indication to me that we had struck a nerve. The EU had done its covert business, as prescribed by its founders, well, but the general public had sensed that something was wrong. We had identified what that something was.

*

The early days are the hardest. Those first life-forms which later became more complex and specialised and evolved into us must have had a hard time. They had to battle against extremes of weather and, pretty soon, against one another. Small wonder that the mythological version in Genesis has one half of the second generation murdering the other.

Political parties are similar. It is little short of a miracle that UKIP survived those first years. You start with a shared conviction that something must be done. Little else necessarily links you, and for every Abel there is likely to be a Cain. In our case, we started with a few airy-fairy academics and retired service personnel, a couple of farmers, a solicitor, an accountant and an angry young metals trader convinced of a destiny beyond the City.

Enthusiasm is a prerequisite, and enthusiasm is nowhere greater than in the fanatical or the personally ambitious. Nutters and the self-seeking therefore hitch rides. Peaceful, orderly, obsequious health and safety officers and those functionaries of borough councils with enthusiasm for nothing who would quite willingly sanction genocide provided that it were tidy tend to stay away. Of course, the big political parties are crammed with criminals, racists, sexists and paranoid conspiracy theorists, but they pass unnoticed amongst the orderly mediocrats. In an embryonic party, just one of these loonies can bring the entire set-up tumbling down.

The founding of a party takes enormous amounts of time and energy. The average concerned young or middle-aged person has little time and his or her energies are already committed to family or to work. Most of our early activists were therefore retired and 'of an age', so giving rise to the popular perception of us as a 'Dad's Army' offshoot of the Tory Party (an inaccurate caricature, as it happens, since we had former Labour diehards and political agnostics amongst our number from the outset, and Sked himself had stood as a Liberal).

Nonetheless, with agitprop *démodé*, local councils emasculated and all politics increasingly regarded as irrelevant by the young, the huge majority of our members in the early years were at least only distantly acquainted with rollerblading.

Nature abhors a vacuum, and, in any new volunteer organisation, there are spaces crying out to be filled and volunteers eager to step into them.

Not all offers of help, alas, are altruistic. There are differences as to means, style and structure. Where leadership is not strong and decisive, fierce rows develop amongst over-enthusiastic members who should be united but whose several backgrounds persuade them of the rightness of their different approaches.

And God and established politicians are overwhelmingly on the side of the big battalions.

Over the years, we have had to fight not just for every second of every official party political broadcast, but for every column inch. Because we were not a mainstream party, we must, it seems, perforce be extremists. There is a sort of logic to this. What just and reasonable cause, after all, would not find advocates in three established parties?

Ours, actually.

I suspect that we could never have survived even the first two years had we not acquired at this point a quiet, dedicated member whose organisational skills were equalled by his honesty and lack of self-interest.

David Lott was the desperately needed officer amongst us enthusiastic amateurs. It may sound like one of those 'Wind Beneath My Wings' tributes, but I seriously doubt that UKIP could have survived those first years and grown up – I seriously doubt that I would have remained on board amidst all the factional in-fighting and plotting – had it not been for David's calming, encouraging, motivating influence and his clarity of vision.

David was a master fighter jet pilot with the RAF. He flew reconnaissance planes, was one of the first to master the Harrier when it came into service, served all over the world in constant battle-readiness at a time when there were no battles to fight, rose to the rank of Squadron Leader and proved himself a superb administrator, managing three squadrons, 1,300 vehicles and a vast array of ordnance.

He retired and took up a job as a commercial pilot with Britannia Airways. He flew for them for sixteen years, soon doubling up as area manager for the north east, before taking early retirement at fifty-three.

He should then have enjoyed his existence in the Borders with his wife Kathy, but he just happened to see an article about Sked in the *Daily Mail* and made the mistake of ringing to express his support.

Within ten minutes, Sked had persuaded him to stand in the 1994 election. David won 4.25 per cent of the vote and, as he recalls with a sigh, 'bang went retirement. This was a new organisation without infrastructure. I just happened to be the mug who had the requisite experience and rang at just that moment. The party has been at the centre of my existence ever since.'

David, Kathy and I met early that year at a UKIP lunch for all candidates in the European election. It was a long lunch. We discussed the party's weaknesses. We envisaged its future. We were aware even then that Sked, though a visionary and charismatic enough in a small and compliant group, was a potential liability.

In his defence, he had never thought beyond establishing a League, revealing the truth, attracting adherents and so obscurely changing the course of British history.

As with Saul's conversion, if you read history a certain way (GCSE gobbets for example), it can read thus. 'The women's suffrage movement encountered much traditionalist opposition but also attracted much powerful support. Dramatic demonstrations, increasing pressure from distinguished writers and intellectuals and the experience of effective female emancipation in the Great War finally prevailed. . .'

There. Simple. Fifty-six years of impassioned battling and brilliantly organised campaigning distilled into a simple sports result.

We knew that it could not work that way. We were mere microbes hoping to mass in sufficient numbers to fell a mammoth.

The EU empire had limitless resources and a hugely efficient propaganda machine. We had no money and desperately needed good media relations if the word was to spread and we were to be recognised and taken seriously. Sked's ease with *New Statesman* and *Spectator* columnists was not sufficient.

We needed a structured hierarchy if there were not to be hundreds of dissidents bidding for the leadership every time something went wrong.

We needed thick skins where Sked's was shuddering and sensitive as that of a thoroughbred filly.

Above all, even if we sang in consistently sweet harmony (which was highly unlikely), we needed a massed choir to shake the building. At present we had only a little glee-club.

David's Luton horse-box, which had been bought for his favourite leisure activities, was converted into a mobile information centre. David drove about the country, parked in market squares or on village greens, pulled out a collapsible table and chairs, piled up the leaflets and, with a few local allies, engaged passers-by in debate. He talked to the local media. That was how many – maybe most – of UKIP's party branches were begun.

More than that, however, David brought his RAF experience of managing hotheads to bear. At Cranwell they had been hotheads because they were young, fit and battle ready. In UKIP they were hotheads because they passionately believed in the cause and had no established hierarchy to keep them in place.

Some of them believed in the cause for the wrong reasons and had their own agendas. Some were no doubt nationalist or racist. Some believed the EU to be a long-established Nazi plot. Some may well have thought that it was a Merovingian plot hatched by gay-lib Knights Templar with highly trained Roquefort cheese-mites, its codes clearly discernible in Beethoven string quartets and the works of Johnny Hallyday. I don't know. Any new party will attract its share of strange bedfellows and, God knows, we had ours.

The vast majority, however, had seen the truth and believed in democracy but, on seeing the chaotic nature of the Party at that stage, either sought to take control or wanted to give up in despair. David created the structure which, I think, had been beneath Sked's attention and beyond his abilities.

I followed David's meandering lead. I was soon being referred to as 'the Billy Graham of the Eurosceptic movement'. For the next ten years, my every free evening and weekend was spent in sparsely attended village and town halls and upstairs or back rooms in pubs, making speeches and spreading the word less formally in the rather better attended bars afterwards.

With the assistance of a few other truly committed new members, including Graham Booth, a successful hotelier in Torbay, and John Whittaker, a doctor of economics at Lancaster University, both in time to become MEPs, the branches increased in size. I made many friends in my travels. We were still broke and still disorganised. Sked reserved media relations to himself.

*

I have just learned an interesting if obvious lesson in narrative. If a working girl has amazing sex, there is no story. If a dull virgin has a halfway moderate shag, it is a foundation for inspiring romances and fairy-tales.

Keep the central characters' lives uneventful. When they are full, the story gets dull.

There is precious little to say about the years between 1994 and 1997 because every day was filled with activity and new, fascinating characters. We were engaged in building a political party nationwide. From dawn to dusk, I risked millions on the exchange. From dusk onward, I made converts and many, many friends. I drove tens of thousands of miles every year. I spoke at meetings all over Britain. I was arguing until the small hours. There were occasional fleeting affairs. Dawn saw me heading back to London.

When I had no other meeting, I headed for Salisbury.

Shortly after the 1994 election, a retired farmer named Tony Gatling rang me to ask if I would be interested in standing there at the next general election. Tony was a founder member of the Salisbury branch and he impressed me from the outset by his commitment. I considered his suggestion for a few weeks and was at last persuaded by the sheer number of letters in the *Times* and *Telegraph* correspondence columns signed 'A. D. Gatling, Salisbury'.

In 1995, I set to work with a programme of leafleting, canvassing and public meetings. Every four weeks, we held a well-organised action day. We rapidly acquired a superb, dedicated team of helpers. With such a programme and such a team, we could surely have won that seat with ease if only people had known who the hell we were. Instead, we had to introduce not just me but the entire party and the entire concept.

This was my first bid at door-knocking and public-speaking on my own account. I was lucky enough to be able to stay with Tony and Mary Gatling in their delightful thatched cottage for weeks on end. I was lucky too to have a first-rate agent and chairman in Malcolm Wood, who has since been a UKIP stalwart in the south west. We drew small crowds. We counted an audience of thirty a triumph. At one memorable meeting in a village called Hanging Langford, no-one turned up. We still did our double-act before retiring to the pub. It was all great practice.

A couple of months before the election in 1997, several of our members received anonymous, libellous letters alleging all sorts of things of which I did not even want to be guilty. That was the start of a campaign which continues to this day.

I already knew that our prospects in the 1997 general election were negligible. I did not care at all. No sooner had Jimmy Goldsmith been elected to the EU Parliament for the French party L'Autre Europe than he decided that he was after all going to serve the cause by means of party politics. He announced the foundation of the Referendum Party, which was to stand for this one election only in every seat where the established parties' principal candidates had not already declared themselves in favour of a referendum on the future of the EU.

Goldsmith's wealth meant that he did not have quite the same problems as we in getting the message across. He simply took out double-page advertisements in all the major newspapers and, as the election approached, sent a VHS tape to five million British homes. The support which he mustered and the prominence of many of his candidates – Mrs Thatcher's economic adviser, Alan Walters, Tory MP Sir George Gardiner, TV botanist David Bellamy, entrepreneur Peter de Savary – merely drew attention to the extent of Euroscepticism in Britain and drew many supporters out of the woodwork.

It was rumoured that Sked and Goldsmith met in the run-up to the election. Sked has since denied that any such meeting took place. The story that I was reliably told is that Goldsmith actually offered to stand down his candidates in seventy-five seats where UKIP candidates would instead stand on 'UKIP/Referendum Party' tickets. Goldsmith was willing to pay all costs.

Sked, so the story goes, refused the deal. This would, alas, have been entirely characteristic. Aside from his insistence on being top dog, Sked displayed a quite unreasonable dislike for Goldsmith and the Referendum Party, who were, after all, natural allies.

6

BIRTH-PANGS

Now the bloodshed started.

Two events – both apparently trivial in themselves – occurred which were to come back to haunt both me and the party.

On 12 October 1996, I was back where it all started for me at Westminster Central Hall. Over 1,000 UKIP delegates turned up for the party's second ever conference.

The buckets were being passed around in hope that a few enthused members might have backed a winner when a benefactor, plainly unconcerned to preserve his privacy, stood and pledged that he would personally match whatever sum was raised. Other patrons had been discreet in their donations. In any language, however, this one translated as 'I have lots of money and seek prominence in this party.'

And that is another problem common to all newly launched parties. They need fuelling and can as well be boarded with grapnels of gold as by mobs of mutineers or troublemakers marooned by other boats.

The grand gesture had in fact cost a mere £4,500 and the cheque took a long time in coming, but, on investigation, it seemed that we could well use the acumen and the energy as well as the cash of Mr Michael Holmes. He had at least £8 million in the bank. He was just fifty-eight. He had worked in the advertising and marketing departments of the *Sunday Times* and the *Evening Standard* before launching his own free newspaper company in 1970. The business had boomed and he had sold it to Reed International in 1987. He had thus been rich and effectively idle for the last nine years.

There is a lovely old adjective which describes me now. It is *hadiwist*, as in 'His tone (or his expression) was hadiwist as he considered Michael Holmes'. It means just what it says. Had I wist that Holmes's retirement until now had been empty, that he had had no passion or interest aside from his family into which to channel his undoubted energies, I might have been less eager to have him on board.

As it was, I was as delighted as everyone else to have a proven and well-capitalised businessman on our team. I was young. I did not feel that I knew enough to challenge Sked, though the volunteer staff in our London office was discontented, ill-informed and totally disorganised and the provinces were all at sea.

John Harvey was a teacher, Gerard Batten a salesman, Graham Booth a provincial hotelier and so on. Why British society is so structured that such practical men must defer to a metropolitan theoretician I do not know, but we did.

Only David Lott had the experience and seniority to tell Sked that the party was a mess. 'I told him that we needed delegation, organisation, staff – help in what we were doing. He was still hogging the limelight in all media interviews and seemed to think that was all that was needed.'

Apparently, Sked made it clear to David that he resented my small successes as a speaker around the country. '*L'etat, c'est moi*' was Sked's attitude. He wanted no rising stars. His invention was running away from him and he couldn't stand it. He just wouldn't listen.'

Holmes appeared to be the means for us to move on to the next stage of our development.

And so, in a sense, he proved, though not as we had anticipated.

*

And then there was the Deavin business – the first direct attack which UKIP sustained. It wasn't to be the last.

Just as an accusation of promiscuity is the first and cheapest made by a woman of a rival, so racism is the charge most readily brought against any contemporary political party and perhaps the most difficult to refute. 'Some of my best friends are Jews' is in fact a perfectly acceptable response to the charge of anti-Semitism, but what defence does not sound patronising and particular, and how can a negative be proven?

UKIP had the added disadvantage of representing the interests of one nation, albeit that nation comprises many races, against the perceived or presumed interests of others, albeit those others also have anti-federalist movements. I will not deny that, amongst our members, there are blazered buffoons and unschooled oiks who have not progressed beyond the 1950s in their attitudes towards other cultures. So there are in the Tory and Labour parties, but they are more easily ignored.

For all that, those who sought to tar us with that brush were in large measure unsuccessful. There was a memorable attempt in the *Guardian* of 30 December 1996. In his desperation, Europhile Liberal Democrat Lord Wallace ended up apparently demonstrating the very vice of which he accused UKIP:

> There are nasty undertones of xenophobia, even echoes of fascism, beneath
> the coalition of malcontents who claim to be dedicated to the salvation of
> England. For a start [??], an astonishingly large number are not truly English
> . . . The UKIP candidate in the Barnsley by-election was Nikolai Tolstoy
> – a name redolent of European high culture rather than the Saxons rooted
> in England since before the Norman Conquest. Sir James Goldsmith, who
> stems from a great European financial family, made his money largely in
> New York, and invests it from Mexico to France.

As Wallace tied himself in knots, the NEC met to draw up its election manifesto. At this point Sked introduced one of his post-graduate students who, he said, was writing a ground-breaking history of post-war Britain with particular reference to Harold Macmillan's government.

This physically personable but otherwise unprepossessing young man's name was Mark Deavin. Sked believed that such a sterling chap would be very useful to UKIP. He even proposed that we take him on as our research director at a cost of £3,000, which we barely had in the coffers.

We all shook hands with our leader's protégé and said rhubarb. Deavin attended two more meetings then vanished. By then, word had reached me that Deavin might be associated with the BNP. I raised concerns with Sked but he said things like 'All nonsense, I'm sure' and 'There'll always be tittle-tattle' and proceeded to the next business.

In April 1997, just a couple of weeks before the election, Radio 4's investigative programme *The Cook Report* telephoned. Deavin was indeed a BNP activist.

My apologies here to the majority of British readers who are all too painfully aware of the BNP and its principles, but a word of explanation may be needed for those hitherto more fortunate.

The British National Party is the slightly more polished and professional successor of the National Front. It is determinedly white-supremacist. Its constitution, until February 2010, required that all members must be 'of British or closely kindred native European stock'. Even then it was only changed because of the threat of legal action. It opposes mixed-race relationships and immigration and proposes financially aided repatriation for law-abiding immigrants and compulsory repatriation for all others.

All such organisations seek to justify their policies with academic research 'proving' that Aryans discovered fire or invented jazz, that the *Wizard of Oz* was covert Zionist propaganda, Auschwitz a naturist holiday camp which suffered technical glitches and so on. Deavin, as their research director, is the guru of such 'studies'.

The BNP is rabidly anti-foreign. Ergo and ipso facto it is also rabidly anti-EU. Deavin's thesis is that the EU is part of a Jewish (natch) plot concocted by 'a homogenous transatlantic political and financial elite [somehow including Harold Macmillan and Stephen Spielberg for all its homogeneity] to destroy the national identities and create a raceless new world order'. The BNP therefore bitterly resents UKIP, which supplies a somewhat saner and more inclusive voice for those who value freedoms and cultural rather than racial autonomy.

Deavin was immediately expelled from UKIP, but the damage was done.

A month later I was to compound it with the worst mistake of my political life.

*

The election went as poorly as I had expected. The country's priority was removing the Tories and replacing them with new, fresh Labour, so there were few stray votes to be picked up either by us or the Referendum Party. The RP contested 547 constituencies, we just 194. They won 3 per cent, UKIP 1.1. Of the 106,000 votes which we won, I, standing in beautiful Salisbury, received 3,332 – 5.7 per cent of the poll and the highest UKIP vote in the country.

I am a bull-trader by nature, but no-one can survive on the markets with blind optimism alone. Nonetheless, I declared then with absolute certainty that we would have MEPs in the 1999 election and that I intended to be among them. I had no idea how I would manage it given that I was already living on four hours' sleep a night, but heigh-ho.

Thanks to Goldsmith and us, the nation had awoken – slowly, groaning and with more pressing things on its mind, perhaps, but it had nonetheless awoken – to the threat from Brussels.

The Referendum Party had caused a host of ardent Eurosceptics to raise their heads above the parapet. These were not just millionaire chums of Jimmy but stalwarts such as the indispensable, infinitely good-natured and inventive, bearded, sea-booted fisherman Mick Mahon of Falmouth and mild-mannered, retired Frinton undertaker Jeffrey Titford, who had bagged 9.7 per cent of the vote in Harwich.

Rivalry is generally healthy but can become asinine compulsion. I have met restaurateurs who seek to put down competitors just down the road, unaware, it seems, that diners, for economic as much as gastronomic reasons, would choose to eat ambrosia every night of the week and that every halfway decent establishment profits from a Michelin star in town. Rick Stein has the right idea. Padstow's reputation has made fortunes for the Seafood Restaurant's neighbouring bakery, which makes great pasties. He has even set up a chippy.

Sked was no Stein. He did not get it.

He not only resented any popularity which my travels yielded but instantly saw Holmes too as a rival and wrote a libellous letter about him to David Lott. He also had a – to me totally incomprehensible – dislike of the Referendum Party.

His fears were self-fulfilling. OK, Sked was neither organiser nor populist, but he was a bright guy who really could have remained UKIP's revered founding father, still explaining the cause to those publications which could understand him, if only he had acknowledged his own failings. He preferred to fight.

Lott, Holmes and I fought back. The alternative was that UKIP sank slowly but surely into the still and stagnant shallows. It might have done just that if the Skedites had prevailed.

We organised a meeting in Basingstoke to which we invited all the most successful Referendum Party and UKIP candidates. Sked had proscribed all such association and instantly announced that all UKIP members were bidden to a meeting on the same evening in London.

At his meeting, Sked effectively declared that Lott, Holmes and I were beyond the pale. His *bella figura* was gravely threatened when Malcolm Wood arose and told him to applause that he could ill afford to lose Nigel Farage, 'the best platform speaker that we possess'.

Down in Basingstoke, we simply made a lot of new friends.

There was still room for compromise, but Sked went ballistic. He summarily suspended then expelled the lot of us without consultation. Open war was declared.

Now that intemperate letter from Sked to Lott about Holmes came into play. Holmes, who was by nature vengeful and had money to burn, began legal action against Sked and threw a libel action into the mix. Sked was repeatedly advised not to defend the action. He rejected the advice. Craig Mackinlay, a founder member and a long-standing loyalist, told him that the libel was minimal but unquestionable, but Sked spent £15,000 of precious party funds obtaining precisely the same opinion from counsel.

I was perhaps still stupider.

BNP spy Mark Deavin rang. He told me that he had valuable information about Sked which might help me in the battle. It had never been his intention to betray UKIP, he said. He had been the victim of a mugging and, when susceptible, had found solace and support in the BNP. Now he wanted to make it up to me.

Thumb in bum, mind in neutral, concerned only with winning the battle in hand, I arranged to meet him for lunch at St Katharine Docks. In my defence, that is how little I considered subterfuge necessary. I met him in a public place much frequented by city colleagues and journalists from nearby Wapping. As ever, I hailed a few passing people and casually exchanged greetings as we talked. Deavin remained apologetic and conciliatory but had no new intelligence to convey. I returned to Farage and Co. a little bemused, thinking that I had wasted a lunchtime.

It was not a waste for the BNP. I had been photographed with Deavin on the street outside the pub, and one of the people hanging around us was proudly identified by them as Tony 'The Bomber' Lecomber, a peculiarly malodorous floater who had done time for possession of explosives and for stabbing a Jewish schoolteacher.

I had been right royally stitched up.

Sked considered his options. Common sense prevails far less often than is commonly supposed and than it undoubtedly deserves. It fares best, I find, when fighting shoulder to shoulder with *force majeure*. Then people start inviting common sense in and asking it to give them babies.

Not to be immodest, Sked was up against 90 per cent of the useful energy and talent in the party at that time. Even those who liked him and admired his intellect conceded that he could not run a piss-up in a brewery. He had to go.

He penned a last, vitriolic edition of the newsletter, anointed Craig Mackinlay his heir and departed back into the academic hinterland.

Even then, there were plenty of members who believed that we had struck too soon or too savagely. Graham Booth, John Harvey, Gerard Batten – all regretted the manner of Sked's departure and thought that he deserved better. John and Gerard even resigned from their posts in protest. All, however, were to be shocked and hurt by the fury which he has subsequently expended on UKIP and on all who remained in the party.

He has become the lazy journalist's easiest source of a space-filling story about UKIP. At every election, Sked has re-emerged on air to accuse

UKIP of right-wing extremism – he who invited Deavin to the NEC – to reiterate the claim that I have been known to drink too much (moi?), to chastise us for non-attendance at the EU Parliament (though this was our long-stated policy), to quote BNP troublemakers and 'certain observers' as to non-existent 'pacts' and to urge everyone to vote Tory.

I suspect that, by appealing, as any democratic political party must, to all and sundry – including, as with any mob, some nutters (welcome if benevolent), ragamuffins and academic duffers (both especially welcome) and downright villains (welcome until so proven and then purged), we had tainted Sked's lovely, pure, nineteenth-century vision of his League and brought him, to his mind at least, into disrepute amongst his academic peers.

But a party is not a private club – though many of today's parties are run as such, and mere supporters are dismissed with sneers as irrelevant cannon-fodder. It is merely an assemblage of people of all backgrounds and intellectual abilities who share certain broad principles.

We cannot and would not blackball members for expressing their views a little coarsely, for wearing dirty shoes or for failing to grasp precisely what Hans von Essen zu Frankfurt und change at Bremen meant in his seminal paper on European union (1936).

Broadly speaking, we believe that an individual has the freedom to live her life as she pleases provided that she harms no-one else, that she may elect whom she will to speak for her local community and can remove that person from office if he fails to do so, and that local communities should, where practicable, speak and act as a nation in her best interests and with due regard for her culture and environment.

And that's it.

It may seem incredible that it is necessary to assert such a principle in Britain, mother of the free and exemplar for the world's democracies, but today all the major parties have a different view. They all believe that our laws should be made and our freedoms constrained by a distant, unelected body of people unknown and unaccountable to us and unaware of our particular requirements. These people are self-appointed and regard themselves as masters, not servants. We cannot sack them.

There are those – the functionaries, the doctrinaire, the natural apparatchiks – who love such government. In denying the citizen choice, it also spares him problems of conscience or individual taste. It wraps him in down, croons lullabies with subsections and tells him not to bother his pretty little head about anything. So long as he abides by the rules, he is in the right. Hence genocides and gulags.

UKIP, however, attracts the other sort – the bolshie buggers who believe that they should be consulted before thousands are killed in their name, who see no reason why they should not strew their brains on the tarmac if it means that they can feel the wind in their hair or risk ptomaine poisoning in exchange for Colchester's or Galway's finest, who consider it their inalienable freedom to cause offence and so accept the freedom of the offended party to bop them on the nose, who believe that they know more than bureaucrats about bringing up their own children and so on.

Inevitably, some of these will have some very weird notions indeed. So? I once had excellent times with members of the Flat Earth Society. I even count some vegetarians and teetotallers amongst my friends.

To be frank, then, I consider that Sked and much of the metropolitan elite, with particular reference to the BBC, are snobs. They do not like to be associated with those who cannot speak in acronyms and cite obscure papers. They mistrust the accumulated and inherited wisdom of the common man or woman. They believe that those who are a trifle eccentric about the shape of the globe, for example, must be stupid about everything else. They assume that inarticulacy indicates empty-headedness. They assume, in other words, that there is a natural ruling class.

Anyhow, it is a source of sorrow to me that, since his departure, Sked has engaged in so sad and so interminable a sulk. Democracy means getting your hands dirty and associating with the common herd. The League in its ivory tower could never have won elections.

We had every intention of doing just that.

*

Even now, though Sked had lost, we had not won. Craig Mackinlay could yet have claimed the crown, maintained our banishment and so killed UKIP. We would then have had to start again from scratch with the New Alliance.

Craig, however, remained loyal to the cause rather than to a faction. He concluded, as we had done, that 'having got this far, we just had to keep this thing going'. He called an election for the leadership.

There were a few enthusiasts who suggested even then that I might have stood and stood a chance of winning. It did not even cross my mind.

First, I was thirty-three years old, with young children and a busy life.

Second, I was no politician. My idiocy with Deavin had shown that. Even as a businessman, I had only ever been a cheery rails bookie, albeit in a dark suit rather than a loud check, not an industrialist or a Goldsmith-style corporate raider, accustomed to devious dealings and hiring and firing. The experience with Sked had been instructive but harrowing.

Third, I could not begin to afford such indulgence. I could not at that point have afforded to take on the role as the Tories' leader, let alone UKIP's. I was earning a great deal, but every penny was swallowed up by my lifestyle, children's education and, above all, politics.

Holmes was the obvious choice. He could not only afford it, but he had ample time and, as it seemed, the businessman's dispassion, so often wrongly characterised as 'ruthlessness', which enabled him to make executive decisions without turning a hair.

Craig Mackinlay and another founder member, Gerald Roberts, stood for the leadership but were too closely associated with the *ancien régime*. They stood no chance. Holmes appointed me party chairman with particular responsibility for attracting former Referendum Party members.

To his credit, Holmes was energetic and an effective fund-raiser. He was like a parody of the eighties businessman, always on the move, permanently barking into his mobile phone.

It was only later that I discovered that Holmes's brusque, peremptory manner might also mark a martinet. The difference between Holmes's style and David Lott's was hugely instructive. Holmes was an organiser. David was a manager.

UKIP was all but unknown. We had just pulled ourselves from the brink of annihilation. The coffers were empty and our perceptible prospects poor. Nobody worked for UKIP in hope of wealth or glory. Everyone was therefore a volunteer, motivated by conviction alone, which is why there was a preponderance of retired people in our Regent Street office (supplied by a founder member) and in our regional branches.

In that these people chose not to vote for the major parties, they were free-thinking and bloody-minded. In that they chose to devote their leisure hours to licking envelopes, setting out chairs, distributing leaflets and so on rather than watching daytime television, they were energetic and determined. These people and these headstrong qualities were our most precious assets.

David was a great manager because, like Mike Brearley captaining a Botham, he recognised this. In the RAF, after all, he had nurtured the wildness of his wild, headstrong men and women even as he had attempted to keep productive order. All his working life had been spent in maintaining such a balance between battle-readiness and passion and the discipline required by peace.

Holmes's style indicated impatience with individuality. It was as though he were running a call-centre rather than a team of eccentric and ardent libertarians. He was even affronted by Mackinlay's gross presumption in having stood against him in the leadership contest, though there would have been no leadership contest without Mackinlay's good sense and lack of personal vanity.

He treated our most indefatigable volunteer at the London office, Tony Stone, like a Dickensian skivvy. 'I was working all hours,' says Tony, 'and Holmes would call whenever he felt like it, demanding to know who had joined and what this person or that had said. Even when I had gone home, he would call, even in the middle of the night. No greeting. No "sorry to bother you, Tony". Just "I need to know this or that" as though I carried the entire membership list and all the members' life-stories in my head.'

In time, I came to see that Holmes was perhaps the only member of the party whose principal motivation was not passion for the cause but his own leadership and amour-propre. This was in large measure my fault. I had seen him from the outset as our saviour. I had swallowed the cliché, very much of that era, of the turbo-charged, go-getting high-flier.

On reflection, I see that that aggressive image, though it plays well enough in the movies, has precious little to do with management skill or commitment. I suspect that Holmes's passion was to prove to himself that he still existed and mattered.

Reared by the notoriously puritanical Plymouth Brethren, from whom, no doubt, though a victim himself, he inherited a mistrust of natural impulse and infantile disorder, he never felt that he belonged at his school where, as a scholar, he was forced to wear a shirt of a different colour from that of ordinary boys. The only time in his life of which he spoke with pleasure was his spell with the Royal Warwickshire Regiment.

He was ideally positioned to note that advertising revenues exceeded production and distribution costs and so to be in the vanguard of the free newspaper market. He was then bought out just weeks before the crash. For all the appearance, then, of being a high-flying, innovative businessman, I think that he was a creature of circumstance who never felt at home amongst schoolboys or on editorial desks, nor was quite certain how he had become a tycoon. Since his early retirement, the highpoints of his life, by his own account, had been daily lunches down at the pub.

Reports of his abrasive, unsympathetic style began to reach us daily as we geared up for the European elections. These were the first to be decided on the basis of proportional representation. We were enormously hopeful.

The Referendum Party was proving a rich seam of talent. Dr Richard North and Heather Conyngham, without whose skills in research and organisation the first years in the EU Parliament would have been totally shambolic rather than merely profoundly confusing, came to us from Goldsmith's team. Norman Tebbit has repeatedly alleged that Heather was working for MI6. All I know is that her dedication and industry over those first years in Brussels did us nothing but good.

I invited Jeffrey Titford, the Frinton funeral director who had done so well at Harwich, to lunch with Holmes and me at Simpson's in the Strand. I explained that we had resolved that, instead of boycotting any seats which we might win at the election as per Sked's plan, we would take them up and use them to investigate an institution whose members were unknown and whose structure and workings were a well-concealed mystery to the British public.

Jeffrey had swallowed the myth that withdrawal from the EU was practically impossible. We pointed out that, on the contrary, the EU needed Britain far more than vice versa and that we had a cumulative trade deficit of £30 million a day in relation to the EU. We expatiated on the practicality of Britain's withdrawal. We dreamed, then, in silence for a few minutes. Jeffrey became enthused. He joined the party and expressed an interest in a more active role.

I liked Jeffrey. His style and personality were the antitheses of mine. He was quiet, meticulous, reassuring, determined. We worked well together.

And suddenly, astonishingly, the turning-point was upon us. The Labour MEP for South Yorkshire resigned. Michael Holmes was convinced that we were not ready to fight the resultant by-election, but David Lott, John Whittaker and I disagreed. John Whittaker even put up the £1,000 deposit out of his own pocket. David moved his horse-box to Doncaster. We had fastened on the pound as the symbol of British autonomy no less than as a means to it. Our slogan was 'Keep the £. Vote UKIP'.

It struck home to the extent that the Conservatives nicked it (all save the 'UKIP' bit) for themselves within months.

Peter Davies, our candidate, won 13,380 votes. The Conservatives had 21,085, the Lib Dems 22,051. There had never been the slightest question as to who would win. This was Labour territory, and Linda McAven was returned with over 62,000 votes, but we, in an inhospitable environment, were in an honourable fourth place which, if a similar pattern were seen about the country, would win us seats in Brussels next year.

I worked flat out, confining my travels now to home ground – the south-east. I was still running my company by day, then rushing off to the endless village halls throughout the region. Jeffrey worked his region with a vigour incredible in one who had retired nine years before. Graham Booth took charge of the south-west in his purple and gold double-decker. Michael Holmes rode on his coat-tails as a candidate for the south-west, but, as leader, claimed the leading spot on the closed list. Graham graciously deferred.

At the same time, I was chairman, running the entire national campaign. David Lott, on whom I had come to depend for logistics, had bought a motor-home and, no doubt with a sigh of relief, had set off to the States for a year-long tour, hoping at last to enjoy his long-expected and well-earned retirement. I did my best to develop a telesales department. I dealt with stickers and banners and the demand, growing daily, for leaflets and membership forms.

I seldom admit such things, but I now conceded defeat. There just were not enough hours in the day for the admin, the speeches, the fund-raising, the socialising and the daily business in the City. In January, I called David, who had somehow been diverted to Australia. I needed his help.

He boarded the next flight back to Heathrow. I will be indebted to him and to Kathy for as long as I live.

Some have surmised that I was already aware that Holmes's volatile temperament, of which evidence now came in daily, was going to cause us leadership problems in the near future.

As ever, some are irritatingly right. I had not time to worry about it much just then, but Holmes was becoming unpopular amongst the active members, and it could not be long before that discontent filtered down to the rank and file.

With David now in charge of the national party administration, I was freed to get on with what I seem to do best. Aside from explaining the nature of the EU and its plans for ever-increasing federalism, this consisted largely in pointing out that the Conservative pledge, that Britain would be 'in Europe but not run by Europe' was a specious, disingenuous nonsense, since no such option exists under the provisions of the Rome, Maastricht, Amsterdam and Nice treaties, all of which the Conservatives had eagerly signed.

That June evening when the election results came in marked a quite extraordinary transition. UKIP had won 7 per cent of the poll, the Lib Dems 10 per cent, Labour a pathetic 28 per cent and the Tories 35.8 per cent. We had three seats, allotted to Michael Holmes, Jeffrey Titford – and Nigel Farage.

At one point that evening, I escaped the champagne corks and the congratulations, the flashing cameras and the television and press interviewers (to whom we were suddenly inordinately interesting although they had ignored our existence throughout the campaign), sat by myself in a plain white room and covered my face with my hands.

I had fought to this point simply because I passionately believed in the cause. I had attained popularity because I liked people and prominence because – well, I felt as though I had discovered a new land simply because waves kept pushing me towards the shore so I had kept on diving through them.

And now I had not a clue how I was going to cope.

Most good stories are *Cinderella* in one form or another. There is misfortune and injustice. Our virtuous, blushing heroine obtains what she has always dreamed of. Further adversities afflict her and her original misery is compounded. Then, by merit of virtue or shoe-size, she triumphs.

I was never cut out to play Cinderella. In June, 1999, I was granted admission to a ball which I had only seen in nightmares in a palace whose very existence I deplored. So far from moving from servitude amongst the cinders to the warmth and glitter of the ball, I had been earning a great deal and disporting myself amongst friends until I attained victory, instantly lost a fortune and henceforth found myself amongst people whom I found distinctly uncongenial.

For at least two minutes, I laughed like a loon.

Then I got down to some serious celebration.

My first live media interview was with Phil Hornby of Meridian TV. 'Well, Nigel,' he said, 'you said you'd do it. Very few people believed it, but you've done it. So, from now on, it's going to be endless lunches, lavish dinners and champagne receptions. Will you be corrupted by the lifestyle?'

'No,' I told him with a shrug and a grin. 'I've always lived like that.'

David Lott drew me aside at some point in the evening. 'Your life's just changed forever, Nigel,' he said.

I nodded. It was an obvious statement, I suppose, but I had never truly considered just how much it was to change. My hobby had outgrown everything else in my life. No less than Antony by his passion for a woman, I had been borne by the surge of my own passion from familiar shores to a new, bewildering, intimidating territory of which I knew next to nothing.

Just how bewildering and intimidating I was about to discover.

PART II

7

NEW BUGS

We travelled to Brussels on Eurostar, accompanied by BBC cameras which nosed in on our table suddenly and unexpectedly. We opened a bottle of champagne, partly just because we wanted to celebrate, partly because it gave us something to do with our mouths other than putting our inexpert feet in them and with our hands other than scratching, nose-picking or whatever.

The cameras were there because we were the wild men from the hills, the hillbillies who somehow made it to Washington. No doubt the producers were hoping that we would attempt to extinguish the steak Diane with the contents of the ice-bucket and all the other clichés of the genre. Astoundingly, we managed to avoid such solecisms.

Although we did not yet know it, we would receive £600 apiece from our new employers for this journey whether we wanted it or not. The cost of the return fare was, I think, £99, but the EU does not care. After all, it is only your money, and we were no longer ordinary people. We were members of the club now – the ruling class.

The complex of buildings which constitutes the EU Parliament (or one of its three homes, since, even at the outset, leaders could not agree where their capital should be, so decided to have two) is vast, impersonal and deliberately intimidating to all save its members whose confidence is thereby enhanced. Its construction alone has so far cost you £700 million and we're still counting.

It was built on the site of a very much cheaper brewery, which was surely a more useful purpose for so large an area of God's earth.

It is a building without a focal point or a narrative dynamic in its design. Millions of things move about you rather than your moving through them. It is like being a flea caught in a monochrome kaleidoscope or a goldfish released into the depths of the ocean, looking about and wondering in which patch of weed and at which of the countless mysterious levels refuge can be fond.

The doorways gaping onto snaking walkways give it much in common with a conventional prison, only here the prisoners all wear suits and mill this way and that, murmuring importantly in many tongues. Where prisons thrum and echo, the sounds here are muffled but nonetheless continuous.

It is the world's worst signposted building. Usually I loathe signs. Believe it or not, I do not need to have the landscape ruined by cartoon screams of 'STOP', 'PASSING PLACE' or 'VIEWPOINT'. A building like this, however, where everyone (bar the Commission) must be seen to be equal and so in identical offices on identical landings, needs more signs than a city modelled on a Pollock painting.

There was no Virgil to guide us through this inferno. We just gawped and wandered in and out of the propaganda shop and wondered if the whole election had in fact been a fantastically elaborate charade and all these bustling Eurocrats were about to point and laugh at the presumptuous British businessmen and chant 'Nanananana' – only in French. It was my first day as a 'new bug' at Dulwich all over again.

At last we found an officious looking man in a uniform, explained that we were new members of the parliament and, after he had flapped through a long, long list, were directed to the right suite of rooms. We realised as we climbed into the bulimic's pill-capsule lift that, of course, this so-called parliament was intended to be a cosy continuum. There was no protocol for new parties. Members died or resigned and were replaced without election.

We were 'inducted' and equipped with identification badges and security passes, then led by an exceptionally pretty Dutch girl to our offices.

I laid down my briefcase and looked around. It was really quite pleasant. There was a desk. There were chairs. There was a bookcase. There were filing-cabinets and computers. I said, 'Splendid. Thank you very much. . .'

'No, no,' she corrected. 'This will be your assistant's office.'

She led me on into a larger room, similarly equipped but with a lot more space, a grander desk, a chaise-longue and a shower. Since we were not permitted to doss there overnight, this seemed to me to suggest an obsession for cleanliness during working hours or, perhaps, a courteous provision for *ententes* so *cordiales* as to necessitate ablution. I shower daily but have never in ten years used that expensive facility in my workplace.

Having distributed Rolodexes and framed photographs of children about our offices, we met up again and wondered just what to do next. We were not even strictly MEPs yet. Whereas at Westminster succession is instantaneous and a constituency is never without a representative, we would only be MEPs if we survived until July when we could take up our seats. In the meantime, the South East, the South West and Eastern regions of England were unrepresented.

As if they cared.

We had no staff, no agenda, no idea what we should do. We had, however, a few contacts with fellow Eurosceptics from other reluctant member-states.

At last we met someone who actually knew who we were. Ole Krarup, a Professor of Law at Copenhagen University who had been an MEP for the left-wing People's Movement against the EU since 1994 arose from his seat and bellowed, 'Ah! Welcome to the charade, my friends!'

And charade it was. Charade it is, its sole purpose to furnish an illusion of democracy.

No measure originates in this parliament. There is no such thing as a Private Member's Bill. Every single directive and regulation is conceived by the unelected Commission, drafted by unelected Eurocrats and handed down to the parliament for form's sake. No such measure is ever rejected for long.

The EU is a serial date-rapist. It does not understand the word 'No' or accept rejection of its advances. When referendums in member-states have demonstrated clear opposition to further integration, the EU has simply poured another drink down the dissenter's throat, taken a deep breath, growled, 'You don't really mean that, my dear', grasped her by her privy parts and insisted that what she really meant was 'Yes'.

So too, should the parliament in some drug-induced fit of rebelliousness actually vote against a Commission motion, it will be subjected to a process known as 'conciliation' whereby the vote will simply be overturned and the original reinstated.

Our total irrelevance was made clear from the outset by the very fact that the parliamentary committees were busy drawing up our agendas on our first day in Brussels. They were working a directive whose first and second readings had already taken place in a previous parliament, but bills do not fall with a dissolution as in any other parliament. They have nothing to do with the beliefs of members. They just keep on rolling along in eternal spate. We, the MEPs, are just interchangeable twigs on the surface. The cast might change, but the plot and text of the play remain unaltered.

*

Our first task was to find or form a parliamentary group. Without a group, we would be 'unattached' – an unattractive proposition because it means sitting alone with only the far right, anarchists and sexual or religious obsessives for company. Within a group, you share briefings, intelligence, speaking time and mutual support. You have a professional secretariat.

Unfortunately, in order to be able to enjoy these benefits, you had to find eighteen members from a minimum of five member-states. These must be broadly congenial – which, in our case, meant anti-EU-centralisation – and, if unconventional, not so barking mad as to cause embarrassment by the very fact of association.

Quite a tall order, as the Tories have recently found.

Fortunately, we had friends not merely in Ole but in Jens-Peter Bonde, the urbane, veteran Danish MEP who had been in the parliament since the first ever election in 1979 and knew his way through the physical labyrinth and its labyrinthine procedures as well as anyone living.

Jens-Peter was another man of the left. He had originally been elected as member for the People's Movement Against the EU before founding the June Movement in 1992. He and his wife Lisbeth Kirk ran the well-informed Eurosceptic insiders' website EUObserver.com. He had monitored our progress in Britain and now introduced us to other natural friends.

Notable amongst these was the charismatic Jean Saint-Josse of the French Chasse, Pêche, Nature et Traditions party. They brought six members to the group. Their principal raison d'être was that the shooting of songbirds in February had lately been banned. They liked shooting songbirds in February, regarding it as just one of many agrarian traditions under threat. More to the point, they disputed that anyone on earth had the right to stop them. We did not share their tastes, but we shared their view as to the liberty of French hunters to do what they would when they would on their own terrain.

Jean was one of the few characters in this institution of ciphers. He was Gallic to his nicotine-stained fingertips. He chain-smoked continuously. His lunches were interminable. He demanded a coffee-cup with the aperitif and then filled it with fag-ends as the meal and the operatic debates wore on and on.

He was to stand in the 2002 French presidential elections. One night two months before the poll, when a British politician would surely have been busy being photographed with a fixed grin as he tried to recall his children's names and the geography of his local church, Jean casually said to me, 'Do you want to come out with us tonight?'

I had nothing else planned, so I shrugged, smiled and accepted the invitation. The presidential candidate took us to a very friendly private hostess club. A couple of years later, Richard North, who had been of our party that night, sensationally revealed to the newspapers that I had been to this apparently disreputable establishment. This was apparently news in Britain.

Similarly, the Combats Souverainistes (Fighters for Sovereignty) of France, the orthodox Protestant Dutch ChristenUnie–SGP and a couple of Calvinists, though all separated by ideology, faith and personality – as was only natural for parties from such diverse sources – were united in their insistence that they were entitled to hold their beliefs.

I am not given to Morris dancing, eating blowfish or hiking about Britain in a beard and a dayglo anorak with a telescopic stick, but, perhaps to labour a point, I will die for your freedom to do these things (even the last, offensive though it be).

I am Christian in the normal English way – I love communing with my ancestors who built the mighty English church and who lie in its churchyard. I like to hear the glorious words which they too heard from 1604 onward and to bellow along to *Hymns Ancient and Modern* (but spare me – and God – all that patronising 'Shine, Jesus, Shine' drivel). I approve of Jesus. He seems a decent sort who liked his wine and the company of riff-raff, knew when to pick up the whip and set about him and displayed exemplary manners with that girl caught enjoying a little light relief.

I have precious little, in short, in common with orthodox Dutch Protestants with supposedly moral views on how you amuse yourself in bed or how you deal with the consequences. Provided, however, that they merely seek to express these views and not to enforce them, I will defend them from those who attempt to silence them.

The parliamentary group system makes for strange bedfellows, but hey, they were no stranger than Flat Earth Society members and they too deplored the unelected establishment which wished to legislate them out of existence, so, on the important things at least, we were agreed.

So we formed the EDD – the Europe of Democracies and Diversities – and thus won, on average, seven to ten minutes' speaking-time a day to be divided between sixteen of us. In a really good week, we UKIP MEPs would be permitted to speak for precisely ninety seconds apiece twice a week.

But then, as we were to discover when we went to Strasbourg, where the actual parliament sits, debate – another notion at the heart of parliamentary democracy – is not permitted here. A Canning, a Fox or a Burke would pass unnoticed – just another functionary, eloquence or expertise irrelevant to the process. Just as he was warming to his subject, his microphone would be switched off and the interpreters in their smoked glass booths would start translating the next poor bloody Spaniard's or Dane's ninety seconds or nip off for a fag.

I sat there with my calculator on that first day and worked it all out. I was allowed to make just twenty-eight speeches a year – forty-two minutes' speaking-time. Once overheads are taken into account, an MEP costs the taxpayer £1,200,000 a year. That works out at £500 a second – a damned expensive sniff or hiccough. A pregnant pause can cost more than a pregnant lover.

Given that, when asked what he does in his homeland, an honest British MEP will probably allude to a certain Fanny Adams who was murdered near Alton in 1867, I suggest that your hard-earned money might be better spent.

Here it has gone into constructing and equipping these monstrous buildings. A further million pounds an hour pays innumerable useless but fat employees. Not a penny goes to representing your views or to defending constituents whose health, freedom, livelihood or life may be imperilled. Such concerns are irrelevant impediments to the great homogenisation process.

The EU is a team, for God's sake. No room for individuals here. You remember the old definition of a rowing team? 'Eight men with but a single thought. . . if that'?

Well, that's what we are meant to be. Unthinking, dutiful oars. What does it matter that stroke has chest-pains or cox's family traditionally hosts a reunion today? How can these compare with the interests of the boat as a whole? This programme can work only if all the players act as one.

When idealists speak dreamily of 'global accord', 'global resolve' and even 'global leaders', supposedly in response to environmental threats whose existence is questionable or to terrorist threats no graver than they have ever been, I suggest that they look at the EU as the model of global government – unaccountable, unresponsive, unconnected to the constituents who entrusted it with power – and consider how and by whom 'global law' may be made and enforced. . .

. . .and shudder.

Today's Blofelds caress doped snow-tigers, not Persian cats. Rosa Klebb wears frocks with little mirrors on them. They both have secret shares in McDonald's and Coca-Cola. They are dedicated MEPs.

So what you have paid for instead of debate is 3,100 specialist committees constantly buzzing in Brussels in the cause of homogeneity, resolving subsections to resolutions which, from the moment that they emerge from the Commission, cannot be challenged or rejected but only modified.

This is consultancy heaven.

The actual parliament sits for just sixty days a year.

Should I say that again?

The actual parliament sits for just sixty days a year – twelve days in the £700 million Brussels complex and forty-eight in the £300 million Strasbourg one.

The rest of an MEP's time is taken up with group meetings, visitor meetings (lobbying and propaganda in any other language) and all these committees. Believe it or not, there is now a Brussels Science of Commitology. The Commitologists have meetings too.

Every fourth week, an extraordinary migration takes place. MEPs and their staff pack the entire contents of their offices into tin trunks. These are transported 270 miles to Strasbourg.

Friends of mine who went to Cambridge University tell me that they used to do something very similar when they were undergraduates. As a joke, they would enter their friends' rooms when the owners were away, take meticulous measurements then shift everything to some improbable spot – the middle of a quad, the roof of King's chapel or the Senate House – and reconstruct the whole shooting-match there, right down to the positioning of the slippers and the replacing of boxer-shorts and porn in the drawers.

This little version of the same joke costs you €250 million a year and it serves no purpose whatever. Occasionally the reform of this absurdity is mooted, but to no avail. The French have had it written into the treaties so that they get their share of the profitable action and the status attached to being a centre of government.

Luxembourg, the administrative centre, also wanted in on the act and is the seat of several more agencies of the Union and the base for 2,000 more staff. The Luxembourg institutions included, incredibly, the parliament's library. Books and documents are needed in a parliament, but it sort of gives you pause when you know that every book ordered costs €50,000.

When first I arrived at Strasbourg airport, I was mortified to discover that there were three channels at passport control: one for European citizens, one for all others – and one for us grandees of the European Parliament, who were swept through without question or delay.

I felt as though I had stepped back in time to the days when the nobility had their own pews in church whilst the peasantry gathered at the back. Then it was an aristocracy. Today it is the mediocracy. The scum also rises.

In the Soviet Union, party leaders had their road lanes so that they were not held up by the common herd in their annoying traffic jams. Oh, and good Lord. With Strasbourg establishing the precedent, John Prescott famously did the same thing on the M4 between London and Heathrow.

A rot spreads fast.

As we step from the airport at Strasbourg, chauffeur-driven, air-conditioned limousines sizzle softly along the kerb. These are European Parliament cars. Should we choose to fly to Baden-Baden or Stuttgart, we receive the same star-treatment. The Mayor of Strasbourg wants the EU to stay here. Ferrying self-important functionaries to and from the airport is a small price to pay for keeping the restaurants, bars and knocking-shops thriving.

This EU Parliament only cost around £300 million to build. As I wrote for the *Daily Mail* when first I arrived, 'The impact is staggering. It looks as if my seven-year-old son has been given a kit with 14,000 tons of steel, 140,000 cubic yards of concrete and every available window-pane in France – then told to construct something silly.

'So the building resembles the mother-ship from *Close Encounters* descending onto the gasometers next to the Oval.'

All that glass inside is meant, so they tell us, to represent 'democracy in motion' and the 'transparency' of the European Union. It sort of does. You can't see anything through it.

When first we arrived there, the air-conditioning was not working. Glass without air-conditioning is called 'a greenhouse'. The temperature was in the nineties. Again there were no signs and there were far, far too few lifts. Those that there were were therefore jam-packed with steaming, scowling MEPs in sweat-darkened shirts and suits which clung to their legs. Sometimes the lifts did not work but got stuck between floors.

Getting up to the right level, the right corridor in this ants' nest colosseum was hard. Getting down again was apparently impossible.

This is a new trick which ingenious modern architects have emulated at Tate Modern. There perhaps it is intended to be a conceptual installation referring to lost innocence. You know. The fruit cannot be untasted or reattached to the Tree of Knowledge sort of thing. Cute.

What message the same device in the EU Parliament building is intended to convey I am unsure, but, having left the ground floor, you can continue to rise or you can sink to the nether regions of the subterranean car-park, but you can never again find terra firma or the exit.

As the lift-doors opened for the fourth time on the lowest level of the underground car-park and I moaned and loosened the shirt under my armpits and once more headed upward, I was put in mind of the legend graven at the entrance to Dante's inferno, *'Lasciate ogni speranza, voi ch'entrate'* – 'Abandon all hope, you who enter here.' Luckily, I spoke this out loud, and an Italian Europhile MP with rivulets of sweat running down his temples and dripping from his nose hastened to tell me the secret. You had to cross a bridge across the atrium to find a lift which gives access to the ground floor.

Freedom!

On the second day, the plenary session opened. The parliamentary chamber or 'hemicycle' is a vision in Euro-blue, a lecture-style theatre with static-free, synthetic-topped benches forming a half-wheel around the presidential bench.

My seat was number 543 of 750. I was given my all-important voting swipe-card. This allowed me, without leaving my seat, to vote on the fates of millions of Europeans of whom I knew nothing. It was also a telephone credit card which allowed me limitless calls free of charge. A useful piece of kit, all in all.

Members started to gabble in various languages. Simultaneous interpreters gabbled behind their screens. We were about to elect a new president. I was wearing my headphones which performed an admirable function but not that which they were intended to perform. They prevented me from hearing the members' brief speeches. I could have laid my head on my forearms and had a tranquil kip for a few hours. No sound came to me at all. I felt that it was my duty to object. Technicians bustled forth. They frowned. They tinkered. They provided me with three new headsets. None of them worked.

I knew that it would make not the slightest difference to anything, but hell, I had worked hard to get here and I wanted to know what rhetorical gems were being scattered by my fellows.

I was not to receive a set of cans which actually worked until a few minutes before the vote, but no-one much seemed concerned, although, in any real election, one vote might have won or lost the poll. This vote did not require my swipe-card. All the candidates were federalists, so I just scrawled 'No confidence in any of these candidates' on the ballot paper. There were seventy-eight other spoiled papers. Nicole Fontaine became president.

That simple.

For all that I had understood barely a word of this cursory 'debate', I had at least understood what I was voting – or failing to vote – for. The following day, however, we got down to the day-to-day business. Now things got seriously scary.

Look. We said from the outset that we would play no active part in the parliament's procedures, that our function was to do what any parliament should do but this one signally fails to do – that is, to make the process accountable to voters in Britain, to monitor its machinations and expose its more glaring cases of corruption and waste. This is not transparent government, but perhaps we can poke peepholes in the cloudy screen which surrounds it.

Nonetheless, we cannot but be aware that we are now theoretically members of the ruling caste. Although our votes here will make no difference to the vast sewer of laws which will spew its contents onto distant shores, they are being passed in our names, and we would quite like to know what toxic waste we are sending home.

Every one of these thousands of amendments to directives and regulations upon which we are invited to vote may drive an honest, hardworking citizen out of business, break up a family, destroy a way of life or a life.

In Brussels, we dealt with the fine points of directives. Here the results are seen in draft agendas, soon to be followed by final draft agendas which often bear little resemblance to their antecedents. So MEPs stand up and make their ninety-second submissions to 'debate', heeded only by the interpreters.

Then it is voting-time, and suddenly a passion for democracy infects the entire building. If Mme Fontaine had announced that she was about to perform a nude pole-dance, the chamber could not fill more rapidly. This may have something to do with the fact that, were members not there for the vote, their daily attendance allowance would be cut by half.

In little more than an hour, before the bored gaze of a bingo-teller president, we may be required to cast 600 votes or more, each having a direct effect on the lives of hundreds, maybe millions of people.

Of course, no-one has the least idea what they are voting for. The three buttons in front of me are all of the same grey and unlabelled. The big parties all obediently vote as per instructions. They have whips with huge offices, research teams and parliamentary tic-tac men who wave their arms about in order to indicate how they should vote. As in a giant Mexican wave, hundreds of hands shoot up into the air or hundreds of fingers press the same buttons.

We, at that time without a research team, had not the faintest clue what we were doing. Someone told us that the middle button was for abstainers, so we kept our fingers on the middle button.

Later on, I confessed my bafflement to some British Tories whom I met in the bar. They laughed and admitted that, despite their huge and experienced secretariat, they had only known what they were voting about on four or five occasions that day. Otherwise, well, they had been told how to vote, so they did.

After that deeply depressing morning session at which we learned that we were mere functionaries without the least autonomy, we staggered out, intent on several stiff drinks and a brisk lunch at a cafe which we had spotted within easy walking distance.

As we reached the front desk, our chauffeur materialised, shepherded us to an air-conditioned Mercedes and whisked us the few hundred yards to the cafe.

Mere functionaries? Us?

Nonsense. We were Hugely Important Persons.

*

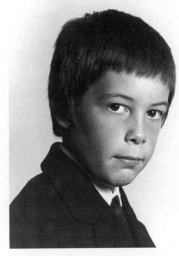

At prep school, aged 5.

Just about to start at Dulwich College. I was terrified.

In the uniform of the Combined Cadet Force, aged 18.

Launching the 1999 European election campaign. *Left to right*
Christopher Booker, fellow candidate Christopher Skeate,
Bill Jamieson and myself.

Making my acceptance speech after winning my seat in
the 1999 European elections.

Speaking in Trafalgar Square against the euro, August 1999 – my first time on a platform with the 'big boys'. Also pictured are (*from far right*) Norman Tebbit, Austin Mitchell MP and Anthony Coughlan, leader of Ireland's anti-euro campaign.

At the launch of the Metric Martyrs campaign, August 2000. To my left are three shopkeepers charged with failing to use metric units: (*left to right*) Neil Herron, Hassan Yusufali and Steve Thoburn.

More campaigns: *above* supporting the Irish 'No' vote on the Nice
Treaty in the European Parliament; *below* outside Westminster against the
European Constitution, with the Conservative MP Bob Spink.

At the Bromley &
Chislehurst by-election,
June 2006, beating Labour
into fourth place.

'Parking our tanks on
David Cameron's lawn'
outside the Conservative
Party spring conference,
Manchester, 2006.

'Farage's Foragers': at the Menin Gate, Ypres, 11 November 1998, to mark the eightieth anniversary of the Armistice.

With the comedian Frank Carson (*centre*) and Paul Nuttall, party chairman, during the 2009 European election campaign.

My favourite pastimes are fishing and golf, but sadly I don't have as much time to indulge in either of them as I would like nowadays. *Above* the catch from a tuna fishing expedition in Kenya, 2001; *below* at Royal Birkdale, February 2003, with my colleague Danny Gillespie on my right and my brother Andrew.

With the late Colin Merton,
a stalwart of UKIP,
in September 2007
(Michael Bloch)

Getting our point across
outside the European
Commission office in London.

And that became my life. I ran Farage Futures — though I had to employ a new man to take up the slack in my absences on duty — I continued to campaign for UKIP at home and to tell the faithful what I had learned, I skittered back and forth to Brussels and to Strasbourg. We engaged Richard North and Heather Conyngham who enabled us to make some sense of what was going on.

Oh, and I got married and we lost a leader.

*

I have never stood on a political stage nor posed for the media with my family. I never will. If, then, they are ever bothered by the media, it is because the media are intruding into irrelevant matters which are none of their concern.

Those are the rules and, with one notable exception, the media have respected them. If, then, I deal cursorily with personal matters, it is not because they are unimportant to me but because they matter too much to be dragged through a rough circus in which it is my perverse pleasure to perform.

So yes. In November of that year, I got married.

I had been in Frankfurt looking for execution business in 1996 when I met Kirsten Mehr, a stunning government bond broker whose brisk efficiency at first sight belied her aethereal appearance. She could have stepped into a pre-Raphaelite painting and no questions asked.

She was posted to London later that year and we furthered, as I think the expression is, our acquaintance. It was an arduous time, and she was, and has been since, fantastically supportive, not in the style of some political wives — fawning and simpering on stage, glittering at my side at receptions and all that — but supplying sanity and stability at home, managing my correspondence (particularly my email which would otherwise overwhelm me) and organising my diary.

Our lovely daughter Victoria was born the following year and her enchanting sister Isabelle five years later.

I am not uxorious, and am glad that my family has not joined me on the tightrope on which I have elected to prance and preen. They have been my safety net, however, and have made my more daring tricks up there less daunting.

If that seems an ungallant tribute, I apologise to those who believe that emotions cannot be expressed without, at the least, an ode. Any odes which I have in me will be clumsily stammered to those who have warranted them in the privacy of home.

*

Maybe it was the limousines which changed Michael Holmes. Maybe he simply blundered. He certainly seemed overwrought. John Whittaker, who had been a keen supporter, found his Sunday afternoons taken up by panicky telephone calls from Holmes, demanding that he send out faxes to UKIP members about Holmes's perceived enemies.

Holmes was unable to take a brief. It is far harder to write short than to write long, and there was much that we wanted to say. Finding ourselves limited to ninety seconds, therefore, we depended upon very careful editing to enable us to get the point across. Richard North distilled our original ideas again and again until only the quintessence remained.

Even I, though something of a natural orator (I find the words 'garrulous gobshite' deeply offensive and how the hell did some get back in here?) recognised this and, for all that I argued with Richard at length, accepted the necessity to take expert editing. Holmes, however, would take the arduously written draft and scribble his own version all over it, apparently wholly unaware that, for everything added, something else must be removed.

When he arose to make his maiden speech, we sat open-mouthed as, winging it without consultation, he called for the European Parliament to be given increased powers.

UKIP voters were demanding Britain's withdrawal from the Euro-Soviet, not the usual palliative and effectively ridiculous policy of reforming it from within, as favoured by every other political party when confronted by the undemocratic nature of the institution and the undeniable corruption of its members. And here was our leader apparently advocating just that!

In fairness to Holmes, his point, if he had been allowed to complete his off-the-cuff ramble, if we had for one moment accepted the necessity or the validity of the EU, if one man's, one party's – one nation's – voice had counted for anything in this giant, unresponsive institution, his point would have been a valid one – that 'the elected representatives should have much more authority over the programmes and policies of this institution'. As it was, he was speaking both nonsense and heresy.

Being an MEP had plainly turned Holmes as it has turned so many others. On 3 September 1999, he turned up at an NEC meeting wearing his EU Parliament badge, identifying him as an MEP.

This should surely have been a joyous meeting and a time for thanks. Entirely thanks to volunteers, we had three members in the European Parliament and were an acknowledged force in the land. Graham Booth, who had not only worked so hard in the south-west but had stood aside to make way for Holmes, was looking forward to a celebratory meeting. Holmes, however, wasted no time in such frivolity but attacked the entire committee for 'leaking' privileged information.

Craig Mackinlay, his deputy, suggested that perhaps Holmes was taking these 'leaks' somewhat too seriously. Holmes drew an envelope out of his pocket and flicked it across the table at Craig. It contained his summary dismissal, which, considering that he was an unpaid volunteer, argued a shaky grip on reality.

Nonetheless, Craig got up and stalked with considerable dignity from the room. Party secretary Tony Scholefield, who had supplied the party with its Regent Street offices, remonstrated with Holmes and informed him that he had committed effective suicide in the party. Holmes had another pre-prepared envelope ready for him too.

This was the tough, go-getting, feverishly authoritarian tycoon at work, only he seemed to have forgotten that he was exercising his authority over a group of mild-mannered supporters to whom he owed a huge debt but who owed him nothing.

To his astonishment and outrage, a vote of no confidence in his leadership was proposed then and there. Of the seventeen people present, nine felt that they had no choice but to vote for Holmes's removal.

Three others, Holmes loyalists, actually voted for his retention. I was livid, but Titford and I, terrified of such mess so soon after our triumph, felt in duty bound, albeit reluctantly, to vote with our leader. No-one in the party believed that we supported him.

Holmes was out. The sense of relief was overwhelming, but the embarrassment for the party promised to be hugely destructive.

We hammered out a face-saving deal. Citing whatever excuse he chose, Holmes would resign with his dignity intact at the party conference a month hence. He would not then stand for re-election. The entire NEC would also step down and would not campaign for re-election until conference was done. Holmes signed an undertaking drawn up by lawyer Hugh Meechan to this effect.

I breathed another sigh of relief. We still had the small problem of getting Holmes to knuckle down as an MEP under another leader or resign his seat, but we were confident that good sense and the interests of the party would prevail.

UKIP's conference opened at the National Motorcycle Museum in Birmingham on 1 October 1999. Here at least, there was a celebratory mood. This motley gang of rebels from the shires assembled to hobnob and congratulate one another and themselves on an enormous achievement. After just seven years in existence, we were the fourth political party in the land.

The first day of conference is the one intended for public consumption. The media and the provincial members with no interest in internal politics are there in force. Richard, Earl of Bradford, who had lately defected to us from the Tories, made a memorable speech. He compared himself with Michael Portillo, declaring, 'After all these years, I am coming out! Ladies and Gentlemen, I am UKIP!' Jeffrey and I also rallied the troops and thanked them for their efforts.

Amazingly, we enjoyed one minute fifty-two seconds of coverage on the national evening news. That was another watershed.

Holmes's announcement would come on the morrow, when crowds were smaller and party business and specific policy would be dealt with. The media headed back home that night, duty done. So did all the loyal members who had just come along for the day to lend their support.

The following morning, Holmes struck.

We had never thought that he would go back on his word. We were totally unprepared. He, however, had carefully prepared his ground.

He swept aside the entire day's agenda and insisted that the conference be deemed an EGM. This was promptly agreed with a lot of bemused shrugging and a show of hands.

I was in the chair but, as one of the three MEPs – and one with strong views on the subject – I at once surrendered it. Hugh Meechan volunteered to take it in my stead.

Holmes told the assembled faithful that yes, he had agreed to resign, but only under undue psychological pressure. He therefore proposed a vote of no confidence in the NEC, insisting that he had been illegally usurped and was still the constitutional leader.

Here Holmes pulled a distinctly fast one. At the time of the European elections, he had asked that NEC members should stay in office rather than standing for re-election for fear that the instability and possible controversy surrounding an internal election might adversely affect our prospects in the broader poll. Now he claimed that, in consequence, they no longer had voting rights and had no right to oust their duly elected leader. Oh, and by the way, the NEC had been infiltrated, root and branch, by the BNP – a claim subsequently proved to be wholly without foundation, but hey, what attack upon UKIP would be complete without that weary lie?

By now, the heckling was so loud that Hugh Meechan was shouting to be heard. Holmes, whose supporters had been forewarned, was confirmed as leader by 236 votes to 35 with fifty-five members, including myself, abstaining. The fact that Holmes's supporters were there in force whilst most other members had happily gone home or were still enjoying black pudding or one another in their Travelodges meant that this was anything but an EGM.

Publicly I kept my head down. This was partly a politician's self-interest, partly a recognition that self-interest and the interests of the party were, in this instance, one and the same. Unity was paramount. When Sked was driven out, it had still been possible to consider the formation of the New Alliance party. Now we had gone too far and achieved too much to have the party riven from top to bottom. UKIP must be preserved, and, whoever won this unseemly tussle, I wanted Jeffrey, David Lott and myself to be there to lead it onward and the bulk of our loyal supporters with us on the journey.

Holmes had behaved shoddily, but we were colleagues for now and, though I was aware that he must not continue as leader and I was in daily – often hourly – contact with the 'rebels', I could not declare for them without forcing every member of the party into one camp or another. UKIP must go on unified, and I was confident that the all-important rank and file of the party-branches would at length withdraw their support from Holmes without prompting.

The rebel faction, though justified, was for now anarchic and uncontrolled. My first fear was that the party's database might be abused, in which case members would be betrayed and would never vote for UKIP again. Back in London the following morning, I sent someone round to Regent Street to secure the computers and filing-cabinets. Tony Scholefield had already been there, using his authority as party secretary, to have the locks changed. As party chairman, I outranked him. I had the doors forced and the locks changed again, and all the sensitive files shifted down to Salisbury where Holmes guarded them.

Holmes branded everyone in the party who questioned his actions an 'extremist'. He conducted a postal poll which, he claimed, showed 90 per cent support for him – not exactly surprising since no-one who did not support him would pay for an envelope and a stamp. Craig Mackinlay had Holmes's bank account frozen. Holmes retaliated by attempting to bring an injunction against the NEC claiming that they were 'time-barred' and giving them just twenty-four hours to prepare a defence.

Although Holmes engaged a QC, the judge-in-chambers decided that the punitive emergency suit, of a type commonly used to prevent gross abuse of copyright, was wholly inappropriate to these complex circumstances. He made it clear that he was displeased with such abuse of process. Craig demanded costs for the defence of a frivolous suit. Holmes, at last getting the message, settled out of court before the claim could go further.

Now was the time for us to move.

Jeffrey and I nailed our colours to the mast by writing a letter in which we stated that we had no faith in Holmes and demanded that he step down. David Lott, John Harvey and I gave the go-ahead to the required twenty-five branch chairmen and women to call a genuine EGM to sort out the unholy mess.

It was held at Westminster Central Hall on 22 January 2000. Some 900 members attended. Norris McWhirter vainly attempted to maintain control.

The crowd roared and wept and shook fists and sheaves of papers. Every speaker was shouted down. I have never, before or since, attended a meeting so constantly close to eruption into violence. One member of the audience suffered a fatal heart attack.

A splinter group under the influence of Rowan Atkinson's brother Rodney – a man obsessed with the notion of the EU as a Nazi plot who had many avid followers in Newcastle and in Oxford – made most of the noise. Poor Norris, himself heavily under Atkinson's influence, nonetheless called for order. Disgusted members were standing, many of them in tears at seeing all their hard work undone by this battle, and storming out.

I too was by now close to tears. Everything for which I had fought and worked was being ripped apart by self-seeking factionalism and idiotic pride. The people now walking out, maybe forever, they mattered. The ordinary advocates of decency and freedom who had sacrificed a precious day off to come up here from Suffolk, Devon, Yorkshire. . . they mattered, not the vainglorious morons up there squabbling for position and power.

I felt guilty too. Maybe I could have intervened sooner and prevented this. Maybe I had tried to be too clever in my bid to force Holmes and Atkinson to show their hands against the will of the members so that UKIP would not drift asunder. Because now UKIP was falling to pieces before my eyes.

It has entered UKIP legend – the way that I leaped up onto the stage and imperiously took control. Hmm.

I leaped onto that stage in desperation. If I commanded attention, it was because I howled for calm as if I had seen my own children preoccupied by squabbling as the car rolled towards the cliff-edge rather than grabbing for the handbrake. It was not the light of authority in my eyes as I yelled 'Enough!' and 'Stop!' It was the glint of fury from behind a film of tears.

It worked.

Maybe it was because so many of them knew me from my travels. Maybe it was because they were curious as to what the weird, flashy 'boy' who had been silent for so long actually thought of the betrayal. I like to think that it was because they had been longing to hear a voice as sincere as theirs and that sheer passion carried the day.

I cannot say that silence fell. Silence lurched at first. Silence staggered. Silence slumped as I spoke. Then silence fell and I spoke into echoes.

Holmes was overwhelmingly ordered by the party to stand down.

Under the list system, an MEP who changes allegiance cannot be removed, even though it was his party not he who was elected. We begged then tried to bully Holmes to do the honourable thing and to leave the seat in Brussels for one who represented the views of those who had elected him. He refused.

He did not need the money and it afforded him no real power, but he had known what it is to be an MEP. He did not wish to lose it. He remained there, sitting on his own amongst the unattached, until at last, in 2002, after a heart attack and a stroke, he yielded his seat to Graham Booth, the man who had won it for him.

In retrospect, I regret my provident temporising. I should, I think, have taken a stand and given a lead sooner. At the time, all that mattered to me was the unity and so the survival of the party.

Whatever my feelings towards Holmes and his towards me at the time and since, he has never once spoken out against Jeffrey, me or UKIP. Temperaments may have clashed and personal loyalties foundered, but, in our very different ways, we have remained united in the cause.

Of course it was not all over. It never is. Even in a work of fiction, those two words, 'The End', are the biggest lie of all.

There had to be a leadership election. I think that I really might have won that one, but now was a time for healing, and Jeffrey was emollient where I was abrasive.

Although Jeffrey too had openly demanded Holmes's removal, I was perceived with some justice as the man who had brought him down.

I was also aware that, after being leader, there was nowhere to go save down. William Hague, the best speaker and the most gifted man in his party, was then leading the Tories. He was just three years my senior, and his destiny was already obvious to me.

So Jeffrey stood and, after a fierce competition with Rodney Atkinson and the timely release of a letter written by Christopher Booker of the *Sunday Telegraph* and his colleague Bill Jamieson, now executive editor of the *Scotsman*, in which they declared that they could not support the party under Atkinson, won the day by a mere 0.4 per cent.

Atkinson vanished off the face of the earth, accusing me of 'dirty tricks' and the party, of course, of 'extremism', nature unspecified. Holmes's supporters faded away or clambered back on board.

And things settled down.

It is not realpolitik. It was not engineered. The lesson of history, however, seems to be that every political party needs a purge, just as many a habitat needs the cleansing but doubtless painful effects of fire. This painful, spontaneous episode saw the party strengthened and those who would place their own convictions, fancies or personal ambitions above the interests of the party and the central cause burned up to make room for new, healthy shoots.

With the assistance of Richard North and Heather Conyngham, Jeffrey and I punched well above our weight in the EU Parliament but increasingly returned to our principal mission – spreading the word in the UK. The party was small and vulnerable. We nursed it at home. We were back in the pubs and the village halls. New branches opened. Established ones grew.

But there is one game in which, more than any other, the decks are marked and the dice loaded against a small party. The media may be critical of the established parties, but they are cosy with them. They too are of the establishment. The media are overwhelmingly liberal but therefore astonishingly illiberal when a new voice is heard in the land.

We made our mistakes, of course, and sometimes deserved media scorn, but, for several years, that scorn was reflex. We simply did not belong.

8

'MEDIA SAVVY'

In October, 2009, I was ranked No. 41 in a list of the 100 most powerful right-wingers in Britain. I am unsure about the 'right winger' bit, preferring to consider myself a Whig, but, if individualism, advocacy of capitalism (which always seems to me a little bit like advocacy of overall wetness in water) and concern for the preservation of established institutions be 'right wing', I plead guilty. The principal reason given for my purported potency, however, was my 'media savvy'.

My what?

My media savvy consists in enjoying a drink or several with journalists and broadcasters, recognising that they, like me, have a tough job to do, speaking my mind and, I hope, being mildly entertaining.

But then, I don't suppose that anyone in politics has tried that technique in quite a while.

When I started out, I had no experience of the media whatever. I have had no training. Despite growing evidence that we were going to win seats in 1999, the national media – and particularly the BBC – tried very hard to pretend that UKIP did not exist. There was a profile in the *Telegraph* with a rather fetching picture of me in a cream suit, and that was about it.

This had been the case for the entire Eurosceptic movement for years. We were simply ignored.

Of course every small party will develop paranoia and accuse the establishment of censorship, but independent analysis after the election demonstrated the extent of the BBC's Europhilia. Stories about Europe concentrated exclusively on the largely fictional split in the Tory party. Labour, it seemed, had no Eurosceptics at all. A party called the Pro-Euro Conservatives of whom no-one has ever heard since received more coverage in that campaign than UKIP.

On the Record conducted interviews only with dedicated servants of the European project – Margaret Beckett, Paddy Ashdown, Jack Cunningham, Sir Leon Brittan (by then a European Commissioner) and Romano Prodi (who had nothing to do with the election at all). Their sole concession to the Eurosceptics was an interview with William Hague – he of 'in Europe but not run by Europe' infamy.

The BBC is meant, as a public service broadcaster, to retain impartiality. It signally failed in that obligation here. It began to be known as the 'Brussels Broadcasting Corporation'.

Even this was not entirely fair, because Brussels thinks that its doings are of paramount importance, whereas the British media like to ignore European elections then bemoan the fact that voter turnout has dropped yet again. The BBC News department afforded 2.5 per cent of its time to the forthcoming poll.

All in all, in that campaign UKIP received 3½ minutes of national coverage out of a total of 624 hours, and yet we won 7 per cent of the nation's votes. Speculation is bootless, but I hazard that, had we received even 5 per cent of the coverage, we might have won a much larger share of the poll.

Radio 4's *Today* programme is possibly the most influential and best-researched current affairs programme of the lot, and, when I am asked with which broadcaster I best like to work, I unhesitatingly name John Humphrys, who puts me on my mettle like no other and draws out the best and worst in his interviewees.

Being grilled by him is like donning white tie and tails for a party. Suddenly the back straightens, the vowels become purer, the consonants crisper and the mind sharper. And, of course, any defects in deportment or thickening about the intellectual waist become more apparent. It is uncomfortable. It is daunting. It is infinitely more fun than 'smart casual'.

I did not approve of him, however, on my first appearance on the programme – my first ever interview on national radio.

It had been arranged that a car would pick me up at 5.30 in the morning to drive me to the London studio. At the last minute, however, I received a call from the BBC. The car could not make it, but no matter. A telephone interview would suit them just fine. David Lott and I sat waiting nervously in my kitchen. The phone rang at 6.55. I was almost immediately on air.

'So, Mr Farage,' said Humphrys, 'I have here a copy of *Spearhead*, the BNP's magazine. You are singled out for particular praise. What's it like to have friends like that?'

How do you answer a question like that without being on the defensive and so appearing to have something to hide? I had thought journalists wise to 'When did you stop beating you wife?' stories, but no. It still makes good copy.

Nothing which I had ever said or written indicated sympathy with the BNP or its so-called policies. If a badger-baiting or Europhiliac magazine had made me its playmate of the month or dish of the day, would the BBC therefore have concluded that I must share their perversions? A lazy researcher had simply heard malicious gossip, noted that we had 'UK' in our name as the BNP had 'British' in theirs and, had, in effect, done the BNP's work for them.

But it was I, not the lazy researcher, who had to suffer.

I spent those 3½ minutes on the ropes.

The BBC may barely have noticed our existence or the threat which we posed, but the dirty tricks departments of other parties were plainly rather more alert. On the Friday before the election, I received a call from my friend Nick Jones, the BBC's political correspondent who was in the end to lose his position for being 'off message'. He was invariably on the side of those who challenged authority, no matter what their political affiliations.

Nick felt it only fair to give me notice that tomorrow's *Times* was to run a piece by Andrew Pierce about UKIP's 'links' with the BNP and that Francis Maude of the Tory Party had already indicated his willingness to comment on air.

It was a terrifying moment. We had waited and worked for so long for this moment, and now, I supposed, some idiotic branch chairman was about to reveal that he and his mates also happened to run the Budleigh Salterton chapter of the Ku Klux Klan or something.

Andrew Pierce rang. It was nothing so dramatic, but it might at the time have been still more destructive. Sked had been singing a favourite tune, now well known to be inspired by injured amour-propre but then still novel. He spoke of Deavin – his protégé, but he preferred to recall my later lunch with the man. He alleged that I had in conversation referred to 'nig-nogs'. The paper had the picture of me with Deavin and Lecomber.

I did something which I have never done before, something which was against my nature. I called the famous libel solicitors Carter-Ruck and appealed for the protection of the law against allegations without substance.

Even as we celebrated our election victory, Carter-Ruck were locked in a battle with Rupert Murdoch and News International which could easily have escalated into a bloody – and bloody ruinous – war.

It was Michael Gove, a *Times* columnist who has since become a Tory MP, who stepped between these two pawing and snorting herd-bulls and insisted that his newspaper end the deadlock. I owe Michael one for that. An apology was duly printed (at the bottom of page 2) and the whole business closed. I still reckon that that *Times* article, though fanciful, cost us seats in Yorkshire and in the north-west.

On the night of the election count, it was eighty-seven minutes into the programme before David Dimbleby deigned to notice our existence, and, as we excitedly awaited results of immediate importance to all present in Winchester Guildhall, Bruce Parker of BBC South approached me with a microphone. He demanded, 'So, Mr Farage, we see that M. Le Pen's party is doing well in France. You must be pleased?'

I usually try to nurse a drink on such nights, but this fatuous, malicious lie posturing as a question sent me seething to the bar where I ordered several large gins before painting a smile back on my face.

I suppose the ease with which I took to the broadcast media was the consequence at once of nature and of nurture. My mind teems with opinions and jokes, I like people and I have always made it my business to understand my opponent's point of view and to observe his or her 'tells', as poker-players call them – the telltale signs of confidence or nervousness.

The diversity of my interests too – ridiculously rare in an age of 'professional politicians' – enabled me to answer questions about business, sport, sex, drugs and rock'n'roll and other subjects of more interest to the discerning public than the intricacies of some impertinent bureaucratic Brussels directive.

So although *Question Time* is easily the scariest programme of the lot, I love it. We genuinely do not know what questions are to be asked or how the audience will react. Again, at first I had to battle against ignorant preconceptions. The producer and his team treated me as an unwelcome token guest, there on sufferance and to be regarded with circumspection, much as if I bore some vile ideological contagion.

On one of those early appearances, I was arguing that the tenuous peace which Europe had enjoyed since World War II owed nothing to a united Europe but a great deal to NATO. A member of the audience, plainly untroubled by the strains of excessive cerebration, gave it as his opinion that a largely British and American alliance all seemed to him 'rather racist'. I confess that I dumbly gawped at this intervention.

At dinner afterwards, David Dimbleby expressed the concern which made the programme so nervous. He said, 'Of course, the BNP question hasn't been answered.'

Nor is it likely to be unless it be asked, but then, save in the minds of the BNP and the BBC, there is no BNP question. There is also, so far as I know, no Girl Guide, Flat Earth or Holy Roller question. We have nothing in common with the BNP. They are racist. We are inclusive. They are authoritarian. We are anti-authoritarian. They hate Europe, to be sure, as they hate all of the rest of the world and a large percentage of Britons. We love Europe but happen to reject the EU.

The all-important fact to them is that we are successful where they are not. They therefore want to be associated with us.

They are not. They never will be.

At the private post-production drinks party that evening, the man with the strangely tranquil brain who had thought NATO racist was drinking with the producers.

To be fair to *Question Time*, they too had been the victims of lies and garish headlines and were, I suppose, nervous. They genuinely believed that, beneath the surface charm and the professed cause, there must be another, secret, nationalistic or racist agenda. Convinced and passionate amateurs were simply a novelty to them.

I resolved then that I must just be myself, express my love of life and my belief in people and so, by degrees, persuade the general public and *Question Time* that we were what we seemed – representatives of millions of ordinary, hardworking people who resented unelected government and would quite like to get back to running their own affairs.

You think that experienced politicians look confident up there on the stage? Like hell they are. They know, as do I, that it is the one programme on British television which causes people to stop you on the street and challenge or congratulate you. So they pace and fiddle and check their notes. They consult their policy advisers to discover just what it is that they think. They mutter retorts to imagined heckles.

I was in the Green Room before my third or fourth *Question Time* when I suddenly realised that I was in fact the least terrified person there.

The professional politicians had to please their masters without alienating the public and vice versa. The celebrities from television or show business – barring the stand-up comics like Marcus Brigstocke – had little experience of thinking on their feet. I had been facing random questions and vigorous heckling for years and I was concerned to please no-one. I have, I confess, made a point since then of ordering a gin and tonic rather loudly and chatting to the bar-staff about just about anything as the audience gathers. I am sure that it makes my fellow panellists feel more relaxed.

Slowly the truth sank in. I had no secret agenda.

I had another advantage. It has long been a staple of the established parties in such forums to make sincere assurances which mean nothing. So the Tory, for example, pledges with tears in his eyes that his party will, if elected, cap immigration or reclaim British fishing-grounds. His Labour opponent knows full well that this is gibberish because no British political party has such power. They have all signed it away under the terms of the various European treaties. He will say nothing, however, because he is about to outline his own exciting but entirely fictional immigration or employment policy.

I know the exact terms of the treaties which prevent such autonomous action, and I have no interest in pretending that these lies are even potentially true. I flatter myself, then, that *Question Time* tends to be more interesting when I am there. Politicians look askance at me and shuffle in their seats. They have to tell something akin to the truth.

I have made some unlikely friends (David Blunkett, for example, enjoys a few glasses of red with a Eurosceptic and is himself deeply mistrustful of European institutions) and have enjoyed some right royal barnies (with Alistair Darling on compulsory metrication, for example).

I have even, though reluctantly, made enemies. I suspect that David Davis may never forgive me for challenging him over his gallant 'stand' on detention without charge for twenty-eight days. He was posing as a champion of freedoms because he opposed the government's proposed 42-day suspension of civil rights. I simply asked him, 'Do you stand for habeas corpus?' to which he had no reply.

I have appeared regularly over the last decade. I knew, I think, that I was accepted when I gave it as my opinion that, after a snowy spell, people should be back at work. Will Young accused me of puritanism. I protested that I was no puritan and David Dimbleby, with a grin, said, 'Ye-e-s-s. Well, before we go too deeply into that. . .' The audience laughed spontaneously. David now looks to me as a source of cigarettes as soon as we leave the stage rather than of extreme views when we are on it.

After that first successful European election, I got myself into more trouble. Paul Henley from the independent film company Mosaic wanted to make a documentary film, funded by the BBC and Arte, about the workings of the EU. Since this exactly reflected our aims in being there, we agreed. For four months, Paul followed us wherever we went in the course of our duties.

The resulting film, *The Enemy Within: Desperately Seeking EUtopia,* was entertaining and hugely instructive. It demonstrated (at huge expense to the licence-payer) the total futility of the intricate system of pseudo-government which (at huge expense to the tax-payer) kept all those thousands of Brussels functionaries in business and put so many thousands of British sole traders and small enterprises out of it.

The BBC did not want to show the film.

Oh, it was shown to acclaim in every other EU country and in the United States, but in its country of origin it was shelved without explanation.

Lord Peter Shore raised the subject in the House of Lords. By what right did a public service broadcaster charged with instructing and entertaining the public presume to censor – to ban – a film made at the public's expense which did just that?

The BBC declined to answer. They conceded. Sort of. They showed the film to the two women, one man and one West Highland terrier with cataracts who watched BBC Knowledge.

And, just in case the terrier was of a sensitive disposition, they issued a solemn warning before it was shown. 'Viewers should be warned that Mr Farage expresses extreme views as part of this programme.'

I did, too. Like 'Have you ever seen so much money thrown away on so little?' and 'No matter what these people do or say, the elector cannot remove them from office'.

Please ensure that no young or impressionable people are in the room as you read this page. Here is an example of my extremism: 'Whatever your vision of the future, you are not going to be able to attain it or even aspire to it unless and until you are free to go your own way. For as long as we are part of this intrusive and ever more powerful Soviet, we can't make decisions for ourselves or determine our own future. What we do with our freedom once we have won it remains to be seen, but we are demanding that we be allowed to take that first step and reclaim responsibility for our own lives.'

Is the suppression of such dissident ranting in the national interest? Or is it pernicious, Soviet-style censorship?

I grew angry. It was not just the production team who had put a lot of effort into the making of the film. We too had done many interviews and had had our first steps in Brussels and Strasbourg dogged by Paul.

I taped the film and, from my office in Redhill quite openly sold the VHS tape at a not-for-profit £5 a throw for the information of our members only. One punter who turned up claiming to be a party member from Portsmouth then revealed himself to be an officer of Surrey Trading Standards Authority, tipped off by a sorry and chagrined former member.

Since the film had otherwise sunk without trace and its makers had not instituted proceedings against me, I had had no idea that I was breaking any law. I merely thought that it was the same as taping an instalment of a favourite television programme for a friend. Apparently I was transgressing four separate Acts of Parliament.

A long, expensive and wearisome battle with the authorities ensued. In the end, it was accepted that I had acted in ignorance and had made no profit so no further action was taken.

The next pre-election assault from the press came in 2004, this time on the Sunday before the election, when the *Mail on Sunday* ran a double-page spread headed, as far as I remember, *The Wild, Drunken, Womanising Existence of Nigel Farage*. For myself and for UKIP, I was unconcerned. In fact, my response was, 'I only wish it were all true'.

We had never set out nor claimed to be plaster saints, after all, but normal people with normal weaknesses, and I have perhaps more normal weaknesses than most. What I did not have was one half of the strength or stamina required for my alleged excesses. Still, I have on occasion behaved a little wildly and I have enjoyed the odd drink from time to time, so what the hell.

My sole reason for concern was that our principal backer at the time was Yorkshire millionaire businessman Paul Sykes, a determined, ascetic man of high moral principle who had consistently urged me to behave better. Monday's edition of the *Mail* carried still worse allegations.

I need not have worried. On the Tuesday morning, Paul rang to tell me that he and his wife were 'right disappointed' that there were to be no more instalments.

In January 2006, I blundered into my very own media embarrassment. Just one week after the Liberal Democrat MP Mark Oaten was exposed as having rented a fastidious Polish former ballet-dancer called Tomasz for 'a gross act of humiliation which only a few punters ask for . . . quite revolting really', the *News of the World* printed a story about me.

This time it was a 25-year-old Latvian girl named Liga whom I had met in the local pub one evening when I was far too well lubricated to occasion a similar effect in her, but I had been flattered and foolish enough to accept her invitation home for a drink.

This is because I am a male of the species and so easily flattered, for which I apologise. She claimed that I was a beast in bed and 'we must have had sex about seven times'. Given the amount that I had drunk on the night in question, the former statement was probably accurate – or would have been had I got to a bed. The second was a physical impossibility.

She was, as far as I remember (which is not much), a sleek and seductive creature, and I will not splutter and expostulate that, after the first bottle, I would necessarily have behaved like Galahad in full armour and been immune. I hope that I would have, but I can give no guarantees.

There are, however, occasional merits to excess. On that night it saved me. I fell asleep on her sofa where, by her no doubt truthful account, I 'snored like a horse'.

But of course, as any nineteenth-century maiden could have told me, protestations of innocence will avail you nothing if you have spent the night with another. The altar or the scandal sheets await you. Liga wasn't screwed. I was.

I don't think that this fantasy did our election prospects any harm, not least because none of the UKIP faithful believed a word of it. It did get me into fearful trouble with Kirsten. She did not find Lothario Nigel after a hard night's drinking credible, but she was furious at me for being so bloody stupid and inconsiderate as to pass out three miles from home. That made two of us.

There have been media heroes in the UKIP story – journalists and broadcasters who, even if not unquestioning supporters, have been open-minded enough from the outset to acknowledge that we represent many of their readers, listeners and viewers and that our cause is just.

Booker and Jamieson knew enough about the EU and its workings and had met enough of its victims to become involved in their own story. They have been crucial elements in our development.

Simon Heffer has always given us a fair crack of the whip and has shared a platform with me at every election in which I have stood. Kelvin

MacKenzie has given me good advice; James Whale and the late Mike Dickin of TalkSport gave our message a priceless platform when those serving themselves or the metropolitan elite declined to do so. James, who is now with LBC, even wanted to stand as the UKIP candidate in the London mayoral election, but Ofcom informed him that he could not be mayor and a broadcaster, and the notion of James sans mike was unthinkable, the thing itself probably dangerous.

Of the national columnists aside from Booker and Heffer, Quentin Letts of the *Mail*, Stephen Glover and early Eurosceptic Andrew Alexander have all been fair and sympathetic to our libertarian message and respected our sincerity. Trevor Kavanagh of the *Sun* and Michael White of the *Guardian* have always treated us as a serious party with a genuine, dedicated and therefore important following.

That seems to me a pretty distinguished roll of honour. In fact, if it had been left to the bright, bolshy, opinionated columnists whose business it is to see *sub specie aeternitatis* and to understand the moods and movements of the nation, we would have had favourable or at least fair coverage from the outset.

It has been the time-serving trendies, more anxious to impress their fellows than to serve truth, who have consistently prejudged us.

We have often been outspoken and careless. Real people often are, particularly when they are angry. We have, however, always tried to answer questions rather than evading them and, if we don't know the answer, to admit it.

But for all my occasional idiocies and those of my fellows, I believe that we have an authenticity and sincerity alien to the professional politician. Maybe one day it will change and we too will be infiltrated by those more interested in glory than in the freedom of the British people.

For now, however, I think that we can assert with certainty that no-one who has battled through the years of routine calumny and derision, squabbling and monetary sacrifice, negligible election returns, wilful neglect by the media and empty meeting halls has done so from anything but conviction.

I think too that such authenticity has nowhere been more clearly seen than on the most democratic and largest platform of them all, more immediate even than *Question Time* and accessible to millions who would never watch a BBC political programme or attend a village hall meeting.

On YouTube, my speeches can be seen for what they are, spontaneous outbursts from the heart – or the spleen – unpolished, unfiltered by sneering comment and captions. I am now daily hailed in person or receive encouraging emails from people of my children's age, here and abroad, who have seen me on the web.

Of course, the other parties have a much larger and certainly a much more professional presence online, but they cannot compete with us. Why? OK. Sincerity? Energy? Roughness round the edges? Anger? Marginalisation? Occasional excess alcohol? The thrill of the unquestionably authentic?

Maybe it sounds absurd to those who merely look at the ages of some of our party faithful, but Clapton and Stephen Stills are sixty-five this year and Jimmy Page sixty-six. Janis Joplin would be sixty-seven.

Labour is over-produced prog-rock with full orchestra, lasers and interminable dreary solos. The Tories are a made-up boy-band doing cover versions for the weenie-boppers and the grannies. The Lib Dems are Enya, an indoors, studio-enhanced celebration of fictional nature.

What you are witnessing and what I feel up there, with all its absurdities, all its strutting, all its occasional discords, is something very closely akin to real, live rock and roll.

*

Those who in future follow in our footsteps and attempt to storm the fiercely guarded citadel of the established parties can rest assured. Play it straight, roll with the punches, shed liabilities as fast as possible – and the jury of press and public opinion will at last give you a fair hearing.

It took us many frustrating years, but, in the 2009 European elections, we suddenly found ourselves afforded the same amount of airtime and media coverage as our rivals. I was party leader by then, and running that campaign.

At last I had a chance to express to the British people without snide interventions or dismissive sneers from pundits the message which so desperately needed to be expressed and the passions which had moved us and motivated our lives for so long.

Because the public share so many of those passions and recognise sincerity on the rare occasions that they see it, we came second in that election.

We were beaten only by the Tories. Their leader, David Cameron, made a stab at sincerity about Europe too. He made two pledges.

The first was that his party would form a new Eurosceptic group — the European Conservatives and Reformists. So far, the ECR's record is shameful. Without their support, that most curiously constituted butterfly José Manuel Barroso, who entered the chrysalis of political power a dedicated Maoist and miraculously emerged a ponderously flapping, right-of-centre social democrat, would not have been retained as EU Commission President.

The second was a 'cast-iron undertaking' that the British people would be graciously permitted a referendum on the Lisbon Treaty.

Here is my Health and Safety warning: Do not let your infirm antecedents sit on a Tory-made bench on a hot day.

Tory cast iron melts at a slightly lower temperature than ordinary people's butter.

Mere months after the election was won, the undertaking was withdrawn. It was replaced by a new one: to, er, reclaim for Britain various sovereign powers. He might just as well have undertaken to give every voter a million pounds and a luxury holiday on Venus, since any such alteration in the provisions of a European treaty requires the unanimous approval of other member-states.

Needless to say, David Cameron knows full well that this will not be forthcoming.

But hey, it sounds good, and we're too stupid to know any better.

Aren't we?

9

THE COST OF FREEDOM

The pre-election attack on me in 2009 had nothing to do with drink or doxies. This time, the *Observer* led the pack with an unimaginative claim that I had 'boasted' of taking £2 million in expenses from the EU system.

> The leader of the UK Independence Party, which wants to lead Britain out of the EU, has taken £2m of taxpayers' money in expenses and allowances as a member of the European Parliament, on top of his £64,000 a year salary.
>
> Nigel Farage, who is calling on voters to punish 'greedy Labour, Conservative and Lib Dem MPs' at the European elections on 4 June, boasted of his personal expenses haul at a meeting with foreign journalists in London last week.
>
> The admission threatens to flatten a bounce in the polls for UKIP that has seen the party climb to around 17 per cent over the last fortnight as angry voters flock to smaller parties regarded as untainted by the Westminster expenses scandal.

The story did not fly.

It did not fly because, as soon became quite apparent to a perceptive reader, I was not boasting about an MEP's expenses but condemning them.

I had been asked by former Europe Minister Denis MacShane how much

I had received in expenses over and above my salary since my election a decade earlier.

The paper pretended that it had engineered a brilliant bit of investigative journalism and had caught me out by ingenious subterfuge in the public interest. My statement, it was claimed, had been 'discreetly taped'. No, it hadn't. The Foreign Press Association openly tapes all its debates with permission and posts them on its website. I was fully aware that I was on the record.

Attempting to indicate the enormous cost to the taxpayer of maintaining a useless and unwanted employee, I told the gathering, 'It is a vast sum. I don't know what the total amount is but – oh lor – it must be pushing £2 million.'

'Last night,' the *Observer* continued, 'as UKIP circulated new party literature saying Westminster MPs had "ripped off taxpayers", Farage, who employs his wife to help run his office and pays her from his allowances, faced a backlash as opponents accused him of hypocrisy. MacShane suggested that UKIP's attempt to pose as more honourable on expenses than other parties had been exposed as shameless and hollow.

'"Far from being the party of the little man in Europe, Nigel Farage's astounding £2m raid on the taxpayer shows he is up there with any other politician, happy to line his pockets with gold."'

And that, *mes enfants*, is how a dishonest news story is created.

Since it is a subject which has been painfully central to the last decade of my existence, tells us a lot about the EU and is seldom truthfully discussed, I thought that I should tell the next section of the story as viewed through the prism of filthy lucre.

*

The common perception is that MEPs are on easy street – underworked, oversexed, overpaid and over there. And so they can be. So most of them are. It all depends how well (for which read poorly) you do your job.

If you do your job for your employers (your constituents) really, really badly, you can live like a movie star. If you do it well, you can damned near go bust.

An MEP's basic salary is the same as that of an MP – some £65,000 per annum (of late enhanced a fair bit since we are now paid in euros and the pound is weak). Considering that I had had to employ a new man in my office at a cost of £40,000 to fill in for me in my absence, I was not exactly crowing when first I arrived in Brussels.

But no matter. All I had to do was play the system.

I at once learned about the travel expenses racket. We were awarded £600 for every return journey to Britain, no matter whether we flew club class, by economy airline, by train or in a shared car. We could have hitch-hiked. As long as we submitted a boarding-pass or 'proof of travel', £600 was paid into our accounts without further question.

I bought advance Ryanair tickets from Stansted for a fraction of that sum. Given that, as I have said, I had indefinite free parking at BAA airports and that a free limousine picked me up on arrival in Belgium or at Baden-Baden, I could easily have pocketed an extra £15,000 a year just for travel home for the weekends.

So soon as this institutionalised corruption was explained to us, Jeffrey Titford and I broadcast it. Since there was no mechanism for returning the money, we agreed that we would not 'pocket' it but put it to good use in funding the victims of the EU.

One such use became almost immediately apparent when, in July, 2000 some sad little undercover officer for Sunderland City Council entered one of Steve Thoburn's three shops in the city and made a 'test purchase' of bananas, criminally advertised as selling at 25p per pound. They *were* selling at 25p per pound. They were, by all accounts, first-rate bananas. The price was a fair one. The crime lay in the fact that they were sold in pounds.

Napoleon and his bureaucrats could not count without using their fingers. The EU wanted to homogenise the whole of Europe, whether the people of Europe wished to be homogenised or not. The infinitely superior Imperial weights and measures system which had evolved for purpose over centuries was thus a tiny tussock in the level playing-field. The EU brought out a fleet of steam-rollers and dreary little people with theodolites and spirit-levels.

Steve Thoburn's customers could count without using their fingers. They actually preferred to use pounds and ounces. So he let them.

Soon afterwards, two further sad little trading standards officers (OK. They were 'only obeying orders', but they must have been sad for all that) arrived to impound Steve's wicked scales. Since these were the tools of his trade, Steve not unreasonably objected. At that, the police were called.

The scales were removed. Steve was compelled to buy dual-purpose scales at considerable expense and went right on selling in pounds and ounces because that was what his customers preferred. If they wanted to buy in kilograms, he was quite willing to let them do that too. He was liberal about these things.

Despite understandable furore at this quite extraordinary, pointless exhibition of what can be achieved by a combination of weak brain and enormous power, Sunderland City Council decided to prosecute.

Now we had the perfect use for our unwarranted travel expenses. We – well, the EU via us – also contributed to the defence fund of a publican charged with selling T-bone steaks on the bone and to fishermen's organisations at a time when thousands were being put out of business. We then told the world what we were doing.

The EU accepted that MEPs routinely pocketed their travel expenses for foie gras and floozies. That they should put the money to good use in their own communities was quite intolerable.

Michael Charmier, director of finance for the European Parliament, summoned me to his office and presented me with a bill for £10,500 for excess expenses – the sum which I had publicly declared that I had thus far donated to causes which I deemed good. I protested that, had I retained the money for my own use, there would have been no problem, that the money was therefore mine and that how I elected to spend it was my business.

Charmier now showed me how the rest of the parliament justified its expenses, at least to itself. 'There shouldn't be any excess!' he objected. 'After all, there are cups of coffee and newspapers to be paid for on your journey!' And, he might have added, excess baggage fees and hospital bills if MEPs insisted on spending £500 on newspapers and coffee on every Eurostar journey.

Jeffrey was presented with a still larger bill.

These were just the preliminary blows intended to soften us up. Now the parliament went in for the kill. We were called in by a quaestor.

Richard Balfe had been a devout servant of the Labour Party but he became a still more devout servant of the EU. He had been so anxious to stand for the position of quaestor (financial overseer or senior prefect) in the parliament that, when his party forbade it, he defected to the Tories.

He was a very shrewd political operator, one of those men who, even in so unwieldy and massive an organisation as the EU, can make things happen.

His first words to Jeffrey and me were, 'All right. Do you both want to be martyred?'

'Martyrdom' in this context meant that we would have to pay the outstanding bills and be under scrutiny day and night thereafter.

'Or', Balfe continued, 'the documents could be "misfiled". . .'

If we accepted a little creative misfiling, we could continue to accept the expenses and to contribute them to whatever cause we would, provided that we did not mention how we had spent the money.

The stinking Golden Delicious cart must not be upset, because beneath that shiny pale-green top layer, the worms are feasting.

It was a very difficult dilemma for us. They had known that it would be.

If we were compelled to repay the money, we would attract a great deal of publicity and cause the EU a deal of embarrassment for a while, but we would be all but spent forces, monitored wherever we went and whatever we did. We would be compelled to withdraw our support for cases which depended on us and which were affording valuable and enduring intelligence to the general public about the practical consequences of European rule.

We conceded.

So now, officially, we drink our excess travel expenses – or rather, we spend them on coffee and newspapers – like every other law-abiding MEP.

The biggest single expenses pot for MEPs is that for the General Expenditure Allowance, which works out at an average £3,500 per month per member. This is intended for running an office in the constituency, 'relevant' entertaining and travelling within the home member-state.

I have been receiving the General Expenditure Allowance for ten years and have never yet had to prove that I have actually spent a penny of it. As it happens, I do not think that even my bitterest political foe will deny that I have been the hardest-working of all British MEPs, continually travelling around Britain (my battered Volvo records a punishing 30,000 miles a year in Britain alone), entertaining constituents and journalists and garnering constituents' tales of injustice and woe.

I spend considerably more than my General Expenditure Allowance, but then, I am known to my constituents, which I believe to be my principal duty since I purport to represent them. Can you name your MEPs or put faces to them? No? And yet they contrive to spend over £100 a day in your very area.

I am afraid that I know plenty of British MEPs who live full-time in Brussels. They keep a single room office in their British constituencies, but it does not cost £42,000 a year.

But they have much more important things to do. If they are working in their constituencies, they cannot claim the all-important Attendance Allowance.

Yes. For clocking in at the EU Parliament, whether they do anything there or no, they receive £270 per day.

Stay in Brussels, then, claiming the General Expenditure Allowance and remembering to drop in on the parliament daily, so proving that it is a working, democratic institution, and you are on easy street.

No matter that your constituents never see you. You were appointed by your party anyhow, not returned by popular acclaim. You cannot lose your seat for abusing your constituents or ignoring them altogether and deciding that, although elected as a Lib Dem, you now represent the Charles Manson Memorial Trotskyite Mass-Murderers' Party. This is not a *representative* parliament. It exists for show.

By living like that, you can easily double your income as an MEP. Oh, and if you buy a stylish little apartment in Brussels on a mortgage, expenses will leave you with a nice capital nest-egg when at last you retire.

Of course, there are other living expenses which must be taken into account. A man or woman must eat. Don't worry. That too is taken care of. Over half of your voluminous correspondence consists of invitations. Every night of the year, you will be bidden to receptions and dinners. So long as you are prepared to accept fifth-rate company in exchange for the Krug and foie gras, you need want nothing more for the rest of your days.

I knew that Tom Wise, one of the new intake of UKIP MEPs in 2004, was a wrong 'un when, two weeks after the election, I told him that there was to be a Gadflies dinner. (In that year, Conservative leader Michael Howard had dubbed UKIP 'cranks and gadflies'. In the great British tradition of adopting an insult as a badge of honour which gave rise to the Old Contemptibles and the Tories' own Vermin Club, I had founded a Gadflies dining-club, which meets once a month in Strasbourg.)

Wise apologised. He had a prior dinner engagement, so he said, with the Sicilian League of Federalists.

I was standing above him as he sat at his desk. Sooner than look at him as I ingested this outrageous intelligence, I looked at his computer. He had stuck a label at the top of his screen. It read, 'HAVE YOU SIGNED IN YET?'

Wise had always been fat and greedy. Now Billy Bunter was let loose in a confectionery factory carpeted with postal orders. We had lost him. I knew then that whatever tenuous loyalty he might have had to the party was gone.

I stated as much, but it was not until the following year that we had it confirmed that Wise had built up 'a surplus of funds'. I instantly raised the matter at the NEC and threatened to resign unless there were an investigation. The results of this investigation were alas suppressed by an excessively loyal leader.

In the end, it was shown that Wise had used £36,000 of his permitted secretarial allowance of £125,000 to pay off credit cards and to buy a car, wines and other luxuries.

Oh, he was far from the only MEP to abuse the system and his predations were small-change compared to some, but a lazy man can live a life of luxury without breaking any of the parliament's rules. In UKIP, which exists not to exploit the system but to drag Britain out of it, such personal enrichment was mortal sin. Wise was in the end sentenced to two years imprisonment for fraud and money-laundering.

For myself, I have no desire to drink tepid champagne with people with whom I have nothing in common. My colleagues and I drink at O'Farrells, the nearest proper pub to the parliament. We have to buy our own drinks, and it is by certain standards a dive, but it is a congenial dive, we can smoke there and anyhow, Farage's First Law states that the quality of a drinking establishment is inversely correlated to the refinement of its décor.

I regard my mission as telling the British people how they are being abused and their freedoms eroded. This involves driving thousands of miles and missing out on lots and lots of attendance allowances. Yes, I pay my wife a small income to handle my correspondence and diary, but she did the same work efficiently for several years unpaid, and would it somehow be preferable that I pay some mini-skirted intern instead?

I stayed in hotels and *pensions* in Brussels and Strasbourg for my first seven years as an MEP. It was only when I was leader of the group and compelled to spend six or seven nights a month in Brussels that it plainly became at once more agreeable and economical to have a reliable base with a change of clothes *in situ*. I very deliberately did not buy, but now rent a flat which I share with my colleague Godfrey Bloom.

When we took the flat, Bloom's theory was that we would at last be able to get early nights. It hasn't worked yet, but it sounds great.

In 2002, I realised that I could no longer responsibly run Farage Futures and fulfil my responsibilities as an MEP. I closed down the company in good health. I ensured that every employee found a job. I thus lost my personal income and missed out on the biggest commodities boom of all time.

I have spent my savings from the metals-trading days. I am now wholly dependent on my income as an MEP. My former colleagues in the City earn more in a month than I in a year.

I think that I can claim, Mr MacShane, that my eccentric passion for freedom, so far from 'lining my pockets with gold', has cost me millions.

I am not out to score political points, but would gently point out in the interests of justice that the Europhile Mr MacShane claimed £125,000 over the period 2001–2008 for the scruffy garage attached to his home which served, so he said, as his constituency office, a further £135,000 in second-home allowances and over £400,000 for staff salaries, as well as some £20,000 or so per annum in Incidental Expenses provision.

The taxpayer also bought him eight laptops in three years, five of them claimed for in November, December or January, a £212 Palm Pilot and three digital cameras worth up to £300 each, and paid more than £8,000 to MacShane's brother's company for 'research and translation'.

I accept that the whole business of MPs' pay is ridiculous. If we want the best candidates, we should pay a sum which reflects their excellence – but only in a parliament which has sovereign power. At present, a GP or a secondary school headmaster earns considerably more, and the member who votes himself or herself a rise commensurate with responsibility will be accused of greed and voted out of office. We have therefore ended up with a parliament of craven, talentless functionaries eager for power within the system and an unworkable fudge whereby expenses substitute for income.

I do not blame MacShane for making the most of a bad system. I would be grateful, however, if he were to acknowledge that I work in a far more corrupt system and have renounced far more in the cause of service to, not domination of, the British electorate, and I will wager that his expenses have been greater than mine with far less cause.

Being an MEP is the only job that I have ever encountered which pays you more the less you do. Thus the system stays intact.

Who wants to get up to do the brightwork, chart-plotting or maintenance when you might thus rock a boat so full of luxuries and privilege? Nah. Better, far better, to lie still in the sunshine, order another drink and not worry about the state of the keel or the course.

That, then, is the principle on which the European Parliament works.

It doesn't.

10

PROS AND CONS

Yes, we are amateurs and oddballs. We have to be, don't we, to stand out from the crowd, to reject protection and the assurances afforded by the party system and to demand freedom to run our own lives?

It would have been so easy to accept Tory assurances that they were on the same side and that no further powers or freedoms would be surrendered.

I flatter myself that I might have done pretty well in the Conservative Party if only I had been willing to found my life upon a bedrock of bullshit.

I might have had the chance to prove it too. In early 2005, I was approached by a Tory Knight of the Shires and asked to attend a meeting at a private house. There, with a mutual guarantee of confidentiality, I was told that Michael Howard would look very favourably upon my application for the candidacy in the safe seat of Tunbridge Wells at the forthcoming general election.

Archie Norman was standing down, and this was my sort of seat. It was close to my home. There were lots of business people, lots of fishing people here. . . As for Euroscepticism – well, why not? The Conservative Party was a broad church. The leader himself was anti-federalist, as I knew. . .

I knew where this was going. Just what, I wanted to know, did tolerable Euroscepticism mean? If it merely meant impotent expostulation against EU excesses to keep the voters happy, Michael Howard could go hang.

Would I be permitted to continue to press for a referendum on membership of the EU, so giving the British people the chance to decide for themselves, for the first time in history, whether they wanted to be ruled by anyone but themselves in the Mother of Parliaments?

Er. . .

. . .well. . .

. . .obviously actual *withdrawal* from the EU wasn't on the agenda and mustn't be mentioned.

Why not? Were the British people unfit to decide their own destiny?

Well, no. Of course not. Not exactly. But that debate was over, wasn't it? Withdrawal was not feasible. Negotiation in order to reform the EU, of course, was splendid.

But the debate was never held! The people were led by the nose into subservience and lied to by Tory politicians. As for negotiation, how can you negotiate without sanction, and what sanction did we possess save the threat of withdrawal?

Oh, come now, old boy. That's all in the past. Can't turn the clock back, can we? And all this withdrawal stuff is really impractical, but you know, we could really use you, and I think that I can assure you. . .

The tyranny of the status quo.

I drained the whisky, which was far too good to be wasted in a cliché, and brought the meeting to a mildly uncomfortable close.

Although this was the first attempt to single me out from the herd, it was far from the first time that the Conservatives had offered a deal. In 2000 our media officer, novelist Mark Daniel, arranged a meeting at the East India Club with their member for Teignbridge, Patrick Nicholls, in order to discuss our standing down the UKIP candidate in his constituency at the forthcoming election.

Patrick was sturdily Eurosceptic in outlook. He had voted against all integrationist measures (save Maastricht). He was a natural ally. His majority in his lovely Devon constituency was just 281. He sorely needed a clear run if he were to stand a chance. If he signed a pledge that he would vote against every measure which increased the powers of Brussels, we were willing in principle to withdraw our candidate.

Of course, Patrick could make no such undertaking autonomously. He had consulted Central Office. The whips had supplied him with a list of 'Eurosceptic' sitting Tories against whom we should also withdraw our candidates. If we agreed to do so – well, who knew what they would do for us?

I took one look at the list and I'm afraid that I started laughing. All the usual suspects were there – the men and women who made impressive noises in Parliament and on the stump in order to win the support of the overwhelmingly Eurosceptic majority of Tory voters but then voted, once in power, for the European project. Even Patrick had to admit rather shamefacedly that the whole proposed deal was based on a fiction. He looked very sad as he left.

He believed, like us, that we should withdraw from the EU, but could not express that view. When we suggested that in that case he should join us (and, with his experience, he would surely have been an MEP in short order), he mentioned that he had been given reason to suppose that there might be 'a red seat' for him if he stayed where he was, and that he could do more good in the Lords than in Brussels. Of course, Patrick lost his green seat, there was no red one and another loyal Tory who had sought to express a valid and sincere view was prevented from doing so.

Unbeknownst to me at the time, Patrick and Mark had independently anticipated a deal which the Conservatives had already initiated the previous month in Scotland. Lord Neidpath, a UKIP supporter, had been stalking with our new leader, Lord Pearson of Rannoch, then a Tory. They had concocted a plot. Jamie Neidpath knew that UKIP needed money. Malcolm Pearson knew that the Tories needed all the help that they could get.

In December, therefore, I received a call from Malcolm, whom I had known for some years thanks to our membership of the Bruges Group. We arranged a meeting at which he handed me precisely the same list as Patrick Nicholls, with the same proposal – that we withdraw our candidates in their constituencies. My reaction was exactly the same.

This time, however, I was invited to amend the list, removing the obvious frauds. I did so. It left a very short list. Malcolm thought, however, that the leadership might still be interested. I was asked what the price would be. I replied, laughing and fully aware that even the Tories could not muster such sums nor explain a sudden deficit of this size in their fighting fund, 'Well, a million pounds would be a good start.'

And that was as far as it went. It was all purely speculative and an interesting opportunity for us to gauge the extent of Tory fears. William Hague got to hear of the whole business and squelched it at once.

The *Times* got hold of the story. It read as though we were Just William or something, strutting with our toy guns up to the local banker and saying 'Giss a million pounds or else'. I was by now becoming immune to implications and was only glad that Tory desperation was being publicly acknowledged. I went off to an Old Boys Golf Society Dinner at the East India Club and of course switched off my mobile phone. When I stepped back onto the street in the early hours, I found that I had received fifty-one voice messages.

Aha.

OK, so, when playing this sort of game, don't disappear. A fairly obvious lesson, I suppose, but a valuable one for all that. For better or, as my family would maintain, for worse, I have made it a rule to be as accessible as possible.

As a matter of fact, we had a healthy fighting-fund for that 2001 general election thanks to Paul Sykes, who financed leaflets, full-page newspaper advertising, billboards and, where necessary, candidates.

I stood in Bexhill & Battle. Some suggested that, as a sitting MEP, I should sit this one out, but you know what I think of some. I love electioneering. Besides, the retiring Tory MP, Charles Wardle, had declared his intention to support me. Charles and his wife Lesley frequently joined me as I campaigned from an open-topped double-decker until it was sabotaged by the addition of sugar to the fuel-tank.

I won 3,474 votes, 7.8 per cent of the total.

We had only won 390,000 votes nationwide, but we had caused a stir and the Tories were thoroughly trounced. They mistakenly attributed this to the European question, which they have in consequence avoided ever since. In fact, William Hague had run with 'Keep the £' – which had addressed only part of the question – and Labour had promptly trumped that card with a promise – never to be kept – of a referendum. The Tories now elected a thoroughgoing Eurosceptic and Maastricht bastard, Iain Duncan Smith, to replace William Hague as their leader.

Although open discussion of EU membership was proscribed, one wing of the party continued to flirt with us. They still wanted to know my price for bringing the Eurosceptic strays back into their fold. My answer was 'a commitment to a referendum on continued membership of the European Union'. Of course, any such deal would have alienated the Europhiliac big hitters such as Clarke and Heseltine. IDS's position was not sufficiently assured for that.

We had acquired our very own 'bastard' in the form of Roger Knapman, a former Tory whip who stood for UKIP in North Devon. He was a very grown-up sort of candidate for us, far more politically astute than anyone else in the party. Plenty of ex-MPs had supported us once they no longer had to conceal their views, but Roger was the first former full-time professional who wanted not only to join the party but to play an active part.

I grew fond of him and his wife Carolyn, and many a plot was hatched in their Devon manor. He was astute, urbane and thoroughly clubbable. I was, frankly, enormously relieved at his arrival. Jeffrey was nearing seventy, his health was suffering and had done the job for which he had been elected.

He had brought peace and some sort of respectability to the party. Membership had risen to over 8,000. He was tired, and had already made it plain that he did not want to remain leader after the 2004 election, nor subject the party to the possibly destructive effects of a leadership battle just before it.

There was no other obvious candidate for the post given that I had no desire for it. I wanted a free hand to prepare for the 2004 Euro-elections and was acutely mindful of William Hague's fate. I was still under forty at the time. Roger seemed a gift from the gods.

He was, too. He was a quiet, self-effacing, self-deprecating leader. He asked for nothing from UKIP. He offered his services and gave them freely. He stood for election to the NEC like any other party member. He stood as leader only after a great deal of coercion and special pleading from me and others. He won unopposed.

Under his leadership, David Lott and I were given a free hand. The number of branches grew exponentially and membership swelled to over 20,000. Much-needed revenue started to flow into the coffers. Roger was unflappable back then and a genuinely nice guy, wholly committed to the cause.

Of course, no man became a Tory whip without the ability to keep his ear to the ground and the will to exert pressure where necessary, and Roger had both.

He is a devious man. I use the word as a compliment. I have a bad habit of letting people know what I think of their views. Roger always listened to them sympathetically and responded politely, but his eyes and ears were always picking up 'tells', and he would be plotting a future use – or occasionally the downfall – of his interlocutor even as he was owlishly smiling and nodding. He was a politician through and through.

On the other hand, unlike so many of that time-serving fraternity, he was outstandingly loyal. He did not pick people up and drop them. He was like certain dogs or children who subject you to lengthy, uncomfortable appraisal before affording you their total trust. The person who rendered service to Roger could rely on him to the bitter end.

It was this unquestionable virtue which in time, I think, became a fetish and was to occasion a rift between us. I too am loyal, and, despite occasional fierce, private arguments over policy, always did Roger's bidding. His loyalty, however, was particular and personal like that of a dog who will serve his chosen favourites even when they go mad and burn down the family home. I was more like the guard-dog who will protect the home – even against its residents.

A certain tension existed even in those early days because of one of the injustices of modern life – image. Roger's slow, pensive manner and his owlish appearance did not play well on television.

I am no Kilroy – in fact, the *Daily Mail* insists that I most closely resemble Mr Bean, and they do not, alas, refer to Sean – but I suppose that the quality sometimes characterised as 'fiery' plays well on camera. No matter that I may suffer *l'esprit de* Jacob's *escalier* on the way home and curse myself for shooting my mouth off when righteous anger or a good joke possesses me. It makes for good television.

Roger felt this injustice keenly. In the Tory party and in UKIP, his contributions had been considerably greater than his public recognition. He wanted to appear on *Question Time* and quite reasonably could not understand why I was repeatedly asked back whilst he was never invited.

He had formerly seemed to understand, however unhappily, that some of us, for no obvious reason, are cursed or blessed with a certain facility or glibness denied to others.

It clearly preyed on his mind. 'But I should be in the news!' he would tell me plaintively.

'Well, do something or say something,' I replied. 'Journalists can't do all the work alone. There has to be a hook.'

One day in 2005 when I was yet again to appear on *Question Time*, Roger rang our Press Office and for a while insisted that, as leader, it should be he who appeared. If he were not allowed, no-one from UKIP would turn up. It was at that point that I started to worry.

I would no doubt have felt something of the same had I been in his shoes. He had a lot to say and he wanted the chance to say it.

It was not this, however – or not only this – which in the end caused us to become regrettably estranged. It was that admirable loyalty which at last became an end in itself. He protested that Tom Wise was a colleague and that we should stand by him. I thought it better to stand by the thousands who had trusted Wise – and us – to expose corruption in the EU, not to go native so soon as we reached the interior.

In 2009, Roger even appeared as a character witness for Wise's defence. I had agreed to appear for the prosecution. By then, he had even left our group in the parliament so that he could keep his own allowances for his preferred lieutenants rather than pool them like the rest of us.

It was not a clash of personalities (well, maybe, in that I can be domineering where Roger was increasingly bumbling and pacific, but the double-act had worked before) so much as a divergence of priorities. My eyes were firmly fixed upon the party's success, to which personal loyalty and cohesion were certainly essential. As time went by, he focused only on the latter.

It was Roger who brought another top professional to our aid. He met Dick Morris and his wife Eileen on a Mediterranean cruise. Dick is an

American political strategist with an outstanding record of backing outsiders and assisting them to win. He had masterminded the victorious campaigns of some forty senators and governors, including one impossibly youthful and good-looking Arkansas attorney-general called William Jefferson Clinton.

With Dick at his elbow, the 32-year-old Clinton won the governorship in 1977. Dick also oversaw his re-elections in 1984, 1986 and 1990. President Clinton then summoned him back in 1994 to mastermind the 1996 presidential re-election campaign. White House communications director George Stephanopoulos said that 'over the course of the first nine months of 1995, no single person had more power over the President'.

The two men shared other foibles. Unfortunately, a couple of months before Clinton's re-election, it was claimed that Dick had allowed a call-girl to listen in on one of his calls to the President. Dick at once resigned.

The two couples got on well on that cruise. Roger outlined UKIP's problems and was surprised to find that Dick was not only a dedicated advocate of democracy but recognised both the threat posed by the EU and the refusal of the media to take UKIP seriously or to acknowledge it at all. He offered his services at a bargain rate. 'This is a labour of love for me – democracy against bureaucracy,' he said.

Dick's analysis was simple and, like most good analyses, obvious in retrospect. We had no need to win over the public. We had already won the argument. Polls showed that the majority of Britons already disliked and distrusted the EU. No other party was even offering the option to say 'No', and the media were conspiring to keep UKIP unknown. Our battle, then, was for recognition and to get across one simple, overarching message. 'We are UKIP and we say "No".'

Simplicity gave us impetus. No more detail. Just, 'Hey! You're sick and tired of people who don't listen to you? Well, we're the people who will give you your voice back.' I was confident that we could increase our seats in the European Parliament from three to eight.

In 2003, I met Alan Bown, an enormously canny former bookmaker who in manner and appearance matched the stereotype of his profession – the wedge of cash, the loud houndstooth jacket with leather patches at the elbows – who had just declared his wish to donate £50,000 to the party.

This is no flash Harry. He has since given us so much more, not merely in money but in practical and intelligent advice. He recognises the necessity for UKIP to be united and to communicate efficiently, internally and externally. It was thanks to his generosity that our telesales agency was set up in an old bookmakers' shop in Ashford, Kent. In time, seven other call centres about the country were to be set up. He pointed out that standard political leaflets were routinely chucked away at election time. He suggested glossy cards instead. Again, he paid for the extra cost.

We were taking expert advice now in the dark arts of electioneering, where formerly we had relied solely on enthusiasm and goodwill, in which we were richer than ever thanks to the party's growth under Roger's temperate leadership. The nine million glossy cards distributed by party members carried Dick Morris's message, loud and clear: 'Say NO to the European Union.'

Thanks to Alan, a further £800,000 from Paul Sykes and innumerable smaller donations, we had around £2 million to spend on disseminating the message. We had billboards all round the country. Heather Conyngham and David Lott were once more doing what they do so supremely well – calmly commanding and co-ordinating operations. It still wasn't enough.

Dick Morris had told us that it was now or never for UKIP. We went for broke. Although the public were interested, the media persisted in large measure in ignoring us. We needed commercial billboards. David Lott had some big decisions to make. With my encouragement and support, he booked billboards, estate agents' boards for roadside and railside fields and high-quality election material. At one point, we were in the hole to the tune of some £450,000 over budget. It was an enormous risk. Today, I am sure, the Electoral Commission would close us down for taking it. Roger Knapman knew nothing of the situation. We were electioneering on a wing and a large number of fervent prayers.

I pillaged the branches' bank accounts. I damned nearly ordered backs of chairs and sofas searched for loose change. Candidates raided their savings, pensioners their piggy-banks. . .

As if fortuitous meetings on cruise-ships had not been enough, a new phenomenon occurred in mid–April and a new performer shimmied onto the scene. This time, it was far from a rough-and-ready crank or buzzing gadfly. It was a slick, polished-to-dazzling dragonfly.

It was a Kilroy.

11

SILKY SKILLS

There are many – and as time goes by, there will be many, many more – who have never heard of Robert Kilroy-Silk. In 2004, however, his perma-tan, orange and glossy as a duck in a Gerrard Street window, his lychee-flesh hair and his long, long fingers which caressed the air, one another and every interlocutor of whatever age or gender, were known throughout Britain.

The son of a Royal Navy stoker who had been killed in the war, Kilroy (as he was generally known) had risen, if that is the word, via academe to be Labour MP for Ormskirk from 1974 to 1986. UKIP has attracted and welcomed members from all quarters of the political spectrum, but Kilroy's dirigiste attitude towards politics in those days – as a means of instructing and coercing the public rather than of serving and representing them – was then the antithesis of all for which we stood.

'Politics', he said then, was all about 'compromises and bargains' and aiming for 'spurious consensus', and the function of government was 'to impose its values on society. Its role is creative: to cast, so far as it is able, society in its image.'

Classic doctrinaire, undemocratic left-wing stuff – the people as tools of the state rather than vice versa, smoke and mirrors and social engineering as instruments of government.

Nonetheless, Kilroy's voting record on all matters relating to the European project was consistently good, and he frequently broke the Labour line. On resigning from politics in 1986, he immediately became compere of a BBC daytime show called *Day to Day* which later metamorphosed into *Kilroy*.

This was one of those patronising 'You may be idiots and freaks but your opinions matter' shows on which people with an urge to be on television relate their intimate stories of sex, spots and social privation to an invited audience.

'Raped a Midget? Damaged by Spoons? Thought No Meant Yes? Bisexual Neighbours? Brought up by Badgers? Suspect That You May Die? Too Fat to Walk? Living in a Cello? Plagued by Big Game?' OK. These are parodies on a witty website of the questions regularly asked by Kilroy to introduce his show, but they are terrifyingly close to the reality.

Offscreen, Kilroy has a habit of hitting people of whom he disapproves and is renowned in television circles as a bully when crossed. 'I have never worked for anybody who was such a bully,' said an ex-producer quoted in the *Independent*, '. . . If guests deviated from what they were expected to say, he would go absolutely nuts. He would shriek, and shriek, and shriek. The air was blue. "You haven't given me a fucking programme. . ." He was nastier to men than women. You didn't want to go into the production meeting because you knew you were going to be publicly humiliated.'

On camera, however, he spent the bulk of this programme with his arm around sufferers from spoon-damage or whatever, sympathetically coaxing out their tales, and only occasionally becoming ferociously censorious on behalf of straight dealing and family values.

This was in keeping with his private life. He was not only married. He was quite the most married man whom I have ever met. His wife Jan, whom he had met when at grammar school, accompanied him everywhere short of – but only barely short of – the gents' loos. How much this had to do with occasional but persistent tabloid headlines about an unacknowledged child by a mistress and alleged advances to fans and colleagues, I don't know.

Kilroy's television fame bought him a stab at a game-show – the notorious *Shafted*, which ran for just three classic appalling episodes – and a column in the *Sunday Express*.

In December of the previous year, he had been on holiday in his Spanish villa when his secretary mistakenly filed a column which had, in fact, already been published earlier in the year. Headlined 'We Owe Arabs Nothing', it was not exactly temperate or scholarly, but it catered, as he no doubt thought, to popular distaste for Islamic fundamentalists.

Unfortunately, Kilroy's style is rather. . . inclusive. He probably had not meant in an earlier article that Ireland was 'a country peopled by peasants, priests and pixies' but only that, according to weary stereotypes and *Finian's Rainbow*, it might be thought so.

So, when he referred to Arabs in general as 'barbarous. . . suicide-bombers, limb-amputators, women-repressors' and declared, 'Few of them make much contribution to the welfare of the rest of the world. Indeed, apart from oil – which was discovered, is produced and is paid for by the West – what do they contribute? Can you think of anything? Anything really useful? Anything really valuable? Something we really need, could not do without? No, nor can I,' (to which my friends and I instantly responded with just one Arabic word, 'Alcohol!') he almost certainly intended, as he was to claim, to refer to 'certain Arab regimes', and it was all the fault of sloppy sub-editors.

Unfortunately for Kilroy, the BBC was rolling on its back and nervously widdling beneath the stern gaze of Alastair Campbell at the time because it had told the truth about the 'dodgy dossier' which had been used to justify the Iraq war and was terrified of the consequences of the experiment.

Now (totally illegally) threatened with the loss of its Charter, the Corporation had instructed its presenters to say nothing controversial at all. The Commission for Racial Equality reported Kilroy to the police, Labour MPs squealed. He was suspended then sacked. He lost £600,000 a year from the BBC. He also lost the oxygen of publicity.

For all the intemperateness and imprecision of the offending article, there was a widespread feeling that he had been treated harshly. He had been writing, after all, in the usual glib shorthand of the tabloid columnist, expressing widespread popular sentiments of the sort all too readily inculcated by censorship. Many suddenly saw Kilroy as an abused 'voice of the people'.

After a touching interview with Lynn Barber in which he bewailed the fact that the BBC had 'disenfranchised' his (long dead) mum by sacking him, Kilroy retreated to his villa in Spain to consider his next move.

It was at that point that Richard Bradford, who had an estate up the coast, invited the Kilroy-Silks for lunch. He already knew of Kilroy's anti-EU views. Intelligence indicated that Jan was already a UKIP voter, which probably meant that he was too. So how would he feel, Richard asked him, about playing an active role within the party? Given his prominence and his parliamentary track-record, it was likely that he would leapfrog up the selection list. He might easily be a candidate in next month's election. . .

Kilroy was very interested.

Richard arranged a meeting for us at his London home. Almost unprecedentedly, I somehow forgot the appointment. Perhaps the gods were telling me something again.

If so, I reckoned that UKIP's guardian angels were also having their say, and I was more interested in listening to them.

I got to know Kilroy (in so far as I can claim to have done so, which is hardly at all) that day in the smoking-room of the East India Club and, later, at Beel House, the Buckinghamshire mansion which he had bought from Ozzy Osbourne. I was impressed. The man was quick, smooth and unquestionably charming. As we spoke, he repeated my best phrases to himself. I thought that this indicated eagerness to learn. He was certainly passionate about self-determination for the individual and for the nation.

I discussed with all our main players the possibility of having Kilroy stand for us. David Lott and Alan Bown approved. Roger Knapman, however, had grave reservations. This was a high-risk strategy. He acknowledged that it would be a wonderful publicity coup, but after the election, what then? Was the man sound? Did he have, in good old eighteenth-century terms, 'bottom'? Would he roll up his sleeves and work as part of the team? He was certainly skilled before the cameras, but he was also known to be egotistical, unpredictable and temperamental behind the scenes. . .

From their first meeting, Roger and Kilroy were viscerally antagonistic. Maybe it was no more than Kilroy's arrogant assumption that Roger was some mere caretaker who would be honoured to yield his position to the great man and Roger's resentment of someone whom he perceived as lightweight and meretricious. Maybe it was the rural Tory against the urban former socialist. For all his dislike for the man, however, Roger allowed me to make the final decision.

For myself, whilst aware of Kilroy's weaknesses, I found him amusing enough company when things were going his way. When his hair was out of curl, it was another matter, but the spoiled – and I had met many of them in my media activities – tend to be less than attractive when in adversity.

Jeffrey Titford was also mistrustful. He told me that Kilroy was using us. As a professional, he said, Kilroy was parroting us, learning key words and catchphrases so that he would belong. His non-specific passions were evident, but where were his convictions? And how in the world could we control him once we had let him in? This, he warned me, was a man with his own agenda. . .

They were right. I knew it, but I was willing to take the risk. If Kilroy fancied another deep draught of the oxygen of publicity, UKIP had been gasping for a mere whiff of it for years. We needed the public to take notice of us and to realise that we represented many views which they shared.

If anyone stood to lose from having Kilroy on board, it was surely I. He was a fine speaker and a master of the media. I might have a few fans, but he would command the worship of thousands.

It has been alleged that I gave Kilroy a pledge that he would be leader. I did not. First, I have no way of giving any such assurance. Second, I had no need to.

It is the conjuror's and the con-man's first principle. Let people deceive themselves. They will always do the job far better than you. If they want to see fairies or hear their long-deceased Aunt Flossie enough, there is no call for elaborate artifice. A drifting dandelion seed or an airlock in the drainpipes will do the job just fine.

Kilroy assumed that he would stroll into the leadership. I nodded and assured him, quite truthfully, that, with a little work and patience, he might well do so. Since he always talked at you, not to you, and never listened, I doubt that he heard the qualification.

He was, after all, no innocent ingénu. As he kept telling us, he was an academic and a far more experienced politician than we. If he chose to believe that his personal beauty, charisma and authority would win him the leadership without turning a single impeccable nacreous hair, why should I dash his illusions? If he really thought that a democratically constituted political party could be given to him, gift-wrapped and bearing a label reading 'To Robert, for being wonderful', was it my obligation to explain to him that it did not – could not – work that way?

I suspect, in truth, that you would be hard put to find a group of people who watched daytime television less and were less impressed by Kilroy than our mob. They tend to be busy people who either laugh or believe that sufferers from spoon-damage should 'shut up, buck up and get on', both crimes in Kilrovia. Kilroy did not believe that there *were* people who were unimpressed by him. I certainly saw no reason to hurt him by telling him the terrible truth.

Had Kilroy served the party and trusted to his personality rather than his persona, he could surely have been leader. He was better known in the country than Michael Howard and probably as well-known as Tony Blair. The man was able enough. He just was not humble enough.

He really did not understand that the party had not been built by Jeffrey, Roger or me but by the fishermen and farmers, the shopkeepers and mechanics, the soldiers, sailors, airmen, teachers, nurses, doctors, midwives, WRVS volunteers, musicians, poets, peers, prostitutes (and those are just the first few categories which spring to my mind) who care enough for their fellows and their freedoms to give up their time to the cause. I might drop dead tomorrow, but the party will, I trust, throw me a salute, a platitude and a bunch of garage-forecourt carnations – and go on.

I think such an idea was beyond Kilroy's comprehension. He had a problem common to many in the media spotlight. He believed that he was the show.

So we met up with Derek Clark, top of our candidates-list in the East Midlands. I did not even need to point out to him how Kilroy's candidacy would help the party. To his eternal credit, Derek immediately volunteered to step down from the No. 1 to the No. 2 spot.

On the campaign trail, Kilroy was brilliant, though his stamina was suspect. He would do an hour of street canvassing. He drew huge crowds and he wowed them. Then he needed a lie-down. The publicity which his candidacy won for us saw instant results in the opinion polls. UKIP was tipped to take 18 per cent of the votes, pushing the Liberal Democrats into fourth place.

Michael Howard panicked. It was now that he launched the 'cranks and gadflies' taunt at us. We were flattered and delighted. He then realised that perhaps he had insulted rather a lot of his own people and, according to the polls, 58 per cent of the public at large who also deplored rule from Brussels, so he made a weird speech in which at last he addressed the subject of Europe.

The Lib Dems and Labour wanted to give away more British powers of self-determination, he said. UKIP wanted to drag Britain out of the EU altogether.

Only the Tories offered 'a sensible middle way', to whit, making proud nationalistic noises AND giving away more British powers of self-determination. Oh, and he hadn't really meant it about UKIP. Well, maybe some of us. . .

Twelve peers, four of them Tories, including Malcolm Pearson and Lord Willoughby de Broke, declared their support for us in matters related to EU integration. Tory MP Christopher Gill, an old ally, published a letter explaining that he could no longer vote Conservative because 'I and countless other free-born Britons want out of this evil empire.'

I suppose the victorious professional politicians who won seats on 11 June experienced some joy. I'm sure they cheered and embraced and congratulated one another on the achievement. I'm equally sure that they experienced nothing to equal the elation and the incredulity which we amateurs, all of us with real lives and proper jobs, knew as result after result rolled in. Godfrey Bloom in Yorkshire & the Humber, John Whittaker in the North West, Kilroy *and* Derek Clark in the East Midlands, Mike Natrass in the West Midlands, Roger Knapman and Graham Booth in the South West, Gerard Batten in London, Jeffrey Titford and Tom Wise in the Eastern region, Ashley Mote and me in the South East. . .

Twelve MEPs. . . 2,650,768 votes. . . 16.1 per cent of the total. . . Tories and Labour given a hiding by the electorate. . . Lib Dems knocked into fourth place. . .

Only one thing marred my joy that night. It was that David Lott was not at my side at the count in Didcot but a strange, bespectacled man who looked a little like actor Anton Rodgers at his most blimpish and whose wife was inexplicably crying as the results were announced.

Just as Kilroy had strolled into his candidacy by merit of television, so David, the architect of so much of our success, had been displaced by Ashley Mote because David worked quietly in the offices (and horse-boxes) whilst Mote was a marketing man and author who impressed the faithful by his pompous speechifying and his impressive publications.

Mote had written a popular book called *Vigilance – A Defence of British Liberty* before he joined the party in 2000. He was therefore 'an authority'. A further book about immigration, *Overcrowded Britain,* was much hawked at party meetings and conferences and cemented his reputation as a good researcher and a pundit to be heeded. He was a busy emailer and a skilful self-promoter. He drafted a petition to Her Majesty requesting that she withhold assent to the Nice Treaty. He persuaded twenty-eight peers to sign it, and, with Trevor Colman, now a UKIP MEP, made a series of videos about the EU which also sold well within the party.

David was too busy selling the party. Mote was selling Mote. Which is why, no doubt, when the list of candidates for the South East was published in January 2004, it read 1. Farage, N., 2. Mote, A. and 3. Lott, D.

Why was Mrs Mote weeping at the announcement that her husband had attained a long-held ambition? I can only surmise that she knew that, now that he had entered public life, the ceiling was about to fall in. Tragic irony was no longer nagging at her. It was clouting her over the head with the rolling-pin. Here they were on what should have been the greatest night of their lives, surrounded by jubilant, honest faces, and her husband's public shame and destruction were inevitable.

The following morning, we met at Didcot station on our way to London for the public celebration of our triumph. Ours was a nodding acquaintance. Mote was aloof in keeping with his perceived (at least by himself) status. He did not join in with the rabble in the bars, but had his own admiring coterie, usually of ladies who had long since crossed contraceptives off their weekly shopping-lists and gentlemen in blazers who were relieved that they had done so.

I told him to buy a first-class ticket so that we could talk in private.

'Look, I've been a lone ranger in this region up till now,' I told him. 'Now that there are two of us, we're going to have to work together. We've got to trust one another.'

It was only for a moment, but he cast me a glance so furtive, doleful and bitter that I suddenly knew that we had a grave problem.

'Oh, absolutely,' he said. 'Right.' And he proceeded hastily to outline his ambitions.

He wanted to focus, once he reached Brussels, on fraud and corruption amongst MEPs.

12

SILK UNRAVELS

Now we started to reap the whirlwind.

It is not like this for established parties which scorn democracy, of course. Their candidates come from 'pools' (clearly postered 'No Diving', 'No Petting' and 'No Bombing (unless the Leader has a bad dream about WMDs)').

In these pools paddle ingratiating, air-guitarist timeservers whose only wet-dreams in youth are about people saying 'Yes, sir' and 'No, ma'am' to them. They generally pubesce, as we understand the term, at the age at which normal humans have mid-life crises.

Only then, when they are members of the Privy Council and have OBEs for conspicuous cravenness, are they found in bed with Greek waiters and/ or misfortunate and very angry weasels. At this point, the party machine pays off the weasel and the offender appears in the media with a supportive family before entering the Priory and taking up evangelism.

We, by definition, do not crave power above principle or we would certainly not be in UKIP. Sorry. You can be a European Commissioner if you have hidden a £370,000 mortgage like Peter Mandelson or embezzled £2 million like Jacques Barrot, but UKIP MEPs must be exceptionally scrupulous about not abusing public funds.

We do have forms which candidates have to complete, declaring criminal convictions and proceedings pending. We have since tightened up our checks on the veracity of candidates' answers, but, at the time, we tended to believe them. We do have CRB checks (now enhanced), but, there is no box to tick in response to the questions, 'Are you by any chance an egomaniac shyster?' or, for that matter, 'Have you any unconventional feelings with regard to weasels?'

Until now, aside from the odd unguarded indication that the leadership was his as of right, Kilroy had behaved. Now, with his position assured by due process, he flexed his muscles.

In public, of course.

That Monday, after a photo-call on College Green in Westminster, we adjourned to 1 Abbey Gardens, the House of Lords press facility, for a press conference. The world's media had been forced to acknowledge us and was here in force. I sat at Roger's right hand, Kilroy at mine. That was as far as normal order of precedence went. I answered questions in a very unsophisticated, jubilant way. Roger, as ever, was cool and dry.

Now it was Kilroy's turn. The microphones and cameras turned and lunged at him. It was like a brand new blonde in San Fernando valley at the final stroke of midnight which announces her eighteenth birthday.

'So, Robert. . .'

A momentary and fetching expression which said 'Moi?', then the long fingers intertwined and the brand new deck of cards which was his smile was fanned.

'What are you going to do when you arrive at the European Parliament?'

'Wreck it,' said Kilroy.

It was the first time that he had presumed to venture from a script which he had absorbed from us. As ad libs went, it was inept and pretty much disastrous.

My heart plummeted. My face just fell. Roger half raised a hand as though he had been about to strike his own brow, then thought better of it. His lips twitched just once.

UKIP has no interest in wrecking anything. If other European nations elect to subjugate themselves to an insensitive soviet, that is their business. If we can inspire them by example or expose the deficiencies of the system, well and good, but our concern is with Britain and the freedom of her subjects to run their own lives.

It was instructive to see a true professional trying to save a bad ad lib. Kilroy instantly sniffed our disapproval and his questioners' glee. '. . .Expose it for the waste and corruption and the way it is eroding our independence and sovereignty,' he continued, grasping now at flotsam from the stately ship UKIP, 'Our job is to go there and turn round and say, "This is what they do. This is the way they waste our money. This is how they all go on the gravy train and spend their time in restaurants and. . . the rest of it."'

Then he adopted his invariable strategy. He switched to petulant aggression in hope that adrenalin would come to his rescue. 'I don't want to go to Brussels. I don't want to be there. I don't want to be bogged down in the committees and all the rest of it.'

Yep. We had a problem in waiting. I still thought that Kilroy would learn. I was not excessively worried. Roger was. He was more experienced than I.

I *was* worried the following morning. I was at City Airport, headed for Brussels and intent upon the problem of forming a new group, when I received a call from Mote. 'Er, Nigel. Yes. Good,' he burbled. 'Um, the *Telegraph* this morning. . .'

'Yes?' I snapped as I presented my ticket at the check-in. I hadn't yet seen a paper today.

'Don't worry about it. It's all political. Just, you know. . . Nothing to worry about.'

'I'm delighted to hear it,' I called. 'Excellent.'

I checked in. I bought a *Telegraph*.

I moaned.

Several people in that departures hall jumped and snatched up their infants. They thought, apparently, that a stray bullock with colic had somehow wandered into City airport. A moment later I was swearing and hitting things and looking around for someone who looked suicidal so that I could offer to help.

Political? *Political?*

We had encountered political prejudice all right, but in what conceivable sense was the factual account of a plea and directions hearing in Chichester Crown Court, relating to nine charges of false accounting totalling £67,000

– in what sense was that political? Or was Mote's claiming housing benefit and income support whilst in receipt of £4,000 per month from other sources a sort of Robin-Hood-in-reverse protest against the welfare system?

All right, so the case was not yet proven and Mote was pleading not guilty, but, even were he innocent as a newborn, by what right had he stolen the candidacy from David Lott by lying? By what right had he betrayed the trust of all those hundreds of thousands of voters and the support of so many hard-working party-activists who had laboured on his behalf with no prospect of personal advancement?

At any point in the campaign, right up to the night of the count, he could have told us the truth and that seat would have gone to David. Mote had appeared at a pre-trial hearing in Worthing in May. Had that come out on the Sunday before the election, all that hard work, good faith and hope – the entire campaign – might have foundered.

It was obvious, of course, why he had lied. His position, income, allowances and pensions were now inalienable. He could even (and did) plead immunity from prosecution. He was an MEP, and there was damn all that we could do about it. He had used the rules to commit daylight robbery.

I continued to curse and seethe all the way to Brussels. I am still seething now as I write.

We withdrew the whip within weeks. Mote, who appeared to have mugged up on every trick in the book to delay the cause of justice, playing the British courts off against the EU Parliament, was to remain an unattached MEP until June 2009.

In August 2007, he was found guilty of twenty-one charges of deception. He had constituents email the judge, praising his wonderful work as an MEP. In his summing-up, the judge said how important it was that Mote should return to his valuable work as soon as possible after serving his sentence.

He was sentenced to nine-month sentences, all, alas, to be served concurrently (had he received a twelve-month sentence, he would have lost his seat and it could have been reassigned) and then returned to Brussels. Throughout that time, he held a seat entrusted to him by UKIP voters and drew his MEP's income.

The first day of the new parliament in Strasbourg was a bunfight. Ten new member-states had just joined the Union. All of Europe's media and many from further afield had gathered to eye up the new intake and to identify new stars. The PR-conscious members dressed as though for the Academy Awards and had pre-prepared mission-statements, at least for their own nation's media, about their noble intentions. The European Parliament is as full of noble intentions as a Miss World stage, and, since Miss World has rather more influence than an MEP, they are as seldom fulfilled.

Of course, Kilroy was our star-turn, which was fine by me. He was doing leader-in-waiting today, and his extempore stuff did not wander far from the great UKIP standard melodies. This was, to be honest, one role which I was happy to hand over. I was running the parliamentary group, and the formation of the new group was taking up all my energies.

The Independence/Democracy group was a coalition of secessionists and reformists – those who wanted out and those who believed that the EU could somehow be reformed. Aside from strategic differences, there were Danes, French, Italians, Poles, Czechs, Swedes, Greeks and a solitary Irish independent to be reconciled to our new union and rules and principles to be agreed. Because UKIP brought eleven people to the party, the chairmanship was shared between me – although a whippersnapper, already something of a parliamentary veteran – and the true veteran, Jens-Peter Bonde.

So I did not expect us to make headlines that day. I chaired a brisk mid-morning press conference. It passed without incident but for Kilroy's face-pulling to the gallery whenever Roger spoke. Later, as I scurried from office to office, and from floor to floor, however, I kept hearing the name of my old friend, fellow battlefield-tourist and new colleague, Godfrey Bloom.

It took me a while to be sure that that was indeed what was being said. The lifts in this tower of Babel were filled with mumbles and gabbling in many different languages and dialects, and at first I assumed that the repeated 'Bloom', even with something which sounded remarkably like 'Goff ray' in front of it, was the Latvian or Estonian for 'directive' or 'committee' or one of those other exciting words which features largely in conversations round there.

When I had heard it in a French mouth, coupled with much guffawing, and in a couple of Swedish, accompanied by tutting, I knew that something was afoot.

It was at a cocktail party that evening that I bumped into Edward McMillan-Scott, quite our favourite Europhiliac Tory, who also represented Godfrey's Yorkshire & the Humber constituency. Edward was beaming and chuckling as he told me the tale.

Stephen Sackur, the BBC's Europe correspondent, had been having a quick word with Godfrey after the press conference when our new secretary-general, Herman Verheirstraeten, said, 'I see we have a space on the Women's Rights Committee, Godfrey. Would you like to join?'

Somewhat to Herman's surprise, Godfrey had accepted the invitation. He is an economist and an experienced businessman and adviser to business who has long sponsored the Cambridge Women's Rugby Union team out of his own pocket and deplores the counter-productive nature of so many blanket regulations which, he said, were hobbling and often killing small enterprises at home.

He was speaking from experience, not expressing a casual opinion, when, regarding maternity regulations, he said, 'No self-respecting small businessman with a brain in the right place would ever employ a lady of child-bearing age. That isn't politically correct, is it? But it's a fact of life. The more women's rights you have, it's actually a bar to their employment.'

Sackur, his acute antennae tingling, had therefore asked whether Godfrey would say the same thing on camera. Godfrey had obliged. What he was saying was in fact unexceptionable, but no doubt Godfrey sensed a certain crackle in the air, and, being Godfrey – ebullient and prone to what they used to call 'bamming', or teasing the easily teased – he proceeded with a bit of improvised jollity.

Denis Healey famously advised, 'When you're in a hole, stop digging.' Godfrey believes in hiring a JCB and seeing if he can attain fresh air as soon as possible – via the antipodes. 'So yes, I'm joining the Women's Rights Committee,' he said, 'though of course, I come from Yorkshire, where women always have their husbands' dinners on the table by six – but I'm concerned that they're not cleaning behind the fridge properly.'

I suppose if he had been more mannered, he would have adopted a stage-Yorkshire accent in order to show that this was a joke, at the expense, if of anyone, of his male constituents *d'un certain age*. Had he been illiterate, he might have added 'lol'. Neither is Godfrey's style. Having lobbed out this grenade (a family joke, as it happens, which did not play in the hypersensitive atmosphere of Strasbourg) he just donned his bowler and set forth for the pub.

The following day, the *Guardian*'s front page shrilled 'Neanderthal!' above a picture of Godfrey, complete with bowler. Other media worldwide followed suit, expressing outrage.

The *incantevole* neo-fascist (the words are not mutually exclusive, or there would be no fairy-tales) Alessandra Mussolini cooed, 'I know the English have a sense of humour about themselves, but I am from Naples and I can say that we women do know how to cook and clean the refrigerator and even be politicians, whilst perhaps Godfrey Bloom does not know either how to clean the refrigerator or how to be a politician.'

Godfrey would not have disputed a word of this, and at least la Mussolini acknowledged that Godfrey's remark had been humorous.

A few weeks later, I was to receive a phone call from Miss Mussolini. She requested a meeting. If an adolescent Farage had witnessed the resultant scene without additional detail, he would no doubt have congratulated me and passed through early adulthood content in the knowledge that any hardships would prove worthwhile.

We sat there over coffee and she flung back that lovely hair and fixed me with those lovely eyes. She covered my hand with hers and she said, 'Nigel, I am so lonely. . .'

'*Yes!*' cheered the adolescent Farage who lurks always at the back of my cranium.

'I'm all on my own,' she purred. 'I want so much to be with you. . .'

I'm sure that the adolescent Farage did not speak the words 'Go on, my son! Get in there!' but he was saying something disgracefully like that. My tonsils were by now tickling, so I cleared my throat and sipped my coffee. Meanwhile, I instructed the adult Farage to bind and gag the adolescent Farage and to tell him to behave.

For once it worked.

What she meant, of course, was that she was fed up with being a *'non-inscrit'* member and would like to be accepted into our group. I had to explain that her policies were, um. . . slightly irreconcilable with ours and that it would not be possible until she too became a libertarian.

Anyhow, on that first day, Godfrey had somehow stolen all the headlines. Kilroy, whose big gesture was to rip up his ballot paper for the election of the new president, had been comprehensively upstaged.

Later, Godfrey expressed more lucidly and temperately what he really felt. MEPs with little or no understanding of business were enacting equal rights legislation whose effect was to put English women out of work, and it was 'no place of Brussels or Strasbourg to come between an employer and an employee'.

Godfrey has since, incidentally, been an effective and conscientious MEP in the only way that we know – reporting back to his constituents on EU absurdities and waste and the erosion of their freedoms and speaking up in the parliament – for what little it is worth – for British small businesses against their unelected drivers as they steer them to their doom.

Kilroy declared his loyalty to Roger, stating, 'I have no ambitions. I have no intentions. I have no desire to be the leader of UKIP'.

*

I grant it. We could have done more that summer.

I am not sure *how* we could have done more. We did not have a huge professional corps to work in our absence, and, from the MEPs to the stalwarts who manned the tea-urns and distributed leaflets, we were drained of resources and energy. I was leading a group in the European Parliament and had no official role in the UK. David Lott had resigned as party chairman. We were focused on formulating strategies, engaging staff and setting up our offices in Brussels, Strasbourg and London. Until Paul Sykes, who was impressed by Kilroy's silky media skills, consented to reopen the coffers, we were all but skint.

Our more active followers were not so impressed. They had supported us through a great deal of thin and the odd notable instance of thick. They had been betrayed too often by self-seeking, rhinestone politicians. The fact that we were real, albeit rough, pebbles was important to them, yet here we were with a dirty great gleaming zircon in our midst. They eyed it with open suspicion.

I had hoped that, during his holiday in Spain, Kilroy might have researched UKIP, its history and the personal histories of its members so that he could more readily have fitted in and understood where they were coming from.

I still sincerely believed that he had the acumen and flair to become leader, if only he could forget the media persona and remember where *he* had come from and what had originally motivated him.

*

Our first engagement of the new campaign was the Hartlepool by-election. This had been called because Peter Mandelson was off to Brussels to be EU Commissioner for Trade.

This is one of the problems with the EU Commission (aside from its being unelected, unrepresentative, autocratic and all-powerful, I mean). When a government nominates a Commissioner, it cannot afford to lose a top man or woman and risk a by-election, so it sends unheard-of quangaroos like Lady Ashton who have never been elected to anything but are simply guaranteed to jump as bidden, or discredited or temporarily embarrassed former cabinet ministers, fretful and discontented on the back benches.

This is how we ended up with Barrot, an embezzler whom I was privileged to expose, and Mandelson, who needed no exposure, having already twice been forced to resign from Blair's cabinet, first because of the minor matter of an undisclosed £373,000 mortgage, then because of the Hinduja passport affair.

'Passport to Oblivion' read the headline when Mandelson resigned for the second time, but that, of course, is not how things work any more. Mandelson's disgrace was a passport from Hartlepool and an MP's salary to the Commission, £182,500 a year and sunshine holidays with some very interesting and influential company.

I always imagine Blair saying to Mandelson, like Lord Lundy's grandfather,

> We had intended you to be
> The next Prime Minister but three:
> The stocks were sold; the Press was squared:
> The Middle Class was quite prepared.
> But as it is!. . . My language fails!
> Go out and govern New South Wales!

Nowadays, an embarrassing colleague is told, 'Go out and generate more than 70 per cent of our laws in Brussels.'

In 2008, Mandelson was back in Westminster, this time as First Secretary of State, Grand Panjandrum, Secretary of State for Business, Innovation and Skills, Lord High Executioner, President of the Board of Trade, Lord President of the Council and Lord Knows-What-Else, still on the same wage, with an EU pension of £31,000 assured – and still taking fascinating holidays.

Anyhow, for now he was off on to Brussels, which left Hartlepool unrepresented, so we asked Kilroy to stand. I believe that he could have won it too. He refused for his own obscure reasons.

Again, this did not endear him to our loyal members. He was also vociferous – and, worse, publicly vociferous – in his criticism of the leadership for its lack of proactive initiatives in his absence.

Kilroy had been cultivating Paul Sykes from the first, and it was surely to Sykes's funding that he referred when, at a press lobby luncheon to which I had been invited by Julia Hartley-Brewer, political editor of the *Sunday Express*, he started spritzing on a theme in the preferred key of 'I'. . .

'I have personally been promised all the money I need to fight every marginal seat in the country. We have the money to set up offices, agents, campaigns when I decide to press the button. . .'

He signed the visitors' book that day 'Robert Kilroy-Silk MEP, UKIP leader de facto'.

Now I knew that we were in trouble. We had a mini-Mosley on our hands.

By now, Roger Knapman's dislike for Kilroy and everything that he represented had turned into a deep loathing. Jeffrey Titford and I laboured for days to broker a meeting between the two men in Brussels. Roger at last consented to give it a go. He waited in my office. . . and waited. . . and waited. . . When I went down the corridor (as ever crowded with television cameras) to summon Kilroy, he announced, 'No, no. Knapman must come to me!'

We who witnessed the scene were astounded. We were rumbustious amateurs who had looked to these two experienced professional politicians to teach us a thing or two. Instead, we felt like kindergarten assistants. 'Now, Roger, play nicely with Robert. . . No, Robert, it was at least half your fault and this is Roger's party, so come along and let's be nice. . . You're both ruining it for everyone else. . .'

Throughout that meeting, Roger was unable to look at Kilroy. He sat with his right shoulder turned towards him and his left foot nervously jiggling. Kilroy gazed at a peculiarly fascinating spot on the floor between them.

Kilroy did not want to play pass the parcel or musical chairs. He was not going to share. That was how the meeting ended, with Kilroy and Jan tutting and flouncing out and Roger still pouting at the wall.

I don't think that Roger ever recovered from the Kilroy experience.

He had never before been leader of anything. Whilst he was steadfast in face of attacks from outside the camp, fighting those within it totally unnerved him.

If the virtuous tend not to thrive, it is not because their virtues inhibit them but because they judge others by their own standards. Roger had done nothing but good service. Being loyal and just, he could not conceive that one of his own was now approaching him, dayglo fangs flashing, spit slobbering from his copper-toned dewlaps, eyes greedily fixed upon his basket and his store of bones. It is a rare politician who understands and anticipates the vices of others yet does not share them.

Virtue, of course, is on display where vices are disguised, and even the most flawed pretend to, or aspire to it. It is just as rare, however, for one with pervasive faults truly to understand it. Kilroy did not understand UKIP's loyalty and common sense.

It was not his fault. He had spent twenty years in the spotlight, from which viewpoint it is nigh impossible to see into the shadows where the researchers and technicians labour to make you shine. Worse still in Kilroy's case, he had had daily contact with common people – common people on camera, under lights, clinging to him as the one recognisable beacon amidst chaos.

Contentious libertarian columnist Nick Cohen wrote perceptively:

> Kilroy embodies in extreme form the power and vices of British television and shows how they can be transferred to politics. His apparently mystifying decision to join UKIP and then storm out when he wasn't made leader at once was politically ludicrous. In politics you have to work your way up. But it was a reasonable way to behave for a man from television. For UKIP to take Kilroy and not make him leader would have been as incomprehensible as *Channel 4 News* taking Jeremy Paxman and not making him lead presenter.
>
> Television is a medium which turns balanced men and women into narcissists. The off-screen staff's job is to do everything possible to make the presenters better than they are: to coach them so they will sound good, cover them with cosmetics so they will look good and flatter them so they will feel good. After a while they can begin to believe that this best possible version of themselves is the true version of themselves . . .
>
> . . . Presenters are meant to treat guests with suspicion and ask the hardest questions imaginable. And rightly so. But it's easy for the celeb to fall from necessary scepticism into the delusion that they are the last honest men in England and the true representatives of the people. Kilroy shows what happens when they do. He is what Paxman would become if he let his grip on reality relax for an instant.'

Only twelve years earlier, another singularly pretty television presenter, David Icke, resolved on very little evidence that he was the son of God whilst Her Majesty, the Rothschilds and, for some reason, Kris Kristofferson were reptiles from the constellation Draco. He has, unsurprisingly, made quite a name for himself in the society in which such things are routinely discussed.

For a long time, I had believed that Kilroy had been diverted by his celebrity but was bright enough to return to reality, to study UKIP and its members and to serve the cause. He had never hobnobbed with us, still less with the party faithful, and it was now clear that he and Jan were determined to follow their own path no matter how far it diverged from ours.

I had created the monster. It was for me to kill it.

I have been accused of briefing against him. I had no need to. I simply let it be known that, if he made a bid for the leadership, I would reluctantly stand against him – and fight to the bitter end.

I was forty, Kilroy sixty-two. I was known to the party. Kilroy had remained aloof from everyone. And, as I say, ours is a party peculiarly unimpressed by surface glitter.

It was not necessary. Now forewarned, Kilroy might still have responded intelligently and become a team-player. And who knows? Within a year or two, with his gifts, he might have ousted me and led the party to great things. This, it seemed, was no longer an option for the Kilroys. They were being cheated of the position which was theirs of right. They must strike now.

It was time for our triumphant conference, this year in Bristol's Colston Hall.

This extraordinary event – the failed Kilroy putsch – has been well chronicled elsewhere. Two days before it opened, we had another triumph which enormously boosted our mood. At Hartlepool, our candidate Stephen Allison took third place, forcing the Conservatives into fourth ('a fucking awful result' said Nicholas Soames). A Labour majority of 14,571 was cut to 2,033.

The Kilroys arrived late. Their big, chauffeur-driven Jaguar purred up to the foot of the steps and they stepped out, for all the world as though they were stars at a premiere. The cameras flashed. The microphones nuzzled up to them. They swept past Roger and other lowly MEPs and led their media-train upstairs to the bar where Kilroy held court.

I have never been so proud of my beloved party of cranks and gadflies as at this conference. The members observed the travelling circus, sniffed and continued about their business. I was on stage mere minutes later, welcoming them whilst Kilroy kept the media occupied.

There was to be an important debate later in the day. For years now, I had been unhappy about our candidates standing against the very few Labour and Conservative candidates who very genuinely and demonstrably opposed the EU and favoured Britain's withdrawal. We had no desire to be responsible for the loss of allies of either party. Our members, however, were quite reasonably mistrustful. They had heard too many protestations of Euroscepticism, particularly, but not exclusively, from Tories, which were followed by abject submission and, on occasion, pathetic and slavish devotion to the Eurosoviet.

We had therefore drawn up a motion which would, we hoped, satisfy honour on all sides. The other MEPs and Paul Sykes and Alan Bown had all given it their approval. 'This Conference resolves to fight the general election in every constituency in the United Kingdom, but should reserve the right, subject only to the approval of the constituency association in question, to reach an accommodation with the sitting Member of Parliament of another party on receipt of an irrevocable undertaking that he/she will oppose further EU integration and will support Britain's withdrawal from the European Union.'

This was plainly pretty much a pointless gesture since no major political party as currently constituted would permit a candidate to sign any such undertaking, but we did not want to be the ones to hinder genuine Eurosceptics, and could truthfully point at the other parties and argue that, if they really meant what they said about opposing further integration, they were at liberty to put their money where their outspoken mouths were.

Kilroy stepped out onto that conference stage – essentially to introduce himself. He was unknown save by repute to most of the people in that hall.

He was brilliant. He soothed. He confided. He made us strain to hear him. He told us in mellifluous tones what we already knew – that we had been led by lies into a Common Market but that the French and the Germans desired a superstate and were working towards that end. He outlined all the wonderful things that we could do with £15 million pounds a day, our net contribution to European government.

We were like children lulled by the same old bedtime story or Catholics by the sung Latin liturgy. Even I who had written some of his best lines was nodding admiringly. He was telling us nothing new, singing no new words, but he was rehearsing the old stuff quite beautifully.

But then, as with his disastrous 'wreck it' intervention at the first press conference, a strange streak of violence emerged in his tone and in his words. It was as though, in his mind, an invocation to destruction rather than an assertion of solidarity or an exhortation to creativity was the most stimulating rhetorical device that he knew.

Ducking the heat of the forthcoming debate by anticipating where he could not be challenged, he declared that no deal must be struck with the Conservatives (not that any such deal had been proposed). 'The Conservative Party is dying,' he said. 'Why would you want to give it the kiss of life? What we have to do is kill it!'

It worked with the crowd just then, though killing a dying creature which might be resuscitated was not an image which I would have chosen, nor did it play well when our largely rural supporters awoke from their trance. Many of them too would have counted themselves members of the Tory family. For all that that family was now dominated by parents under the influence of noxious substances, they had residual loyalties. Amongst these was our principal financial supporter, Paul Sykes. Nor had anyone proposed a deal with the Tories. The carrot which we were proffering was intended for anyone bold enough to take it. . .

The debate took place after lunch. I knew that we had lost it before it had started. I also knew that battle was now joined. And that Kilroy was history.

Dick Morris and I had chatted over lunch. Dick could read all the signs. He had witnessed Kilroy's performance and talked to the party members. That afternoon, he made a speech warning of the danger of 'messiahs' who leaped aboard small parties and attempted to steal their souls.

Kilroy did not hear it. He was presumably back at home. Having tossed his burning taper into the powder-keg, he was just waiting for the explosion surely to come. That evening, the entire party met for a convivial dinner and a lot of drinks in a hotel. All the MEPs, the NEC, the branch chairs and the party enthusiasts were there. Two places were left empty at the table for the Kilroys. I glanced frequently at the doors, expecting yet another entrance – this time with what? A flurry of cloaks? A flourish of trumpets? A roll of thunder and a flash?

Nothing.

This was surely Kilroy's chance. It had still not occurred to him that, in order to win the party leadership, he might need to befriend the members in person or show an interest in their views. He relied on his fame to do the job for him.

He resorted to the only thing that he understood – omnipotent television. I was in my shirtsleeves in my hotel room, running late and once more struggling with the cufflinks, when *Breakfast with Frost* came on, and there on the screen was my colleague, languidly discussing our domination.

'I would like to be leader of UKIP,' said Kilroy to Sir David. 'I think I could turn it into very effective electoral fighting-force . . . What everyone tells me they want is for the current leader to accept the inevitable and to stand down . . . During the last June elections, the current leader told me and others that he would stand down after the election, but then of course he got a massive election result and probably liked the size of his new train set and now he's changed his mind. That's fine . . . Now, you will think me arrogant and presumptuous and I'll get accused of all those things, but of course I think it would be better. Otherwise I wouldn't want to stand.'

I set off for the hall.

Oh, how I love our bloody-minded, self-reliant, determined, loyal, passionate, companionable, hard-working, funny members. I could have hugged every damned one of them that morning.

They had all seen Kilroy's interview or heard of it from friends. They thought it funny. They thought it ridiculous. They thought it irrelevant.

They got on with UKIP's business.

Paul Sykes was so angry at Kilroy's death sentence to the Tories and at UKIP's consequent determination to oppose even Eurosceptic candidates that, two days later, he withdrew all support for us.

Even then, Kilroy did not get it. Even I, who had been well aware that Kilroy had been making up to Sykes and that Sykes was hoping that the Tories would return to sanity, could not quite work out just who had been playing whom. Sykes had been encouraging Kilroy to press for the leadership. Had Sykes been endearing himself to the Conservatives when he approved the motion at Conference? Had Kilroy struck out on his own with the 'Kill the Conservatives' business? And if so, how could he still suppose that Sykes would support him?

There was now a Channel 4 interview so memorably cringeworthy as to rival *Shafted* at its best.

Paul Sykes had openly declared that he was leaving UKIP because of Kilroy, yet Kilroy still somehow persuaded himself that Sykes's argument was with anyone but him. I have met with plenty of selective deafness in my time, usually in relation to the questions 'Who's buying?' and 'Isn't it your round?', but this took the entire Huntley and Palmer Luxury Teatime Selection.

In order to run for Parliament in the East Midlands or to win the party leadership, he announced, 'I will have more money than I can spend. Paul and I want the same thing. We both believe in UKIP.'

'I don't believe in UKIP,' said Sykes. 'I believe in the message on Europe.'

'Well, I'm pretty confident that if I want him to help in the East Midlands, he would help,' persisted Kilroy with a little laugh.

'Not in a general election, I wouldn't,' snapped Sykes.

Comprehensively embarrassed and bemused, Kilroy explained the interview away as some sort of marital tiff. 'Paul and I go way back,' he later told the *Telegraph*. This was untrue. I had been working with Sykes since 2001 and had arranged for Kilroy to meet him only this year. 'It's very strange that he's decamped. All last week he was going to help fund the general election campaign if I was in charge of it.'

So had he and Sykes fallen out?

The article continued: 'Mr Kilroy-Silk laughed loudly. "I can't get the man off the phone. He wants to fly me up to the north-east in his jet this weekend to campaign against the referendum on regional assemblies."'

*

That should have been the end of it. Kilroy persisted, though never by the means which the average contender would have adopted. Never once in all the time that he was with us did he visit the other MEPs in our offices. Never once did he join us in the bars. He did not battle for popularity or credibility. He assumed them as though he were heir apparent.

He had, he said, 'been told by every senior member of the party' that they would like him to be leader. 'I am told there is a vast majority of the party that would like that to happen.'

Er, yes. . . Except that all the MEPs and 70 per cent of branch chairs declared for Roger Knapman. We were, he said, 'a self-selecting cabal', though he was the only MEP selected by mutual agreement between the NEC and the MEPs.

Roger quietly appealed to him to play his part in an interview on Radio 4. 'The party leadership was determined by one person, one vote, so there could be no straight handover. If I were to resign, then other people would put their hats in and, quite frankly, I wonder why at Robert's age he wants to do it, because I think the vast majority would go for somebody like Nigel Farage – the next generation. It's one thing to be ambitious. He must start to think about being a team player. I think Robert is beginning to understand that politics is a bit more serious a business than he might have been engaged in for a while, but he must understand that we can't forever tolerate people who cannot toe the party line. We have disciplinary procedures. It is not a question of that as yet.'

Pure Roger. A dart aimed unerringly at Kilroy's softest spot – his vanity, another at the absurdity of his former calling, a reminder of his isolation, a veiled threat. . . Masterly, and for Kilroy, I assume, infuriating.

And the blessed Alan Bown, thoroughly fed up with the whole business, stepped in with a pledge to make good any deficit occasioned by Sykes's withdrawal. He also warned that he would withdraw all funding unless Kilroy's leadership challenge, now unquestionably defeated, ceased.

On 27 October, despite Jeffrey Titford's as ever pacific efforts, Kilroy resigned the UKIP whip, hoping to stay on as a UKIP independent. The party rejected this compromise. Kilroy still believed that he could become leader by general acclaim. On 3 November, he demanded an emergency general meeting as early as possible and announced that he would be leader by Christmas, though the party's constitution requires seventy days' notice of a leadership ballot. It was a little like watching a would-be pirate yelling, 'I am the rightful captain!' from the water as the galleon sails on.

In January 2005, he left UKIP and founded his own party, Veritas. I predicted to Brendan Carlin, then on the *Telegraph,* that it would last for six months. Kilroy contested the seat of Erewash. He came fourth and barely saved his deposit. On 29 July, he resigned as leader of his own party but continued to sit as an independent in the EU Parliament – or, rather, did not sit but retained his seat – until 2009, when he did not renew his candidacy.

I am frequently asked – most frequently by myself in the still watches – whether I did the right thing in accepting Kilroy as our representative.

The long squabble unquestionably tarnished the UKIP brand, but it also made millions of people aware of us and of our cause. There is, I must confess, an irrepressible streak of vulgarity in me – perhaps there must be in any trader. If taking on Kilroy was the equivalent of installing glitter balls and painting the gallery shocking pink in order to sell a product in which I believed, so be it.

There was always a chance that Kilroy would come good and rediscover his old dedication to justice and the common touch which is his birthright. Since I had no desire to lead UKIP and wanted talented colleagues, I had very much hoped that this might happen.

There was a danger – there was always a danger – that he might run amok and do enduring damage, but I was aware of that from the moment we met, and made sure that the tranquiliser-guns were at all times loaded and cocked and that he could be contained.

All in all, I think I that I can say, as Churchill did of alcohol, that we took more out of Kilroy than Kilroy took out of us.

If that sounds a little cold and Machiavellian – well, perhaps the impulsive, ardent boy was growing up at last.

13

BULL-BAITING

Europa was a Phoenician girl who was raped by a bull.

The bull seemed domesticated and harmless, so she went trustingly and without resistance with him to Crete (well, I don't know. Maybe there was a shortage of likely young Phoenician men at the time), where he revealed himself to be the permanently priapic Zeus and had his wicked way with her. Presumably she resisted, but neither bulls, randy gods nor European Commissions heed the protests of mere mortals.

There are precious few creatures which can bring down a horny bull. In fact, until Europa's friends and relatives can get their act together and unite, her future looks leathery, sticky and distinctly uncomfortable.

But the one beast who can cause the bull grief and distract him from his intrusive predations is none other than the humble gadfly.

So we will just keep on nipping at that thick and rather revolting hide until the poor old girl's friends at last wake up and ride to her aid.

We made a strategic decision in 2004 that our mission henceforth was twofold. Whilst we would continue to buzz and nibble at the doped and deluded at home, we would also harry the bull about his nefarious work in Brussels.

Now that I was vice president of a group, I had more prominence and speaking time in the hemicycle. One of the few occasions when we can challenge a Commission is at the moment of its formation. The parliament must technically approve the new Commission.

This is not as democratic as it sounds since we cannot vet or veto individual commissioners but must accept or reject the entire motley crew, and the chances of an entire parliament of pre-prepared delegates from twenty-seven countries doing that are roughly the same as those of my winning next year's Derby. On foot.

As already stated, Commissions tend to be peopled by redundant politicians, irrelevant but obedient flunkies and big players who are temporarily too hot for high office at home.

Thus is constituted our new monarch – because, make no mistake, this is what we are talking about. What else do you call an unelected power which is the source of all laws, permits no debate and forces through laws when there is any objection?

This is no benign constitutional monarch like our own, a safeguard against political excess in turn subject to the constraints of a mighty people in Parliament. Here, as Sir John Fortescue said, 'that which pleaseth the prince hath the force of law'.

We fought a fierce and bloody civil war in Britain to be rid of so arbitrary and capricious a monarch as this. Now our politicians have invited one back again.

So it is surely our duty, until we wake up and insist that we govern ourselves again, to examine the people afforded such power?

Non, non, M. Farage! That is not how this parliament is meant to work at all. This is meant to be a mere formality!

Otherwise, how is it that neither the Conservatives nor Labour nor any of the big groups with their huge, well-equipped research departments came up with the dirt about Commissioner-designate Jacques Barrot?

Shall I tell you where we obtained the information which rocked Europe? On Google is where.

Anyone seeking a little light entertainment can view the event on YouTube, though they will miss the comedy in the aisles and the still more engrossing sequel.

Just to set the scene, the original appointment of this Commission had been delayed, largely because the Italian nominee, Rocco Buttiglione, had been deemed unacceptable because of his traditionalist Roman Catholic views regarding the family and homosexuality. The delay and the alteration to the original proposed Commission was taken by some to be proof that the Commission was indeed democratically constituted.

This was strange but entirely characteristic. Buttiglione's only crime was to be honest. In common with many millions of his countrymen and other Europeans, he was a Christian with conventional, to me misguided but perfectly tenable views as to the sanctity of sexual relations as a means to propagation. It would be a very strange and unrepresentative parliament in which these views were not represented. When asked, he frankly avowed his beliefs but undertook that they would not affect his judgements in the course of his duties.

Secularism, however, has become as dictatorial as Catholicism in its time. Communists may become members of the Commission but not Catholics – nor, of course, Eurosceptics.

For some reason, the BBC swallowed this nonsense and ran a series of interviews asserting that this proved the EU to have come of age.

This, then, was a great celebratory love-in, a group hug between all the group leaders, who were now satisfied that they had a perfectly lovely Commission to feed them laws to pass on to their people.

At 10.30 p.m. on 18 November 2004, after all the big groups had had their say, I arose to give a brisk but damning account of a proposed Commission which the president, Mr Barroso, had declared to be 'of high quality'.

'Let us conduct a human audit. I am mindful that audits are not very popular in the European Commission, and their auditors – if they do their job properly – get fired [a reference to the fact that the EU's Court of Auditors can only validate 5 per cent of the Commission's disbursements and had refused to sign off the Commission's accounts for twelve years in succession, and to Marta Andreasen, now a UKIP MEP, who, on her refusal to sign off accounts which she believed to be dubious, was promptly suspended then sacked for 'violating Articles 12 and 21 of staff regulations, failure to show sufficient loyalty and respect'. Yes, there is your modern Stuart monarch at work!], but nonetheless, here goes.

'From France, we have Mr Barrot, who will take on Transport. In 2000, he received an eight-month suspended gaol sentence for his involvement in an embezzlement case and was banned from holding public office for two years. . .'

Barroso smiled a thin, fixed smile. I was vaguely aware that a funny little Frenchman named Jacques Toubon appeared to have discovered a rare case of spontaneous combustion in his underpants. He sprang up, shouted, '*Cessez, M. Le Président! Cessez!*' and started running up and down the aisles, growing redder and redder. I felt sorry for him of course, but speaking-time was precious, so I just raised my voice:

'From Hungary, we have Mr Kovács, who will take on taxation. For many years, he was a Communist apparatchik, a friend of Mr Kádár, the dictator in Hungary, and an outspoken opponent of the values that we hold dear in the West. His new empire will produce taxation policy and he will look after the customs union from Cork to Vilnius. Are the EPP group and the British Conservatives really going to vote for that?'

Toubon was by now nigh convulsing. It crossed my mind that he really should excuse himself and go and sit in a basin somewhere more private, but the French were ever expressive of their manifold misfortunes. I inwardly shrugged and raised my voice still further.

'From Estonia, we have Mr Kallas, who for twenty years was a Soviet party apparatchik until his newly acquired taste for capitalism got him into trouble. However, to be fair, he was acquitted of abuse and fraud but convicted for providing false information. He is going to be in charge of the anti-fraud drive! You could not make this up!'

'From the UK, we have Mr Mandelson, who will take on the trade portfolio. He, of course, was removed twice from the British government, but, to be fair, he is one of the more competent ones. . .'

Other Frenchmen were apparently trying to attend to M. Toubon, which was as it should be, only Toubon seemed in his delirium to be playing some sort of human Pacman. Every time the others drew near him, he seemed to change direction, plaintively maintaining his cry of '*Cessez! Ah, cessez!*' It was all quite touching really.

'From the Netherlands, we have Mrs Kroes, who will take on competition. She is accused of lying to the European Parliament. These may only be allegations, but they are made by Mr van Buitenen and should be listened to.

'Ask yourself a question: would you buy a used car from this Commission? The answer simply must be "No!" Even if they were competent and even if this were a high-quality Commission – sorry, Mr Barroso, but I do not think it is – we would still vote "No" on the political principle that the Commission is the guardian of the treaties, the Commission is the motor for integration, the Commission initiates the legislation that is damaging our businesses across Europe so badly, the Commission is the embodiment of all that is worst in this European Union. The Commission is the government of Europe and is not directly accountable to anybody.

'Please, when you vote, take note of the fact that twenty of these Commissioners have already said that they intend to attempt to implement the Constitution *even before it has been ratified by member-state governments!* In the face of such breathtaking arrogance, nobody in the Independence and Democracy Group will vote for this Commission.'

My first thoughts as I sat were, of course, for the unfortunate Frenchman – a former Minister of Culture, I recalled – with the smouldering Y-fronts, but it was all right. He was sitting again, still puce, his arms flapping, surrounded by solicitous members as he explained his symptoms. Other members were whispering the details to Mr Barroso, who looked properly concerned.

Speaker after speaker now arose to accuse me of lying.

The head of the EPP accused me of bringing shame on the entire parliament, which somehow recalled Newcastle and coal-deliveries. Lib-Dem Graham Watson, whose devotion to the EU over years would, if only it had been given to the British people, have made him a truly great public servant, told me that I had 'behaved like an English football hooligan.'

And I honestly did not know what I had done, save tell the truth about men and women presuming to control the lives of many millions of honest, otherwise unrepresented people.

I stood to speak again, but was checked by the president of the parliament, Josep Borrell (a Spaniard who, it will be recalled, considered participation in World War II a qualification for having EU institutions in your territory, and forgot that the Danes and Finns had fought gallantly where his own nation, although rendering aid to Hitler, had remained staunchly nonbelligerent). 'Mr Farage,' he said, 'I am asking you to withdraw your words so that they can be struck from the register. Otherwise, you will have to face the full legal consequences. . .'

Hang on.

I would have to face legal consequences for enumerating the transgressions of people who, so far from facing the consequences, were about to be the outrageously powerful and highly-paid lawmakers for an entire continent?

By now slightly uncertain, I replied, 'Mr President. Everything that I have said I believe to be true. If I be proved wrong, I will not only withdraw but apologise.'

More bustle. More swivelling eyes and gesticulation. More disapproving glares from Watson, now looking like a pampered Pomeranian displaced from his mistress's bed and glaring at the interloper.

At last, the news filtered through. Barrot had indeed been convicted of embezzling £2 million from government funds and siphoning them into his own party's funds, but President Chirac had granted him an extraordinary form of amnesty – a sort of Time Lord pardon – which attempts to expunge whole chapters of history. Barrot's conviction had happened in fact but. . . er. . . not in law. It was a criminal offence to mention the event.

Since I was on French soil and uncertain that, in a pseudo-parliament, I enjoyed the privilege which is a prerequisite of democracy, I returned to my hotel that night and actually checked the contents of my sponge-bag, just in case I was about to be borne off to the Château d'If.

Over the weekend, I saw a very excited M. Barrot on television, declaring that the full weight of the law would be brought to bear on this dreadful Mr Farage who had committed so grave a crime.

Group leaders, however, became more and more temperate in their announcements. They had plainly been doing their research.

I returned to the parliament on Monday to be greeted with nervous smiles. It turned out that even Mr Barroso had not been aware of Barrot's criminal record. Barrot, like Mote, had failed to declare it when examined. Barroso owes me a vote of thanks. He has somehow consistently neglected to express it. The Socialist and Liberal groups in the parliament even – somewhat furtively – congratulated me.

Opposition, of course, was futile. Barrot was made a vice-president of
the Commission and, in 2008, Commissioner for – wait for it – Justice and
Home Affairs.

This brief includes immigration. We therefore have a foreign criminal in
charge of deciding which foreign criminals may live here.

Figures.

*

The First Great Battle of Europe was now underway.

There will be others, but this was what Churchill would have
described as 'the end of the beginning' of the war between the people and
the politicians.

The politicians were to win – by cheating.

Twenty days before I caused a stir by exposing Barrot, representatives
of the twenty-five EU member-states had appended their signatures to the
draft EU Constitution.

This had long been a cherished dream of federalists – the laying of the
cornerstone of a United States of Europe, ruled by the Commission.

Modelled on the US Constitution, it was to replace all existing treaties
with a single document, turn the Charter of Fundamental Rights into a Bill
of Rights for the entire continent and supplant the autonomy of individual
member-states over their own destiny with qualified majority voting by the
entire community. In other words, individual nation states would no longer
be able to make foreign or home policy decisions without the agreement of
twenty-four other nations, many of them rivals. Valéry Giscard d'Estaing
was the Sun King of a heliocentric European Convention which drew up
the Constitution.

Labour MP Gisela Stuart was a member of that Convention. She testified
in 2003 that 'the Convention brought together a self-selected group of
the European political elite, many of whom have their eyes on a career at
European level, which is dependent on more and more integration. Not
once in the sixteen months I spent on the Convention did representatives
question whether deeper integration is what the people of Europe want,

whether it serves their best interests or whether it provides the best basis for a sustainable structure for an expanding Union.'

Of course not. What on earth has the will of the people to do with the EU?

The Laeken Declaration, which set up the Convention, is quite open about the Constitution's purposes. Its claims to democratic validity are based on that infantile demagoguery, the unsubstantiated 'Everyone says so!'

> The unification of Europe is near . . . The image of a democratic and globally engaged Europe admirably matches citizens' wishes. There have been frequent public calls for a greater EU role in justice and security, action against cross-border crime, control of migration flows and reception of asylum seekers and refugees from far-flung war zones. Citizens also want results in the fields of employment and combating poverty and social exclusion, as well as in the field of economic and social cohesion.

To give the federalists on the other side of the Channel their due, they have always been quite frank about their intentions. British politicians, however, have been disingenuous. . . economical with the *actualité*. . .

Oh sod it. They have lied through their teeth.

*

First we were told that there was no Constitution. This was where Andrew Gilligan, later to be forced to resign from a pusillanimous BBC for truthfully reporting the 'dodgy dossier' with its 'sexed-up' 45-minute warning, invoked the loathing of Tony Blair and Alastair Campbell.

It was not the first time. Gilligan's record is exemplary and heroic. If honours were given for public service – that is, for service to the public, not service to self-important, soi-disant public servants – he would surely by now be a duke.

He started out by publicising the contents of leaked Ministry of Defence reports showing that RAF bombs had consistently missed their targets in

Kosovo, that rifles and radios had failed and that a £1 billion overhaul was needed if RAF jets were to drop 'smart bombs' – that, in short, our troops were woefully ill-equipped for the battle (for democracy!) in Iraq.

Defence Secretary Geoff ('Buff') Hoon, a former MEP who, it turns out, was not even consulted about Blair's decision to go to war, stood up in Parliament and declared that Gilligan's report was rubbish. He demanded a public apology. Unfortunately, a National Audit Office report confirmed Gilligan's findings. Hoon's public apology has yet to be received.

In 2000, as defence and diplomatic correspondent for the *Today* programme, Gilligan reported on a document being drawn up at an Italian university on the command of the EU Commission. Professor Alan Dashwood of Cambridge had been asked to contribute his expertise, said Gilligan, and it had all the hallmarks of a Constitution. The government had assured us that in no circumstances would it countenance a Constitution.

Rod Liddle, Gilligan's editor, later recalled, 'All hell broke loose. The BBC received three furious complaints, almost identical in tone and content, from John Williams, the head of press at the Foreign Office, a pencil-necked EU bureaucrat called Jonathan Faull and a certain Alastair Campbell. Andrew Gilligan was attacked by Godric Smith, one of Campbell's Downing Street scullions (though purportedly an impartial civil servant!). "Gullible Gilligan," he told the lobby hacks, "falling for the Eurosceptic agenda."'

Yep. Gilligan was getting the UKIP treatment. Naive, fanciful, paranoid, credulous, scaremongering, dumb – that's us who presume to question the pledges given by British governments.

In November of that same year, Keith Vaz, Minister for Europe (a confirmed Eurosceptic until in office), also derided the very notion of an EU Constitution and those who believed in its existence. He told the House of Commons that 'if a telephone directory were published in Brussels, the Honourable Gentleman would believe that it was the forerunner of a European Constitution. We are not going to have such a constitution, so I am happy to deny categorically his statement.'

Plans for the draft Constitution were announced by the government within a year.

On 16 October 2000, the *Irish Times* correctly stated of the EU Charter of Fundamental Rights that 'there is good reason to accept this text as the basis for an eventual European Constitution'.

Vaz, however, informed us that the ECR 'will be no more binding than the *Beano* or the *Sun*'.

The EU Commission surely missed a natural star in property-flipper and serial 'failure to disclose' merchant Vaz, soon to be sacked as Europe Minister for his part in the Hinduja passport affair (the Commission had already acquired one Briton who liked to keep dodgy deals to himself, and they could not be greedy), is at the time of writing chairman of the Home Affairs Select Committee and a Privy Counsellor.

And who better, given their similarities in function, to counsel privies?

Vaz's place was taken by Peter Hain, another notable non-discloser who later clean forgot about a donation of £100,000 to his campaign to be deputy leader of New Labour. Hain had plainly been carefully briefed, because, although he sat on the Convention drawing up the Commission and presumably knew its contents, he described it as merely 'a tidying-up exercise.' Coincidentally, Foreign Secretary Jack Straw used precisely the same phrase.

This was not how we nor leading lawyers saw it. Martin Howe QC, for example, said, 'A constitution would be to turn the whole EU system upside down. At the moment, states confer powers on the Community through treaties. But the effect of a constitution would be to limit the powers to the states, turning them into local councils that are not allowed to do anything unless authorised to do so.'

Some tidying up.

But then, Hain's view of the Constitution changed with the sympathies which he expected of his particular audiences.

For the general public listening to the *Today* programme, he was once more consolingly dismissive. 'This is not a major change. There is no need for a referendum.'

In the House of Commons, he was a little more circumspect. 'I am not saying it has got no substantial constitutional significance. Of course it will have. . .'

In the *Financial Times,* a well-known Europhile title read by his chums, however, he finally told the truth. 'Our task is nothing less than the creation of new constitutional order for a new, united Europe.'

So nice to hear him being honest – well, truthful – at last.

The ability to fit the right person to the right job is crucial in management. Anthony Blair is plainly brilliant at it. In a fresh, new, bright-eyed 'people's party' elected to battle sleaze, how on earth did he manage to find Vaz, Hain and Mandelson, all to be forced to resign for putting their own interests or those of their cronies above their duty to the people but all still in high office – to sell the European federalist cause? Or were they the only people so unhandicapped by silly scruples – about democracy, for example, or service to their employers, or Britain – as to accept the job?

So now it was acknowledged that a Constitution existed and it was evident that it represented not 'a tidying up' but the surrender of Britain's hard-won right to rule herself.

I earlier suggested that Dante's 'Abandon hope, all ye who enter' might be graven above the doors of EU institutions, but the EU itself would probably choose for its motto, 'Softly, softly catchee monkey' – or, since that is a reminder of British colonialism, its rather peculiar German equivalent: '*Mit Geduld und Spucke fängt man eine Mucke*' – 'With patience and spit you catch the gnat.' Where spit comes into it rather than a rolled up newspaper, I am unsure, but the concept is the same, and we, the people of Europe, are the irritating midges, we the monkeys.

So it may be months or years before a directive has legal force in member-states, and it is often years after that, when the people have done with their expostulations and outrage and have assumed that the whole thing was a Eurosceptic myth, that the laws are enforced for the first time.

The commonest reaction, then, to EU treaties once signed is 'What were you worrying about? Nothing much has changed, has it? Has the sky fallen in?' followed by a certain amount of smug tutting and tittering.

And no doubt you would get much the same response if you had objected to the pit-bull being allowed to wander unmuzzled and unleashed around the home, or a loaded gun being left in the children's toy-cupboard.

What is the EU Constitution? Well, listen to Valéry Giscard d'Estaing, the man who supervised its drafting. He should know. 'The Constitution, and law adopted by the Union institutions in exercising competences conferred on it by the Constitution, shall have primacy over the law of the member-states in. . . the competence to co-ordinate the economic policies of member-states . . . the competence to define and implement a common foreign and security policy, including the progressive framing of a common defence policy [and exclusive competence] for the conclusion of an international agreement. . .'

So, in other words, we as a people lose the ability to set taxes or interest rates, to form alliances, to make – or to remain outside – deals or to make – or to remain outside – wars. We sign away our democratic sovereignty over our own destiny.

This may or may not in time mean a European army. 'If you don't want to call it a European army, don't call it a European army. You can call it "Margaret", you can call it "Mary Ann", you can find any name, but it is a joint effort for peace keeping missions – the first time you have a joint, not bilateral, effort at European level. . .' said Commission President Romano Prodi in 2000.

It certainly consolidates for once and for all the surrender of common law to European regulation, and so (I here demonstrate a seldom-acknowledged debt to my long-suffering English master at Dulwich, because it seems that Richard II tried the same trick, and was quite properly usurped for his pains) Britain,

> . . .bound in with the triumphant sea
> Whose rocky shore beats back the envious siege
> Of watery Neptune, is now bound in with shame,
> With inky blots and rotten parchment bonds:
> That England, that was wont to conquer others
> Hath made a shameful conquest of itself . . .
> Thy state of law is bondslave to the law.

'A single European state bound by one European constitution is the decisive task of our time,' said German Foreign Minister and one-time political extremist Joschka Fischer back in 1998.

This was to be the moment and means of its attainment.

It seemed evident to us that only the people were entitled to authorise the overthrow of the entire British constitution – particularly since so many of their purported representatives were bent upon sanctioning it.

If, we argued, our leaders were elected to office and entrusted with temporary power by the democratic votes of their constituents, if they were paid by those constituents and so employed by them to represent them and their interests in Parliament and if they were bound by the same rules as those whereby they were elected, how in the name of God could they claim the right to change those rules in perpetuity, regardless of the electors' will?

To revert to Richard of Bordeaux:

> . . .take from Time
> His charters and his customary rights;
> Let not to-morrow then ensue to-day;
> Be not thyself; for how art thou a king
> But by fair sequence and succession?'

It is as though the fans owned a football team and stadium, appointed a manager and then saw him assume ownership, dismiss the players, sell off the ground for building plots and share the profits with his cronies. It is as though directors of a mutual building society were to privatise its assets without the consent of its owners.

I would have thought all this incontrovertible and inoffensive enough. If the shareholders see sufficient profit in selling out, they are at liberty to do so. If they don't wish to do so, well, the board of directors recommending demutualisation must accept their masters' decision. They can always find another job.

In North Korea, say. Or any borough council.

And anyhow, the Laeken Declaration had told us that 'the image of a democratic and globally engaged Europe admirably matches citizens' wishes', in which case the Commission had nothing to fear by putting their assertion to the test.

Well, so we thought, so thought children who knew how games must be played and so – they said – thought the Tory party. So had thought Blair, back in the days when he was merely a lawyer seeking political power: 'If there are further steps to European integration, the people should have their say at a general election or in a referendum,' he had said back then.

We had a two-year deadline by which the Convention must be ratified. Between us, we piled pressure on Blair and Co. to allow the British people their say.

Blair at least cannot be accused of lying or concealing the truth for personal gain. He told the British people an untruth, certainly, in order to plunge them into a futile war which killed and maimed many, and he did not like to bother his employers by seeking their consent, but yes, whilst you would not buy a used skateboard from Vaz, Hain or Mandelson, you might mortgage the family home for a used Ferrari peddled by Blair.

He is generally smooth and persuasive, and all that hackneyed 'It touches me here' and 'Don't tell anyone, but I'm an ordinary guy with ordinary feelings' stuff plays extraordinarily well when he does his version.

I think that I am the only person who has ruffled the Blair calm and caused him to scream in anger in a public place. He did not look quite so persuasive then.

In general, however, he is the most dangerous of all salesmen. He believes every word that trips from his lips.

He is also, to mix metaphors, a weathercock. Blow him – if you see what I mean – and he spins, right wing or left on show as the conditions dictate.

Initially he was 'on message'. 'I can see no case for having a referendum on this,' he said in May 2003. (Hang on. How is it possible for a man to maintain a case and then, a few years later, to 'see no case'? Ah. There's the Blair magic for you.) 'And, indeed, in relation to many of the allegations made about the impact of the European convention, they are indeed scaremongering. . .'

He was equally adamant on the subject five months later when he told Parliament, 'There will not be a referendum. The reason is that the Constitution does not fundamentally change the relationship between the EU and the UK . . . There is a proper place where this Constitution can be debated. It is Parliament. . .'

Wow. Parliament a proper place for debate. Even that was a huge concession. British troops had been in Iraq for six months as Blair spoke.

'. . .It has to pass through both Houses of Parliament and I think it is preferable to do that than to have a situation, as I know some of the Conservatives and Eurosceptics want, where we literally for the next few months in the country debate the intricacies of the Constitution.'

In so far as this gibberish can be picked clear of its incomprehensible wadding ('literally for the next few months in the country'??), I think that it means, 'The British people may have elected me, but they're far too stupid to decide their own future and I might not have a majority there, where I have one (just) here.'

But at least by March 2004, the debate was no longer about a tidying-up exercise. 'In any debate in the country [??] the choice is absolutely fundamental. It is between those who want to renegotiate Britain's essential terms of entry and those who believe Britain's future lies in Europe. And I believe that is a debate we can and will win.'

Hang on. Last year, the constitution did 'not fundamentally change the relationship between the EU and the UK'. Now it is 'absolutely fundamental'. Heigh-ho. Anyhow, let's have that debate.

Er, no. By 17 April, the wind had veered. Blair was back on message. 'Our policy has not changed and if there is any question of it changing, we will tell you.'

The wind backed. Blair spun. Three days later, on 20 April 2004, he announced that there would be a referendum after all. This was in fact a purely opportunistic tactical move. By this volte-face, he not only shot the Tory fox but blasted it to smithereens. The Tories had to pulp their entire run of election addresses for the forthcoming election on 10 June.

He made it clear that he was merely playing games the very next day, incidentally indicating that he was now a true Eurocrat. He had no intention of actually being bound by the referendum. Should the British people be so impertinent as to disagree with their servants, 'we will be in exactly the same position as, for example, Ireland after its rejection for the first time round of the Nice Treaty, which means if we were in government we would sit down obviously and have to discuss the way forward with other European countries'.

This means, in Blairspeak, 'Don't bother. We'll find a way of disregarding your will either way.'

Nonetheless, with a little help from the Tories in their quest for 'clear blue water', we had attained the concession. We were to have our referendum. Blair's political jockeying left Chirac in France no choice but to follow suit.

Blair may have stymied the Tories, but it availed him little. We were the only party to make substantial gains in those elections. The public had rumbled the others.

Spain was the first country to have a referendum. Unsurprisingly, given the extent to which she has benefited from the Union ('If Spain had been out of the European Union, by now we would be an extension of north Africa,' said Josep Borrell, and she has long been the largest net beneficiary of EU transfers, not to mention British fisheries), 76 per cent of the derisory 43 per cent of Spaniards who bothered voted 'Yes'. I addressed a rally in Madrid on behalf of the 'No' faction, but we had little chance.

Then, on 29 May 2005, came France's turn. The 'No' side was desperately short of cash, so I organised a whip-round amongst the MEPs. Each of us receives some €50,000 per annum from the 'information budget', which is intended for the promotion of the MEP and the dissemination of knowledge about the EU. We were disseminating information about the EU, even if it was not the information which they particularly wished disseminated. Between us, we raised €200,000 which we handed to Philippe de Villiers, president of the Vendée and head of the 'No' movement.

Five days before the referendum, I scored a major coup.

One of the team, the indefatigable and inventive Gawain Towler, had suggested that I submit a written question regarding the hospitality and holidays which Commissioners had received since their nominations.

We received no official answer. The Commission met, as ever, in strict secrecy, claimed a right of privacy and declared that there had been no impropriety. A public-spirited Commission vice-president, however, leaked the truth to Die Welt. The Commission's president, José Manuel Barroso, had spent a week on the yacht of Greek shipping billionaire Spiro Latsis.

There is no reason, of course, why the charming Mr Barroso, a former Maoist social democrat, should not cavort on gin-palaces with one of the world's richest men, but it had surely been more tactful not to have done so just a month before the Commission approved a €10.3 million contract with Latsis's shipping company.

It also emerged that the ubiquitous Peter Mandelson had spent New Year's Eve on *Octopus*, the yacht of Microsoft's co-founder Paul Allen, off St Barthélemy.

Again, it may well have been that their conversations on that festive night were merely about yachts, of which Mandelson has since, though a socialist, shown himself to be an aficionado and of which *Octopus* is a notable specimen, boasting two helicopters on the top deck (one up front and one at the back), a 63-foot tender (just one of seven aboard), a pool and, er. . . two submarines.

It would again have been better, however, had Mandelson not had his dubious record and had Microsoft not at the time been the subject of a major EU investigation. The Commission had the previous year fined Microsoft £355 million for abusing its near monopoly in the software market. The Commission was still battling with the company, of which Allen was a major shareholder, as to how they could verify compliance, and had the power to impose a daily fine of five per cent of Microsoft's huge global turnover.

In such circumstances, although no impropriety was or is alleged, it is clearly inappropriate that a Trade Commissioner should be linking arms and singing 'Auld Lang Syne' with the company's founder.

These revelations caused a sensation. For once, MEPs of all political complexions and origins were shocked at their secretly self-appointed masters' total disregard for the electors. I had to muster the signatures of just 10 per cent of them to compel Barroso to appear before the parliament, there to face examination and a motion of censure.

Given the number of members who had expressed their disgust, I thought that it would be easy enough to find seventy-five, but, of course, the great machine ground into action. A Maltese socialist who had signed the petition mysteriously withdrew. It was then announced that all Socialists who signed would be expelled.

The British Tories were also forbidden to sign. To their enormous credit, six of them defied the whip and signed notwithstanding. The gallant Roger Helmer had the whip withdrawn in consequence.

For all this, I got my signatures. The Commission could not for once bully its way out of at least some accountability. I was still an inept virgin as far as parliamentary procedure was concerned, but our secretary general in the Ind/Dem group, Herman Verheirstraeten, works the parliament's arcane mechanisms with the same – to me mystifying – skill and ingenuity as an eleven-year-old with his laptop. He somehow worked it so that the debate would be held in Brussels just four days before the French were to vote.

It was a scene reminiscent of a real democratic debating chamber. There was excitement and bustle – a rare sense that we, the members, might make a difference. As with the election of the Commission, there could be no censure of individual Commissioners but only of the entire body. In a scene which, I fear, will be seen again in far darker days, all twenty-five Commissioners were on parade. I proposed the motion of censure.

Barroso continued to plead that his holidays were nobody's business but his own. In a dazzling rhetorical flourish which I last encountered at prep-school, he sullenly informed an awestruck world that 'Mr Farage would never be found on a luxury yacht because he has no friends!'

I reeled, I can tell you.

Roger Helmer had discovered that he was permitted to make interventions. Here was one man to whom we are always delighted to yield the floor. 'Does Mr Farage agree that the EPP Group has tried to stop us from supporting the motion and that this has been supported by the leader of the British Conservatives, Timothy Kirkhope, and does he not think such action reprehensible?'

I simply said, 'Yes.'

There was much laughter, and Roger was at once booted out of the EPP.

We lost the debate, of course. That had been a foregone conclusion. British media coverage was minimal. That had been a foregone conclusion too. They just sort of whistled and thrust their hands in their pockets and talked about the weather or something. Throughout continental Europe, however, the whole story was massive. After the Barrot affair, it seems to have established me as the public voice for the millions of Eurosceptics throughout the continent.

On the Sunday before the referendum, I addressed 7,000 passionate French activists at a rally in Paris. My French is, frankly, *épouvantable* (or bloody awful – one of the few words which I have somehow picked up), and I can only pray that my accent was a little less shameful than that of arch-supranationalist Heath. I read a text prepared and rehearsed with my staff. When in doubt, I returned to my mantra, '*Dites-leur NON!*'

A kindly commentator named Michelle Draye recorded that I had made my speech in '*un français parfait*'. I worry for her hearing, but love her for her optimism.

I returned to France on the night when the results were announced. I smiled weakly at Barrot who was also there. I refrained from asking him just how it felt to have misappropriated just less than the Great Train Robbers and to have been rewarded not with a life sentence but with a huge income, pension and mastery over a continent. I was too busy praying.

God bless the bolshy, determined, truculent, independent French. We may on occasion curse them because we have so often been the victims of that truculence, but, unlike so many of our countrymen and women, they know how to stand up for their own. They had suffered for centuries under an autocratic monarchy and oligarchy. They did not want to accept the domination of a far less elegant but equally impervious version.

Sixty-two per cent of them had turned out, and 55 per cent of them had said 'No'. I was that night kissed by a vast number of French women – and men, there were lots of delightful and this time voluntary European unions and we did wonderful things for the French balance of payments, particularly that of the Epernay region.

Three days later, the results of the Dutch referendum were announced. The Brussels parliament was in session, but we organised a small informal party in the Press Bar. The result was better than even we had hoped. Some 62 per cent of the Dutch people – who, like the French, have memories of obedience to force majeure and do not like it – had voted. An overwhelming 61 per cent of these had delivered a resounding 'No'.

Again, the champagne corks popped and the cheers rang through the building. Our small, informal gathering rapidly became a large and chaotic piss-up.

We had done it!

No fewer than 64.3 million French citizens and 16.4 million Dutch had been asked if they wished to cede self-determination and had democratically stated that they did not. In a sane and decent world which played by the rules, that was the end of the Constitution.

I was brimming over with champagne, gratitude and goodwill, but I swear that I was not crowing – or not outwardly at least – when I saw German arch-federalist and socialist Jo Leinen on the corridor, walked out to him and offered him a glass of champagne. I was simply being gracious in victory.

'Bad luck, Jo,' I said. 'Come and have a drink with us anyway.'

He fixed me with a glare and made a noise as though they were moving a piano on bare boards down in his gut. 'You may have your little victory tonight,' he said softly and very precisely, spitting out the words in soft chunks, 'but we have fifty different ways to win. . .'

He stalked on.

The blood drained from my face and neck as I watched him go.

I knew that I was no longer living in a Europe which respected the will of the people, but I had never realised that its leaders could so explicitly reject their employers' clearly stated desires.

Leinen the socialist and lover of the people had just declared that he despised the people. He and his friends belonged to an autonomous, totalitarian ruling class. The people were wholly irrelevant.

The rules stated that all member-states must ratify the Constitution if it were to proceed, so why, after so unequivocal a rejection, did the Luxembourg referendum proceed? Lord knows. Perhaps the Commission wished to claim that the score was 2-2, for all that Luxembourg's total population is a trifle smaller than that of Croydon.

In Luxembourg, as in Spain, we thought that we had no hope. Fifteen per cent of the entire duchy's GDP comes from the EU institutions on its soil. Prime Minister Jean-Claude Juncker threatened to resign should the people vote 'No'. The media were unanimously in favour. The parliament had already voted 'Yes'.

Jens-Peter Bonde and I paid a visit to see if we could lend a hand. We discovered the 'No' faction to have no funding and no infrastructure. At the meeting which we addressed, there seemed to be just a motley but charming collection of libertarians with widely different and sometimes very odd agendas.

We underestimated Luxembourg and the sturdy independence which had kept her autonomous and fighting for freedom for so long, even when invaded. The 'Yes' faction won, but only by 56 per cent. Considering that 40 per cent of the population consists of first-generation EU and eastern European immigrants, this is a remarkable and far from unequivocal result.

At this point, the EU appeared to concede. The Czech and Irish referendums were cancelled and those declared in Portugal, Poland, Denmark and the UK indefinitely postponed.

And now they started playing dirty.

14

LIARS, CHEATS AND FRAUDS

In December 2005, Britain's six months' tenure of the EU's rotating presidency came to an end and Blair came to the parliament.

I confess that, when he had come six months earlier, I had been impressed. The parliament did not like Blair. He had stuck with America in his (not demonstrably Britain's) venture in Iraq without first asking the permission of the EU. Britain still remained outside the Eurozone. Blair was a heretic. Some day soon, he could be branded a criminal for such disgraceful autonomous behaviour. At present, he was just an unpopular dissenter.

He was brilliant. He sold himself as an ardent pro-European. We must encourage the people of Europe, he said. We must speak their language and not become entirely alienated from them. Under Britain's presidency, the EU would get rid of unnecessary regulations and reform the Common Agricultural Policy. . .

Much to Blair's surprise, no doubt, I did not subject him to the habitual Farage barrage. If, I said, he was successful in deregulating the economy and in translating its words and actions to the people, I for one would support him.

Even members of the group later accused me of treason, but I not only meant every word – had Blair indeed succeeded, I would have shaken his hand – but I knew that he was destined to fail and to fail ignominiously. Every least alteration to parliamentary protocols requires unanimity, and the prospect of unanimity was nil.

I was still impressed by Blair at a lunch later in his presidency. Here was a man who could think on his feet. He nursed a single glass of wine throughout, though the carafe remained in front of him. In the end, I became fed up with such 'bogarting' and had to ask, 'Pass the wine, please, Prime Minister.'

He looked mildly surprised, but he passed it.

At the end of the presidency in December, Blair returned to the parliament to report. For once, seating was ad hoc rather than hierarchical. The UKIP members behaved like stereotypical Germans with beach-towels. We rushed into the chamber so soon as the doors opened and occupied all of the second row. Godfrey Bloom wore a deerstalker and carried a meerschaum. When asked why, he explained that he was looking for the French concession.

None of Blair's declared intentions had been fulfilled. He was haggard and ashen. The sparkle in his eye had faded and sunk back like a lately brilliant fish thrown back dead into the ocean in accordance with Common Fisheries Policy. He had been up for most of the night, arguing with Chirac, attempting to salvage something – anything – from the presidency. He was no longer impressive.

Now I let him have it. I pointed out that, so far from reducing regulation, he had overseen the passing of a further 3,350 legislative acts, that there had been no sign of economic reform, that he had pledged that there would be no surrender of the British rebate but that he had signed away £7 billion of it and that, so far from reforming the CAP, he had extracted a tentative commitment that the EU would review spending on agriculture in three years' time.

'Why should British taxpayers pay for new sewers in Budapest and a new underground system in Warsaw,' I demanded, 'when our own public services are crumbling in London? . . . Your budget deal is game, set and match to President Chirac. No cheese-eating surrender-monkey he. Unlike you, he stands up for French national interests not some bizarre notion of Europe, and he has outclassed you and outplayed you at every turn. . .'

Everything which happens in the hemicycle is filmed, but for some mysterious reason, the official film of Blair's response has vanished. Those who saw it, however, will testify that the man simply lost it. He turned crimson. He screamed. He pointed at the Union Jacks which stood on the desks before us and yelled, 'You – you sit behind your country's flags but you don't represent your country's interests. We're in 2005, not 1945! We're not at war with these people!'

This last reflects Blair's greatest folly. He believes his own rhetoric about modernity. Maybe he reads history, but, if so, it is as many a tourist wanders an historic site, sincerely believing that those who built its buildings and lived amongst them were perforce savages, moved by emotions which we have somehow miraculously outgrown. When asked what his food strategy was, he merely blinked and said that 'Britain has no food strategy' because, of course, plagues and wars and fuel blockades and the like are things of the past.

In the modern era, there will always be beans from Kenya and pre-packed grated Reggiano Parmesan from Italy. If Britain should run short of wheat, she can always get it from Canada or Poland. Time has stopped. We have reached a Brave New World where everyone believes in peace, justice and equality.

He does not realise that 1914 and 1939 were really quite modern in their time, and that the less educated people thought then too that they had attained the highest development of humankind. He does not realise that every man-made building, alliance and empire must crumble into its constituent parts and that preparedness, now as always, is all that we can offer in the way of guarantees of safety.

I pray with all my heart that all nations will be mutually supportive friends. I believe it slightly less than I believe in Father Christmas.

And there, I think, lies the greatest difference between us. The EU is built on wholly unwarranted faith. Architects tell us that even in the great Gothic cathedrals whose components have been carefully selected and fashioned for their functions, 'the arch never sleeps' – that there are constant strains pulling this way and that – and even these must one day fall.

So too an alliance such as the United States, built with the consent of all its people, can exist for centuries but will still one day founder. The European Union is a Lego construct, forced together by an impatient child regardless of the shapes and colours of the pieces. Its components strain against one another before it has even been completed.

Blair, Barroso and the rest of them, like the child builder, see the magnificent palace in their minds' eyes but forget that the arch never sleeps and that ill-assorted pieces will not adhere for long.

But then Blair's contribution to modernity, his Ozymandias-style memorial and, by his own admission, the symbol of his government was a gigantic, £789 million glass-fibre fabric blister on the banks of the Thames.

The Dome's life expectancy is sixty years. I'll bet it outlives the European Union.

I have since flayed Gordon Brown, who sat stolidly chewing the cud and looked like an impatient preacher attempting to ignore a resonant fart in the middle of his sermon, Angela Merkel, Nicolas Sarkozy, who schmoozed all the usual Europhile suspects (Cohn-Bendit, Watson, Schulz, Daul etc.) and had them wriggling in their seats like excited puppies, but came back at me fiercely again and again and plainly enjoyed the debate because later, at the Elysée, he preferred to enjoy cigars and talk with the man who had given him hell – now there's a politician for you – than with the more deferential. Sarkozy likes a cigar and respects an enemy.

None of them ever lost his or her cool like Blair.

*

After its defeat at the hands of the people, the Commission had declared that a period of reflection was needed. A 'group of wise men', soon to be known as the 'Amato Group' after its leader, former Italian Prime Minister Giuliano Amato, spent really quite a long time preparing an alternative text.

Which was, ingeniously, precisely the same.

There were the same number of new competencies, the same number of powers of veto withdrawn. The all-important difference lay, as Amato pointed out, in the title, which they changed from the 'Treaty Establishing a Constitution for Europe' into the far racier 'Treaty of Lisbon'.

'The good thing about calling it a treaty', said Amato with relish, 'is that we don't need referendums.'

OK. It wasn't precisely the same. They got rid of the preamble, which had always been incomprehensible and superfluous drivel, and the official anthem and flag, though these have, needless to say, returned without constitutional authority.

They performed a lot of tricks by referring to previous treaties and sort of incidentally giving their provisions force of law rather than bothering to spell them out here. All that the leaders of member-states had had to read when they signed the eventual treaty was a hotch-potch of amendments which required referring back to the previous documents referred to. The European Council forbade the consolidation of all these clauses, though this had been unanimously requested by MEPs, until the treaty was safely signed. There was therefore no parliamentary scrutiny.

And that was it.

What had been Part I of the Constitution, with nine parts, now became Titles I − IX. Then there is a Title X, and Part IV of the Constitution is here rendered as Title XI. The European Council forbade the consolidation of the countless amendments into one comprehensible document, though this had been unanimously requested by MEPs, so none of us could actually read it.

This was cheating.

Forgive me if I here become a trifle fanciful, but governments perform, I suppose, much the same role as parents. The children are too busy playing and learning to worry about exactly how there are meals on the table or money in the bank, so they entrust to their parents a deal of power and the freedom of the family's assets. They trust to natural benevolence and mutual interest.

Of course, the amount of power claimed by parents and granted by children varies widely with different cultures and ages. We no longer accept arranged marriages in the West − though, provided that there be benevolence and insight on the part of the parents and the bride and groom have power of veto, parents may be better judges than the young in the throes of oestrus. Where there is no such benevolence and the parents are greedy for themselves, they claim licence to prostitute their own child.

That is what the Europhiliac politicians have done with their trusting daughter Europa. They made a secret deal with the old bull for her violation in exchange for gold and power.

They did it first by straight subterfuge. They groomed us, booked us into a double room with him – well, he's a nice, harmless old chap, he's loaded and you're sure to come out of it with a pretty present, dear, and two rooms are much more expensive. . .

We got pawed and slobbered over and very badly screwed. And it was our parents, not we, who were driving around in a flash new car.

We sulked. We wanted to play the field, to party, but still we believed that our parents must have our best interests at heart. They kept taking us off to stay with the old pervert and hiring us out to accompany him to social engagements. They gave him the care of our jewellery and other inherited property. At last, when they thought that we were too beaten down to resist further, they sent out the wedding invitations.

We arrived at the altar. We did our best to be dutiful, but took one look at the drooling brute and ran for our lives.

So they arranged a new wedding. They soothed us. They loved us, didn't they? And, to prove it, they had found this dashing young fellow who would still allow us to associate with whomsoever we would.

He had a different name. He wore a bright new coat. They did not allow us to see his face until we reached the altar-rails. And at the very moment that we saw that glazed eye, the telltale dribbling from the dewlaps, the church-doors slammed shut behind us.

When Jeffrey Titford and I had first entered the EU Parliament, we resolved that we would behave – at least in the chamber – like English gentlemen, and comport and disport ourselves with courtesy and propriety.

Up till now, I had kept that pledge and had abided by the rules, however I despised the principles of those imposing them. Now the power-hungry eurocrats had broken their own rules and, whilst deriving wealth and power from them, were cheating the people of their right to democratic rule.

The gloves were off.

As the Commissioners tutted and the ushers manhandled me over the next months, I wanted to shout at them, 'Don't you get it? That is how it works, you bloody fools! Deny people a voice and the power to work change and first they become irresponsible and idle because they are reduced to impotence, then they start to hit out and to scream. And they are right to do so!'

Whilst the Amato group was deliberating as to the exact font which should be used in the new edition, the correct spelling of 'Lisbon' and other matters of similar importance, Roger Knapman's term of office ended and I stepped with remarkably little argument and tentative enthusiasm into the leadership. My enthusiasm was for the battle ahead which promised – and proved – to be more passionate, public, time-consuming and exacting than any in which we had thus far engaged.

The tentativeness? Well, I was still apprehensive about doing anything quite so grown-up, but we had a good team to assist in the admin, Roger had left a party with a large, well-organised and largely unified membership and I was confident that I could get on with the front-of-house stuff so necessary at present without too many kitchen fires.

On 12 December 2007, the day before the treaty was to be signed in Lisbon, the rowdyism started. As Felipe Gonzáles, the Spanish Prime Minister, entered the hemicycle to the usual sycophantic applause, eighty of us from across the ideological spectrum arose with placards and banners bearing just one word: 'REFERENDUM'. We chanted just one word: 'REFERENDUM'.

Over and over again we shouted it whilst totalitarian MEPs tutted and sneered and officials sent ushers scurrying uncertainly about the chamber to contain us, to confiscate banners and to prevent cameras from recording the event. We were scattered about the chamber, which made it hard for them. REFERENDUM! REFERENDUM! REFERENDUM!

Gonzales tried to speak, but again and again had to stop. Ushers gathered up banners only to hear another outcry elsewhere and to rush off again. It went on and on. REFERENDUM! REFERENDUM! REFERENDUM!

Oh, it was fun. The BBC and ITV, to their shame, almost totally ignored it, just as they were almost totally to ignore our friend and fellow banner-waver Dan Hannan's brilliant demolition of Gordon Brown in March 2009. You can, I am delighted to say, still see both events on a public service broadcast medium, YouTube.

Yes. We had broken the rules of civilised debate. We had brought demonstration into a place where there should be debate, but the self-appointed rulers of Europe had broken the rules first. They had prevented debate, so all that remained to us and to the people whom we had pledged to serve was demonstration.

Later that day, the servile ideologues had their say.

What is it about these people that they all spout the same words at the same time? Is it like that Darwinian phenomenon whereby, I am assured, monkeys on Madagascar started washing their yams in the sea for added salt intake at the same moment as their distant cousins on the African mainland, though there can have been no contact? Or could it just possibly be that they had all received similar briefings from on high?

The EU was being accused – and justly – of using totalitarian techniques to suppress democratic debate, so Martin Schulz, chairman of the Socialist Group, stood up and told the parliament that our conduct had resembled that of the Nazis in the Reichstag. Then up popped our Liberal (?) Democrat (?) friend (?) Graham Watson, who repeated his trusty football hooligan line, then compared us to the Nazis in the Reichstag. He also demanded that the president expel us.

It was left to Danny Cohn-Bendit – no stranger, God knows, to demonstrations – to supply the supposedly tolerant line. No, no, he said. Just because we were mad and 'mentally weak', there was no call to expel us physically. There were 500 other members who were sane. This parliament was surely big enough to cope with a few dissident madmen. . .

We were disciplined for being undisciplined – or, rather, thirteen of us were disciplined, including an Austrian nationalist who had actually been in Frankfurt on the day.

Although I had been very audibly and visibly there and the president had identified me as a ringleader, I was mysteriously spared. A few weeks later, I was forced to stand up, raise a fist and declare 'I am Spartacus!', at which many of my colleagues did likewise – to the total bemusement of the president.

I flew to Lisbon that night, tried in vain to grab a couple of hours of sleep and was at the glorious sixteenth-century Hieronymites Monastery in Lisbon in time to witness the signing of a treaty which no signatory had actually read. Gordon Brown, of course, turned up five hours late for the ceremony, so it was left to David Miliband to sign on his behalf and that of the entire British people. Security appeared to be non-existent. I buttonholed Miliband as he set off up the steps. 'Remember your promise,' I said. 'We have to have a referendum.'

He smiled weakly.

Those were the last words spoken to him before he scrawled his name on a document which bound Britain into a soviet without the consent of the people whom he claimed to represent.

I sincerely hope that they – and his residual conscience – ruined his one big day.

*

From that point onward Dan Hannan and I resolved that we must use the tactics of the great Charles Stewart Parnell. Neither of us is exactly a procedure man, and I certainly never thought that the day would come when I would go everywhere with the EU Parliament's rules of procedure under my arm. We resolved, however, that we would use every procedural rule, every point of order and every opportunity for filibustering to register our protest.

But this was not Westminster nor any democratic chamber where the rules are more sacrosanct than the members or any principle. We might have known.

The new president of the parliament, Hans-Gert Pöttering, simply wrote a request to the parliament for the right to silence any member whom the Speaker or president deemed to be obstructive to 'the procedures of the House'. Again, rules were not intended to apply to the divinely appointed masters. They demanded arbitrary powers. The parliament surrendered yet another guarantee of liberty.

Outraged, Dan now joined Roger Helmer in the outer darkness where all Conservatives so sinful as to fight for liberty must go. His microphone was hastily switched off by a vice-president, but he spoke on regardless.

'An absolute majority', he said, 'is not the same as the rule of law. I accept that there is a minority in this house in favour of a referendum. That there is a minority in this house against the ratification of the Lisbon Treaty. But this house must nonetheless follow its own rule-books. And by popular acclamation to discard the rules under which we operate is indeed an act of arbitrary and despotic rule. It is only my regard for you, Mr Chairman, and my personal affection for you that prevents me from likening it to the *Ermächtigungsgesetz* of 1933, which was also voted through by a parliamentary majority.'

This was a far more apposite reference to Nazi Germany (though Dan had specifically refrained from making it) than that which our critics had used. Hitler's 1933 'Enabling Act' allowed the cabinet to enact legislation, including laws deviating from or altering the constitution, without the consent of the Reichstag. The Reichstag approved it – in large measure because the opposition was already in gaol.

This time, however, because the allusion referred to the establishment, not to a minority, the EU suffered a serious fit of the vapours. The Conservatives became apoplectic (the distinctly silly Christopher Beazley even stood over Dan and invited him to 'come outside'. Joseph Daul, the head of the EPP group to which Pöttering himself also belonged, at once demanded Dan's expulsion.

French farmers' leader Daul already disliked me. In fact, he had been threatening to sue me for a year or so. He had somehow never got round to it.

Yes. Yet another one, I'm afraid, again right up at the top. . .

Back in January 2007, when he was named the EPP's new leader, I had thought it worth mentioning to the parliament that Daul had been under investigation since 2004 for 'complicity and concealment of the abuse of public funds' (€16 million or £10.6 million) by French farming unions. There was no suggestion that Daul had personally profited, but his alleged complicity was surely a matter both of public interest and of concern to those who were about to elevate him.

Daniel Hannan was, unsurprisingly, expelled from the group on 19 February for presuming to tell the truth and for making – or rather for not making – a comparison which our opponents had lately made about us to obsequious applause and official approval.

The following day, we were thoroughly childish. Our staff dressed up in chicken suits and we in the chamber wore T-shirts in matching yellow bearing a picture of a chicken and the legend 'Too Chicken for a Referendum'.

Well, we had to attract the attention of the media somehow.

In my time, there have been many costumes seen in the parliament buildings. It is, after all, an acknowledged weapon in the protestor's armoury. Climate-change activists, for example, have worn death-masks and black cloaks and have been treated with due deference. When our staff, however, dressed up and cavorted in the lobby a bit to draw attention to the cowardice of the Commission in declining to face public opinion, they were harried, pursued and threatened with disciplinary action and arrest.

A memorable note was delivered to me in the chamber. It read, 'Your chickens are being arrested. Please can you help?'

I ran out into the lobby and attempted to reason with the officials who by now had the chickens cornered.

I was interviewed by veteran ITN correspondent Jim Gibbons. I told him that the parliament was now resorting to totalitarian methods, that we had been accused of being mentally ill and of being Nazis and that all that we were in fact doing was seeking the consent of the European people for the actions of its soi-disant parliament. At this, the head of audio-visual services in the parliament stepped forward and told Jim, 'I don't want you using that clip. We're not here to record dissent.'

My jaw dropped. Jim blinked and stared. Here was blatant totalitarian censorship in action in the middle of western Europe.

Fortunately a senior BBC correspondent showed a little more articulacy and presence of mind than I. Shirin Wheeler, the daughter of the great Sir Charles Wheeler, briskly told the Jacques-in-office, 'Very well, if that's your attitude, the BBC will withdraw from the European Parliament.'

There was a bit of stammering then.

The would-be Brussels Beria gulped and sadly bethought himself that he had not yet been granted that degree of arbitrary power.

It had been an aberration, it was later explained, an excess of zeal. . .
Unfortunately, that sort of thing is highly infectious.

*

One by one, the professional politicians in member-states acceded to
the EU's demands and ratified the Lisbon Treaty without reference to
their citizens.

Only four nations held out – Germany (who managed to extort an
admission that Basic Law had precedence over the European Court of
Justice), Poland (who saw no point in signing until the Irish had approved),
the Czech Republic – or, rather, one man in the Czech Republic, President
Václav Klaus (who declined to sign for a long as he could, and first obtained
an opt-out for the Beneš decrees) – and Ireland.

The Irish have known much of oppression and cherish their freedom. In
accordance with common sense and principles of fairness, they hold that no
change can be made to the Constitution without the explicit approval of the
people. They rejected the Nice Treaty in 2001 and accepted it in 2002 only
after they had obtained an opt-out from any common European defence
policy and established the primacy of the Dáil in any further integrationist
measures.

They must once more ratify the treaty by referendum or it must die.

Since Nice, of course, the Celtic tiger had all but transformed Ireland. A
combination of a superb educational system, native savvy, low interest-rates
and massive grant aid from Brussels had seen a gold-rush. A stable, largely
rural and frequently black economy had morphed into an international
boom which was the envy of the rest of Europe.

Admittedly, some of the smooth new highways being built to replace
pot-holed byways actually led nowhere in particular, property prices soared,
immigration was managed with staggering insensitivity with tiny rural
villages suddenly having their populations all but doubled within weeks
and the despised 'Foxrock Fannies' were suddenly the kings and queens of
the castle that they had always believed themselves to be, but the folding
stuff was there in plenty.

It takes more than that, however, to make Ireland meek and compliant.

The 'Yes' contingent denied that the treaty had constitutional significance. Just in case there should be any democratic dissent, Taoiseach Brian Cowen stated that any member of the Fianna Fáil parliamentary party campaign declaring against the treaty would be expelled, The media were all but unanimously yes-men.

The executive council of the Irish Congress of Trade Unions, demonstrating that they had learned something from the EU, voted to support a Yes vote but omitted to consult members of the individual unions. In fact, the Technical, Engineering and Electrical Union (TEEU) advised its 45,000 members to vote 'No'.

Kathy Sinnott, an independent member of our group, led our 'No' campaign. Millionaire Declan Ganley, founder of the pan-European party Libertas, ran his own campaign. Sinn Féin were opposed to the treaty, the Greens undecided. Otherwise, we had no support amongst the professional politicians.

Once again, we mustered such money as we could from MEPs and from the information budget. We printed a glossy leaflet which was distributed to every household in Ireland. We visited as often as we could.

Some 53.13 per cent of the electorate turned out for that referendum, and 53.4 per cent of them voted 'No'. Cowen paid me an enormous compliment by saying that 'Nigel Farage and a few extremists subverted the democratic process in Ireland'. He did not deign to explain how, by public speaking on behalf of an under-represented majority, I had contrived to 'subvert the democratic process'.

OK, it was close, but it was a 'No'. Had the 'Yes' faction won, it would have been an irrevocable sanction.

But as with Nice, as with the Constitution, the EU demonstrated that it does not understand that word. When someone else looks like winning the game, it simply changes the rules.

As ever, the serial date-rapist took a deep breath, administered a huge dose of Rohypnol and moved in once more. This, by the way, is a model which we will soon see replicated in our courts.

The Lisbon Treaty allows for the appointment of a European public prosecutor who will have the power to arrest and charge British subjects.

The model for the new European justice will be the French, under which there is no such thing as double jeopardy.

As I write, Dominique de Villepin, President Sarkozy's bitterest opponent, has just been acquitted of conspiracy to destroy Sarkozy's career by linking him to arms dealing – this despite the fact that Sarkozy publicly declared de Villepin 'guilty' during the course of the trial.

The public prosecutor (or, rather, his master Sarkozy) did not like the verdict so, without any new evidence being adduced, he has declared his intention to appeal it. De Villepin, though not guilty, must now face a retrial until they find a jury which agrees with the prosecution.

As for the Irish vote, the Commission played safe. They resolved that the second referendum would take place after the 2009 European elections. By then, Declan Ganley was wiped out as a political force. Kathy Sinnott had lost her seat. The European Commission ploughed millions into the 'Yes' campaign. Furthermore, the Irish Referendum Commission now resolved that its original purpose was not appropriate in this case.

In 1995, Patricia McKenna had won a Supreme Court case which established that it was unconstitutional for taxpayers' money to be spent on promoting just one side of the case in a referendum. The Referendum Commission had therefore been set up to ensure that information about both sides should be disseminated equally in the media and elsewhere.

In this instance, however, the McKenna judgment was set aside on the grounds that there was just so much information about the merits of the treaty to be disseminated whilst the 'No' case was, well, just 'No'.

Opposition to the treaty was wiped out. When I returned to state the case, I discovered that I had become a villain.

The Irish government had played the same well-worn, dog-eared cards. I was no longer a passionate volunteer coming to Ireland free of charge and without prospect of personal benefit in order to advocate independence. I was rather a devious foreigner, an absentee landlord imposing his alien will upon the poor, foolish Irish people.

And yes, of course, I was a fascist as well, or, more precisely and cautiously, according to Europe Minister Dick Roche, I was 'a modern imperialist . . . from the same gene-pool as the National Front' and 'an extreme nationalist'.

Once, believe it or not, this calumny – what Vladimir Bukovsky has called 'the European gulag' – hurt me. It is the most cowardly because the most unanswerable charge. This is the problem with making a crime of a purported character trait. You can refute a charge of a specific act, but not of a conjectured predisposition or sympathy.

If you try, even if you have half-German children, work daily with people of all nations and spend your life battling for freedom of speech and the self-determination of all peoples, they'll only perform a semiotic analysis of your words and conclude that you are a genocidal sexist in your time off.

At length I recognised it for what it was – a cheap playground jibe for those so devoid of intellect as to be unable to confront you in debate, the equivalent of chiding someone for being fat or ginger-haired, an irrelevant taunt which by implication associates the speaker with an approved majority and casts you into the ideological gulag.

Over fifteen years, I had learned to shrug it off and get on with the business in hand, in part because that is all that you can do, in part because honest conviction and anger and care for people rather than principles will shine through. I was annoyed only for Ireland, which deserved much better.

That the people of Britain no longer believed this nonsense was demonstrated by the results of the European election of 2009. Hundreds of parties have come and gone in the past century. None has started with so little and gone on to achieve so much as has UKIP. I remembered that first election at Eastleigh, where I had barely squeezed ahead of Screaming Lord Sutch. Now I was leading the party which had come second in a national election.

We took 16.5 per cent of the votes cast, Labour 15.7 and the Lib Dems 13.7. The Conservatives came first with 27.7 per cent, which translated as twenty-five seats to our thirteen. The people had started to acknowledge what the fight was really about – their enfranchisement – and had recognised, I think, that we, fallible and sometimes amateur as we were, were not part of the self-serving, self-perpetuating cabal of professional politicians who scorned them.

The Irish campaign wore on – hopeless now, because the credit crunch had hit and Ireland naturally clung to what had once been the provider of so much wealth. That the inability to set their own interest rates as members of the Eurozone will eventually cripple them was theoretical only. Once, briefly, the streets had seemed paved with gold, the Liffey had brimmed with rather revolting Chardonnay, property prices had made millionaires of smallholders and the Foxrock Fannies had exchanged their gold slingbacks for Jimmy Choos. If they obeyed the Commissioners, maybe they would once more be rewarded with wealth.

And indeed, Barroso visited Ireland on 19 September 2009 and announced a €14.8 million grant for former workers at Limerick's Dell plant. I rummaged in my wallet and could find no more than the price of a few drinks with which to win over the voters of Ireland. The fact that Dell had moved the plant to Poland at a cost of 1,900 jobs to Limerick was only tenuously linked to EU membership. The EU was still Father Christmas.

Add this to the brazen lies circling – EU law would not supersede Irish law, vote 'Yes' for jobs, the treaty had no constitutional significance etc – and the sudden silence of many who had vociferously advocated a 'No', and it was a hopeless cause.

There were some entertaining moments. At the Reuters debate in Dublin, I managed to skewer Dick Roche, the man who had uttered that weary slander, and to expose a shill in the audience. For those who have led lives untainted by such things, a shill is a player at an open game of poker or chemmy who is covertly playing for the house, so substantially altering the odds. The EU has many thousands of shills scattered amongst the population, particularly where there are young, impressionable minds to be moulded.

An unkempt, earnest, bespectacled questioner with a distinct resemblance to Worzel Gummidge arose from the audience and announced herself to be a professor at University College, Dublin. She started her question – or, rather, her speech, for I could detect not a single interrogatory in the entire thing – and I sat back and relaxed. It was like listening to a gruesome bedtime story for the hundredth time.

It went on and on. . .

. . .and on. . .

I knew at once what she was. Every one of the sentiments and phrases used was familiar to me. I suppose I should have interrupted her, but she was giving me a breather from a torrid debate, and it is really quite instructive to see an expert tying a slipknot at her own throat.

When I was given to understand that she had finished, I simply said, 'I assume that you are a Monnet professor?'

There was no reply. The good professor looked over her shoulder, then seemed to have noticed something interesting on her rump, then demonstrated a hitherto unsuspected concern for her coiffure and ran her fingers though it. Then she was ready for the inevitable. She gulped. She said, 'What?'

'I said, "I assume that you are a Monnet professor?"'

'I have that honour—' she started.

I just laughed.

Amidst her ramblings, this woman had advocated frankness and honesty. Yet she, purporting to be 'a citizen and a voter' had not deigned to tell the audience that she was handsomely paid by the EU to disseminate EU propaganda in the guise of learning, or, in the official version, 'to stimulate universities throughout the world to explain the European Union model for peaceful coexistence and integration as well as European Union policies and external action.'

Just how great seats of learning – by definition impartial – can bring themselves to endorse such propaganda (just try substituting 'USSR' – or even 'British government' for 'EU' in the above mission statement and see how it reads), I fail to understand, but there are over 400 such professors in British universities, all paid by you to teach the party line.

I will search my wallet again, but I am pretty sure that I cannot manage anything similar for the alternative view.

I suggest that all Monnet professors should henceforth be compelled to preface lectures and publications with the words 'The following cannot, alas, attain the high, dispassionate standards of academe because I must serve my paymasters, advocate the cause of European integration and side with all EU policies and external action. I apologise, but I have a mortgage to pay.'

Should they fail to do so, their lectures should be boycotted by all students who value honesty, freedom and the integrity of academe.

Having nodded to all the very familiar faces in the rent-a-mob crowd outside, I wandered through the corridors of Dublin Castle on the day that the results came through. I looked at the portraits of the past British governors of Ireland and saw in my mind's eye the smiling face of José Manuel Barroso at the end of the line. The Irish had fought so gallantly for freedom and autonomy. Today they gave it away again.

The Czechs now had no excuse not to ratify the Constitution – sorry, the treaty.

The Battle of Lisbon was over.

We had won many battles but we had lost the war.

Or had we? In the course of that campaign, we had demonstrated to millions their irrelevance to those advancing the EU project. We had exposed dishonesty and downright disregard for democracy. We had forced supposed leaders of member-states to show their true colours, and they were not those which the peoples of Europe wore on their shields. In defeat, our army had grown a thousandfold.

The war goes on. The people are now aware of its nature. It is not a war between left wing and right nor between nationalists and internationalists. It is far more fundamental than that. It is the struggle between a formerly sovereign people and a coterie of professional politicians who have claimed sovereignty for themselves and wrested it from them by deceit and bribery.

At the last, it goes still further. It is about the individual's freedom no less than the individual nation's to define and govern him or herself without intervention from a self-proclaimed and self-perpetuating mediocracy whose only excellence appears to lie in the prodigious ability to remember acronyms and whose only loyalty is to tidiness, homogeneity – and power.

Thanks to Lisbon, we are entering a second protectorate in which neighbour spies upon neighbour and nothing is immune from regulation. Political correctness and conformity in accordance with safety regulations and an apocryphal ecological gospel are the new puritanism. It is no less killjoy and intrusive than the original version.

As with the protectorate, the Soviet Union, the Warsaw Pact, the Yugoslav union and many others, it will not survive without the wholehearted consent of its constituents. It has not that consent. It cannot hold.

I only pray that we can break it up intelligently and calmly now rather than wait until our children must once more fight for freedom at terrible cost.

The battle goes on, and we all have our parts to play.

15

NO FAREWELL

If the journey from unknown, eccentric little party to second in a national election seems an implausible one, that of Nigel Farage from restless City trader to spokesman for a popular movement across Europe seems, to me at least, still more incredible.

I won't be disingenuous and pretend that I have not fought long and hard for the triumphs which the party and I have attained. I have given every waking hour and a fair proportion of the sleeping ones to the cause.

I can honestly state, however, that no part of the journey was planned at the outset. My every movement along the way has been reactive, not, as the Americans would say, proactive. I have not had my eyes fixed upon some illusory shining city on the hill. There has always been another outrage to address, another election to fight, another blunder to mop up, another smirking prat to be corrected. Once I had taken this road, one new challenge simply led to another. He who rides a tiger cannot dismount.

Am I glad that I took up tiger-riding?

Oh, hell. The disadvantages have been many. Had I stayed on in the City, I think it reasonable to suppose that I would now be rich and looking forward to secure retirement in some delightful part of the country. Instead, I have an aged Volvo and three children still being educated, I have just remortgaged the same home in which I have lived for twenty years and I suppose that I may be fortunate enough to spend my retirement years in a dinky villa in Worthing.

I would certainly have devoted far more time to my family whom I have sorely neglected. In politics I have worked seven days a week for fifteen years. On the rare occasions when I am at home, I am usually in my office at the bottom of the garden.

I have also neglected my other hobbies. I would have continued to play golf. I might even have been pretty good at it by now. I have not played in seven years. I suspect that my handicap today might exceed my highest cricket innings. I am pretty sure that any cricket innings would be lower than my handicap was back then. I would have fished all over the world, not merely in the Channel or the Irish Sea when I can steal a few hours away with the children. I would have caught big game, not merely bass.

I will not be taking a holiday this year.

I may appear blithe and dismissive, but the treachery of Mote, Wise and a few others whom I worked hard to advance only to see them turn rogue caused me acute pain and made me question the worth of working for anyone much.

On the other hand. . . on the other hand. . .

OK. I would have disgraced myself in the modern City. At the risk of sounding like an old fart at forty-six, the compliance culture has taken all the fun out of trading. Everyone must behave and conform. When I visit nowadays, I find orderly people sitting quietly at computers, sending emails to colleagues sitting just ten feet away. They no longer hurl jokes and abuse at one another like civilised people. With three new regulatory authorities about to be imposed by the EU, I fear for the future of the City itself.

I might have survived it for a decade, I suppose – a decade of making a great deal of money, growing daily more frustrated and drearily drunk and at last succumbing to a stroke or, at best, prosperous retirement. As it is, I may be poor, but my waistline is precisely the same as when first I joined UKIP.

In politics, people can still talk and flirt and argue. In ten years as an MEP, not a single day has been the same as any other. I have met many fascinating people, great and humble, and have enjoyed discourse with some of the best – and worst – opponents of our age. I have never had to take up crosswords to keep my mind limber.

I did not enter politics out of philanthropy but rather as an extension of my own annoyance and resentment at having inherited freedoms infringed by power-crazed idiots spouting gibberish. It gives me particular pleasure, then, to know that we have empowered many others and caused them too to doubt the authority whereby such people presume to grant us rights where we can manage perfectly well with innate freedoms, thanks. If you grant us rights, you assume the right to take them away. We do not grant you that.

The disgraceful Lisbon process has demonstrated to many that democracy faces a huge threat. Opposition to the EU's growth has become mainstream, awareness that we can resist widespread. I am proud of that.

I allowed my hobby – my passion – to run away with me. Sometimes I have huddled in the saddle, clung on for dear life and prayed that it would tire and bear me back to the comforting confinement of home. Sometimes, I have leaned forward, given it a crack down its withers and urged it on, whooping at the speed and the feeling of the wind in my hair. It has taken me to many fascinating places and presented me with many daunting obstacles. Sometimes I have flown over them, sometimes barely scrambled through.

Thus far, I have just about managed to stay in the saddle and enjoy the scenery.

I have achieved so much. I have achieved so little. In terms of popular understanding that ours is a common battle – freedoms v. rights, British self-governance v. European oligarchy, democracy v. totalitarianism, people v. professional politicians – we have made great strides. In terms of driving back the massed forces of European bureaucracy and the mass of laws and lies which attempt to homogenise the world, there is so much further to go.

Next on the agenda is fighting bull – and the rapist bull – at Westminster. I believe that UKIP Members of Parliament will serve at the very least to remind their fellows of all parties of their duties to those who elected them, and that there are many in both houses who will side with us and may even join us when once the provisions of Lisbon begin to bite. The British media continue to treat everything that happens in the European Parliament as foreign news, though its antics now affect every aspect of our lives. They will not be able to ignore us in Westminster.

We must destroy the hegemony of the established parties in order to reflect the enormous diversity of interests in the country. Lifelong professional politicians reflect no interests save those of their own kind. This will mean altering the electoral system and the ridiculous mess which is the modern upper house.

Our role – to represent the people against the politicians, to demand self-determination for the nation, to expose arrogant cheats, to fight the bull violating Europe and bull in general – will become more and more important in the next few years. The mediocracy is becoming more and more complacent, the international political freemasonry barely bothering to pretend that there are differences between their parties and ideologies.

We will break free of the European soviet and begin once more to deal freely with the world on our own terms and subject to our own laws. I have no doubt of that. The only question now is when.

If I have brought that day closer, I will be able to sit in my dinky Worthing villa and gaze out across the Channel towards my former workplace with something like satisfaction – provided there's a decent pub nearby.

16

RUMINATION. . .

The most dangerous politicians depend upon the Great Lie.

Once the Great Lie has been ingested, it readily and rapidly grows into doctrine. Then a political preference becomes a religion, its champion a demigod and any aberration heresy. The politician excuses himself for abominations because he has seen the way clear to that shining city upon a hill. He has a duty to follow that path and to shepherd or lash others onto it for their own good.

The Great Lie is just this: one day, time will stop.

For Christians, it is the New Jerusalem, for Marxists, the Worker State, for romancers, the Happy Ever After, for buyers of cosmetics, Eternal Youth, for childish idealists, John Lennon's Magic Roundabout Elysium where there are no countries, no religions (and hence, presumably, no cultures or loyalties) and all the people live (half-)life in peace.

Ooh ooh.

When we have followed the prescribed course of treatment and so attained the ideal, there will be no more human greed, overvaunting ambition or rival lusts (by ordinance, I suppose), bacteria will be stopped from breeding, dogs from fighting, cancers and weeds from growing and volcanoes and stomachs from grumbling and Death will have no Dominion.

It is, of course, irresponsible gibberish. It serves only to make life's rich and only occasionally disgusting stew (with oh, such delicious dumplings) appear unsatisfactory and affords nearly infinite power to the man with the hastily scrawled treasure-map.

Yet it is hardwired into our culture.

Jesus's teachings and Marx's analysis of economic history were fine. The leaps of faith whereby these were turned into the Great Lie, however, initiated centuries of totalitarianism and intolerance.

But who wants to worship a god or vote for a politician who says 'It's going to be pretty much the normal shitty mess, but we'll muddle through and try to keep it as fair and as much fun as possible', when the other guy is promising eternal houris and foie gras to the sound of trumpets?

'Happy Ever After' actually means 'These two young people have fulfilled their biological duty to the race by mating. They are thus, like spent salmon drifting back downstream, of no further interest to us. The End.'

Shakespeare was at least truthful with his Romeo and Juliet. Time stopped for them. They died. Bernstein's Maria, however, lived on, and presumably grew fat and slatternly and had countless children by a man whom she nagged continuously about not being as good as that whatsisname who died. Who wants to see that movie?

As for Lennon's imagined nightmare world, by what grotesque means is its survival for more than a split second to be assured? Brutal regimentation and compulsory unsexing, I assume.

'All is flux,' said Heraclitus, but 2,500 years on, in the era of moving pictures, we still choose to see our worlds in static images.

Our personal growth is chronicled as serial stasis – infant, child, adolescent, adult, parent, old fart, dead. Our moral identities are similarly chronicled. We are heroes or villains, madonnas or whores, brilliant or stupid, heterosexual or homosexual.

Psycho-analysts have even made a profitable pseudo-science out of such paradigms.

Of course, we are aware – or should be – that a whole person is like a composite image made up of superimposed film-cells – that the little girl is – or should be – gazing out through the cataract-misted eyes of the old woman and the slut constantly causing the Madonna to wriggle on her throne, that the villainous can be virtuous and vice versa and that a still picture of someone engaged in sexual activity with his or her own gender tells us precisely nothing about that person but that he or she has healthy sexual impulses and felt that way in that moment.

We also know the truth – none better than I – of Woody Allen's aphorism 'How do you make God laugh? Tell him your plans for tomorrow', but, so soon as we look back on the random, rambling, ramshackle events of a life, we seek a linear route which makes sense of the senseless.

We turn our lurches into curlicues, our stumbles into features of design. We discern pattern where at the time there were only chaos and impulse. We find the origins of this in that, and ascribe our fortunes to our misfortunes, bad parenting or even the positions of the stars at the moments of our birth. We look for a 'So that's why!' moment which will reduce us from free agents into helpless flotsam.

We call that 'making sense' of the random. In fact, it makes nonsense of it.

I don't spend much time looking back. This exercise is a rare indulgence for me. Although I know all the above and have built my entire career on spurning and challenging the Great Lie, I confess that, when I first examined my childhood and upbringing, I could not resist looking for just such snapshots in the album which would 'explain' me to me.

I have signally failed. No doubt psychiatrists will find a hundred telltale indications. That is their dubious business – making paradigms of the infinitely diverse – but, as far as I am concerned, I can blame no-one but myself for what I have done, what I have thus far become.

That a middle-class boy of no great academic distinction should become a city trader is predictable enough. That he should veer from those rails to become a conviction politician, however, is not, nor can I find a single scene, a single specific factor in my distinctly average 1960s and 1970s upbringing to indicate that the child was father – in more than a generic, self-evident sense – of the man.

Until that point, I was just another Englishman of what was once the yeoman – a bolshy, perverse specimen, perhaps, but commonplace enough – leading a conventional, dissatisfied, materialistic life, just occasionally enlivened by lusts or yearnings, sorrows or joys.

I was one of millions of Britons brought up holding freedoms dear because they had lately stood in great jeopardy and had been saved only at enormous cost.

I read, as did many other children, Enid Blyton's tales in which nice middle-class children and dogs enjoyed the liberty of their green and pleasant land and were good friends with the local bobby, Ronald Welch's books in which foreign enemies were routed and wicked barons done down, 'trash mags' – the scruffy, crumpled, small-format war magazines in which the entire German language was distilled into '*Achtung!*', '*Englander Schweinhund!*' and '*Aaaaaagh!*' as 'Jerry' bit the desert dust – and all those wonderful stories, drawing on English history, which my father too had read and which remained on our shelves – A. E. W. Mason, Rafael Sabatini and, above all, Stanley J. Weyman.

These iniquitous propagandists corrupted me for life by implying that England was – or had been – a singularly just and agreeable place in which to live and had achieved a huge amount in terms of technology, the arts, sport and, perhaps above all, in the laws and institutions upon which she had built.

EPILOGUE

It was Economic and Monetary Union (and the firm conviction that it must fail) which first drew me into this all-encompassing, lifelong battle. From 1990 onward, I have warned that the euro could not work. I was branded a Jeremiah and a xenophobe. Now even the most pacific financial commentators accept that this absurd fancy is doomed.

It affords me little pleasure to prove to have been a Cassandra.

The death knell of the euro has already sounded.

It is fitting that it should first have been heard in Greece, the birthplace of democracy. It is as though an alien, artificial organ were being rejected by the body politic.

Hubris was ever punished by the fates, and the euro was the grossest hubris. Never in human history has a currency union held without political union. Again, these historical colonialists who regard the past as an undeveloped foreign country have assumed that they can buck the trends of millennia.

It has taken just eight years from the launch of the euro for the first fatal fissure to appear. Greece will no doubt be bailed out for now, but why then should Spain — the fourth biggest economy, currently attempting to cope with 42 per cent youth unemployment — not default too? Why should Portugal, whose GDP plummeted by 2.9 per cent last year, why should Ireland, why should Estonia or Latvia not be similarly rescued from the consequences of inept Franco-German interest rates? And, if they are not rescued, why should they not get out?

The people know how best to cultivate their own gardens. They will claim the right to do so. We wild flowers – known to the EU as 'weeds' – do not recognise legislation ordaining the levelness of playing fields

The original justification for the EU's foundation and the last-ditch, though wholly unsubstantiated, justification (NATO surely has a better claim) offered to this day for the destruction of democracy is that it somehow preserves peace. 'What is worse than war?' they ask, to which human history has always had just one answer: 'Tyranny.'

The temporary masters of the EU have identified with and invested in their project so much that millions must suffer for their silly dream. My fear is and has always been that, when at last a servile member-state government attempts to enforce its masters' will rather than that of its people, that people, denied any other voice, will resort to civil unrest and at last violent revolt.

The history of insensitive imposition of immigration should tell us too what happens when neighbour is suspicious and resentful of more prosperous and unrepresentative neighbour. If that suspicion and that resentment are turned towards France and Germany, for whose benefit ECB one-size-fits-all interest rates have been designed, we will have recreated the very situation which this fairy-tale construct was intended to prevent.

And all for nothing save an outdated reverie and a few power-hungry politicians, fearful of having to face their electorates to win their status and their wealth.

In September 2009, I stood down as UKIP's leader. I am proud of what was achieved during my spell at the helm and delighted that I could hand to Lord Pearson the wheel of a respectable, respected and orderly vessel with a confident and daily growing crew.

I wanted the time and the freedom to do what I do best and what I believe must be done.

I will stand against the Speaker of the House of Commons, John Bercow, in his Buckingham seat.

I am aware that Bercow has held the seat for thirteen years and enjoys a 13,000 majority.

I am also aware, however, that the revolution will come one day soon, that the downfall of professional, self-serving career politicians and the return of people to Parliament and Parliament to people is nigh, and I can think of no better place for it to start than Buckingham and no better head to throw over Westminster's walls than Bercow's.

This is the ultimate career politician. He makes the Vicar of Bray look consistent.

Loose cannons are notoriously dangerous, but, with luck, their size keeps them lumbering somewhere amidships. Bercow is too tiny and too eager to be a cannon. Call him rather a loose cannonball, careering hither and yon with every pitch and yaw, bouncing over his less ambitious colleagues to be the first to smash into the hull. Whatever ideology appears to enjoy favour, Bercow's principle appears to be 'Think of the policy you first thought of and double it'.

When the Tories were in power, he was a luminary of the far-right Monday Club, an advocate of apartheid and of the hanging of Mandela.

All together now:

> And this is law, I will maintain
> Unto my Dying Day, Sir.
> That whatsoever King may reign,
> I will be the Vicar of Bray, Sir!

Then the tide of public opinion shifted. The boat lurched to port. Tories and Labour alike accepted that they must mildly adjust their positions. Not Bercow. He gleefully bounded across the deck to become the ultimate New Labour luvvy. He opposes all immigration controls. He oversaw the first Speakers' Conference for thirty years, calling for parliamentary quotas for female, black and disabled MPs – social engineering regardless of popular will.

> And this is law, I will maintain
> Unto my Dying Day, Sir.
> That whatsoever King may reign,
> I will be the Vicar of Bray, Sir!

The rumours of his impending defection to Labour were cut short only by the success of his long-sought aspiration to a position not usually considered an object of aspiration. His politically expedient appointment to the Speaker's chair meant that he could stop 'flipping' his London and Buckingham homes in order to avoid paying you and instead afforded him a fine grace-and-favour apartment on whose refurbishment £700,000 of your money had already been spent. Within weeks of his appointment, Bercow had spent a further £45,581 on bigger televisions and similarly important things.

On his appointment, he openly stated that he was relieved to have left the Conservative Party.

But hold it. The people of Buckingham had elected a Conservative representative.

There is nothing shameful about changing your mind and admitting that once you were mistaken. I grant that apostasy can be honourable where founded upon principle, and I am delighted to have been able repeatedly to tell the misinformed that Buckingham's principal river did *not* derive its name from its MP and to recommend him as an ideal MEP.

There are two factors which, for me, overwhelmingly show Bercow to be a professional people-pleaser and timeserver. The first is the coincidence of shifts in power with shifts in his views. The second is that he set out to be a politician when espousing causes fundamentally different from those which he now holds. In other words, he did not enter politics with the aim of serving liberty, democracy or the deprived only to discover that these causes were better served by other means. He entered politics because success and power seemed more attainable there than in a proper job.

Buckingham deserves better.

We all deserve better.

So I hope to initiate a sea-change in Buckingham. I will hope – and damn the impossible odds – that together we can put out an historic signal which will never be forgotten and will cause all the established parties to raise their snouts from the trough and consider their true function.

That signal will read: ENOUGH!

Enough of corrupt, self-seeking politicians with neither experience nor understanding of the lives of their constituents, enough of rule by an undemocratic urban elite purporting to serve you and me but in fact serving only themselves.

We still live in a democracy.

We pay you.

So serve.

I was blessed with relative prosperity and respectability, both of which had wobbled a bit in my early childhood.

I was blessed with a quick eye and brain and a body which did in large measure what I bade it to do. These gave me entrees to the intellectual and sporting worlds, but were not good enough in themselves to ordain my vocation nor to cause me to excel. I had no predisposition to excellence though I had abundant energy, so I skittered and gleaned. I was driven by directionless impatience.

I enjoyed being with good brains but marvelled at their occasional stupidity. I enjoyed the cavalier attitudes and courtesy of the gentry but was incapable of being laconic for more than a moment. I relished the vigour and transparency of my fellow-traders with their Essex twangs, but with them missed the uptake of allusions and the subtlety of manners and conversation.

I had done well. At twenty-one, when I suddenly and unexpectedly took up beetle-vaulting, I was earning some £200,000 a year. Although I had been nigh ceaselessly active, I cannot claim that I had actually worked particularly hard — not, at least, if work means hardship. People were and are my passion. Trading and communicating were therefore blithe fun for me — liberation, not bondage.

Aside from that energy and that gregariousness, perhaps the only thing which gave any indication of my future career was that damnable bloody-mindedness and libertarianism which had for some reason moved me to generally righteous anger since childhood.

Maybe this was the last remaining vestige of the illusions which my grandmother had planted in my father in that fancy name — the swashbuckling freebooter.

INDEX